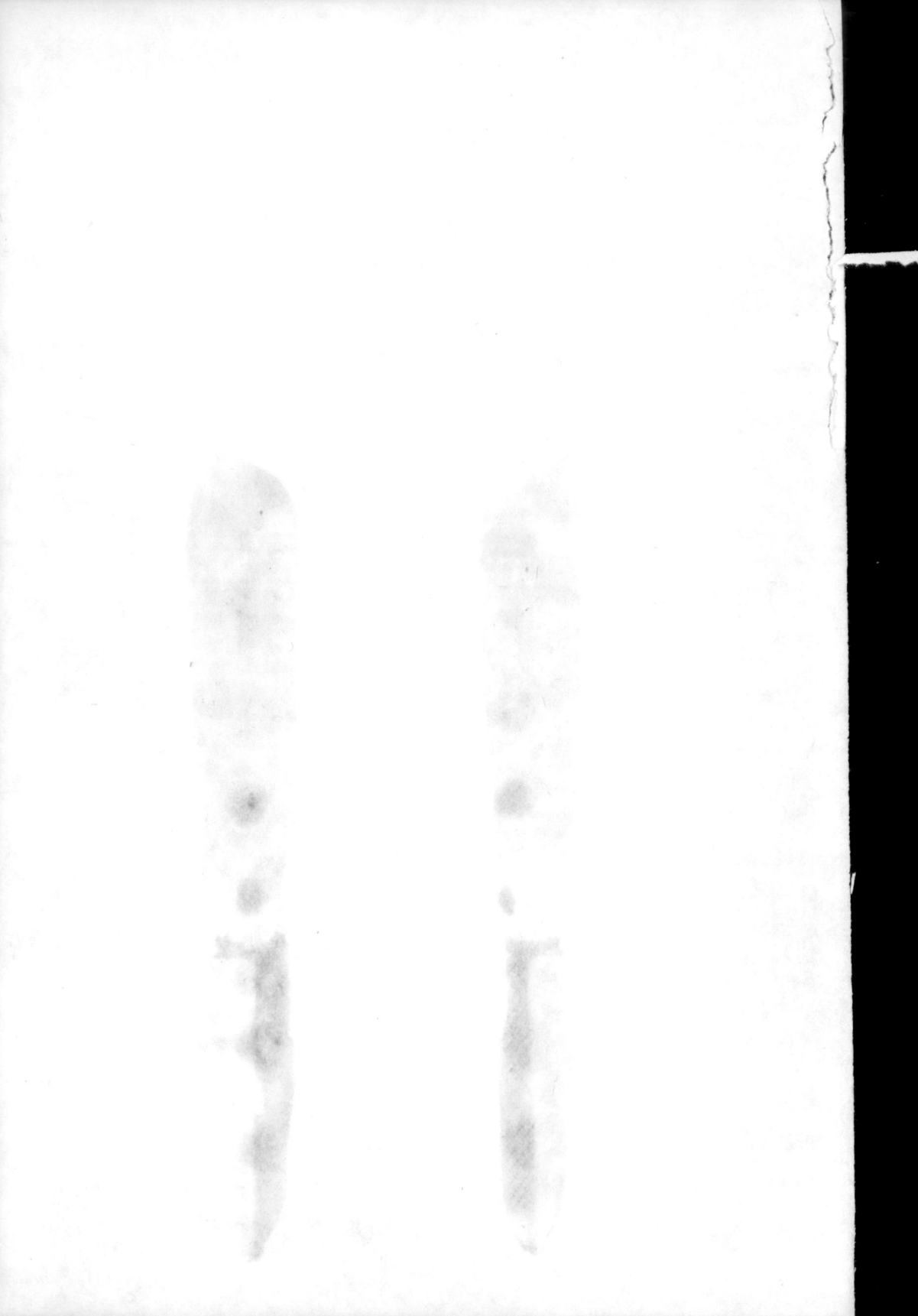

AMERICA
COMES OF AGE

A Da Capo Press Reprint Series

THE AMERICAN SCENE
Comments and Commentators

GENERAL EDITOR: WALLACE D. FARNHAM
University of Illinois

AMERICA
COMES OF AGE

A French Analysis

By André Siegfried

Translated by H. H. Hemming
and Doris Hemming

DA CAPO PRESS • NEW YORK • 1974

Library of Congress Cataloging in Publication Data

Siegfried, André, 1875-1959.
  America comes of age.

  (The American scene: comments and commentators)
  Translation of Les Etats-Unis d'aujourd'hui.
  Reprint of the 1927 ed. published by Harcourt,
Brace, New York.
    1. United States—Civilization—1918-1945.
2. United States—Race questions. 3. United States—
Economic conditions—1918-1945. 4. United States—
Politics and government—1901-1953. I. Title.
  E169.1.S58   917.3'03'91   68-16244
  ISBN 0-306-71025-0

Published by Da Capo Press, Inc.
A Subsidiary of Plenum Publishing Corporation
227 West 17th Street, New York, New York 10011

AMERICA COMES OF AGE

AMERICA
COMES OF AGE
A FRENCH ANALYSIS by
ANDRÉ SIEGFRIED

TRANSLATED FROM THE FRENCH
by H. H. HEMMING
and DORIS HEMMING

New York
HARCOURT, BRACE AND COMPANY

Published, April, 1927

TRANSLATORS' INTRODUCTION

IT is doubtful if any generation has been so absorbed with its own history as are the people of today. Never in a single decade were our ancestors confronted with events so momentous, intriguing, and replete with sudden changes as those brought about by the World War. Modern men and women are still interested in the history of the past, but they read it in the hope of finding in it the secret of the present, and even of the future. They are captivated by the baffling task of studying the changes while they are still taking place, and of sounding the depth of the currents that are still only uncertainly seen on the surface. The task of the contemporary historian is more difficult than that of the historian of the past, for it is hard to "see the forest for trees," and almost as hard to appreciate the viewpoint of the people of another country as of an earlier generation of one's own. This wealth of contemporary research may provide a treasure-trove for the historian of the future, but it is inspired by motives that touch us more closely. The unforeseen and far-reaching problems that are now looming up make the results of scientific study not only intensely interesting but vitally necessary for the guidance of those in authority.

The greatest steps into the future are being taken by the United States, for life moves quickly when either individuals or nations come of age. In *America Comes of Age,* Professor Siegfried describes the American people, perplexed with domestic problems of no mean importance, being suddenly thrust into maturity. The discovery of mass production in industry by such men as Ford and McCormick is introducing a new civilization with a standard of living

higher than anything dreamed of hitherto. Almost against
their will they have become leaders of the white race and
have been forced to assume economic responsibilities that
have always been borne by the older nations of Europe.
Their new relationships with the outside world have come
at a time when they are intent on solving a serious racial
crisis that has developed imperceptibly with the peopling of
their rich empty country. The influx of Latin and Slav
immigration that swept across the Atlantic during the twenty
years before the War now threatens to alter the very composition of the American race. Against this the descendants
of the original Anglo-Saxon Puritan stock are defending
themselves with grim determination. In the West they are
haunted by the fear that their solution of the "Yellow Peril"
may be only a temporary expedient, and in both the North
and the South the negro question has entered on a new and
more urgent phase since the War.

These are matters of moment, with a bearing upon each
other and upon the affairs of other countries that is exceedingly complicated. To analyze them requires long study
of the reactions of peoples and nations in the spheres of psychology, economics, and politics. M. Siegfried's survey of the
present situation in America and the events that led up to it
gives evidence of remarkable penetration, an uncanny sense
of underlying influences, as well as the careful research
needed to prove the reliability of his observations.

America Comes of Age cannot be classed with the superficial books that have been thrown off by the many European writers and thinkers who have made brief lecture tours
in the United States. Professor Siegfried's six months'
tour was not spent in lecturing, but in talking to people of
every class, creed, and colour, and measuring the "Weight
of the Imponderable," as Bismarck might have described
the subtle influences that are today shaping the destiny of
the American nation. Nor yet can his book be described

as "America Through French Eyes," for although he writes
with all the lightness and dexterity of a Parisian, he has
tackled his subject as an unprejudiced economist and sociolo-
gist who holds no brief for any school of thought, not even
for his own country. His frankness and his eagerness to present what he considers to be the truth may seem disconcerting to those who hold contrary views, but no one can chal-
lenge either his impartiality or his determination to think
clearly and speak courageously.

M. Siegfried comes of a distinguished Alsatian family
which has long been noted for its great political insight.
Ever since he graduated in 1898 he has devoted his life to
the study and teaching of economics, and for many years
has been a professor in the Ecole Libre des Sciences Poli-
tiques of Paris. He has already published books on Great
Britain, Canada, and New Zealand. Since the Armistice
he has been attached to the French Foreign Office as an economic expert, and in this capacity has taken part in the various meetings of the League of Nations, and also in the
Inter-Allied conferences at Brussels, Barcelona, and Genoa.

He first visited America in 1898 during a trip around the
world in which he studied Canada and the United States,
Mexico, China, Japan, Australia, and New Zealand. Since
then he has travelled to America on five or six different occasions, once as secretary-general to the mission under General Pau which the French Government sent during the War
to Canada, Australia, and the United States. His last visit
was in 1925 when he toured nearly every State in the Union
for the *Musée Social,* at whose request this book has been
written as part of a series analyzing post-war conditions in
the leading countries of the world.

H. H. HEMMING.
DORIS HEMMING.

CONTENTS

PART I: THE ETHNIC SITUATION

WILL AMERICA REMAIN PROTESTANT AND ANGLO-SAXON?

PART II: THE ECONOMIC SITUATION

PART III: THE POLITICAL SITUATION

CONTENTS

CONCLUSION

PART I

THE ETHNIC SITUATION

Will America Remain Protestant and Anglo-Saxon?

CHAPTER I

THE essential characteristic of the post-war period in the United States is the nervous reaction of the original American stock against an insidious subjugation by foreign blood. Negroes and Asiatics are of course strictly debarred from the white race, but even in the latter the fusion of Anglo-Saxons, Slavs, Latins, and Jews is still far from complete, and at times merely amounts to a juxtaposition of peoples. As every one knows, there is no real American race, although the Americans as a whole pride themselves on their original stock, which was Anglo-Saxon and inherently Protestant. Their forefathers were the pioneers of a continent, pioneers whose outstanding characteristics were optimism, unbounded self-confidence, and success.

In spite of their power and wealth, however, the Americans are now beginning to have doubts, not about their ability or their future prosperity, but about the ingredients of their race. They are dismayed by the heterogeneous elements which they feel growing up within their body politic—Catholic, Jew, and Oriental, all of whom they feel to be out of sympathy with their traditions. They have a vague uneasy fear of being overwhelmed from within, and of suddenly finding one day that they are no longer themselves. Like other nations before them that have travelled the same dangerous slope, they are trying to maintain their unity of spirit by insisting impatiently that their centre of gravity still lies in the Anglo-Saxon and Puritan stock. The War accentuated but was not the original cause of this reaction.

It arose from the new type of immigration that has been arriving during the past forty or fifty years.

The peopling of the United States has been accomplished by three waves of immigration from Europe and Africa, each one leaving a distinct layer or stratum of population. In the eighteenth century the thirteen original States on the Atlantic seaboard were almost exclusively British and Protestant, but the social constitution in each case, in the South, the centre, and the North, was fundamentally different. The four New England States were built up by Puritan Dissenters from England, whose strong personality left an indelible mark on the whole American civilization. So persistent indeed is this influence that even today it is impossible to understand the United States unless one fully appreciates the Puritan spirit.

In the centre, around New York and Philadelphia, were four other States where, in addition to the main population of English and Scotch, there were Lutheran peasants from Germany, Protestants from Ulster, and the Dutch. Both here and in New England it was a case of real colonizing by the people. The various classes of society all came from the same ethnic source, and production was carried on by men who regarded one another as equals.

In the five colonies of the South the situation was entirely different. Owing largely to their hot climate—almost tropical for Europeans—these States were developed not by middle-class colonists but by gentlemen of Anglican religion, rich planters who did not till the soil themselves, but at first used convict labour and, after the middle of the eighteenth century, negro slaves imported from Africa. Even today we must not lose sight of the fact that these were colonies of exploitation, or "plantations" according to the expression of the time, and that in them society was rigidly divided into water-tight compartments according to the various races and castes. Nevertheless, both in the case of the Yankees in the

North, believing in democracy and equality, and of the gentlemen of the South, conservative and aristocratic, they were all British and Protestant; and even after obtaining political independence they remained English in culture.

In the nineteenth century, after the close of the Napoleonic wars and especially after 1840, an unprecedented wave of immigration from Europe to the United States took place. From the end of the War of Independence to 1840, the immigrants numbered slightly less than a million. Between 1840 and 1880 it is estimated that 9,438,000 foreigners, of whom nine-tenths were Europeans, landed in the United States. The terrible Irish famines, the German revolution of 1848, and above all the appeal of a virgin country, were the principal causes of this great movement of population which continued to supply the New World with a type of colonist similar to the early pioneers. These were genuine settlers who went on to the land and opened up new territory. Their origin, however, was not quite the same as before, for though they were mostly Nordic, they were no longer almost entirely British and Scotch. During the decade 1871–1880, 91 per cent. of the immigrants came from northern and western Europe, as compared with only 8 per cent. of Latins and Slavs. Of the total, 32 per cent. were Germans, 24 per cent. English, Scotch, and Welsh, 19 per cent. Irish, and 9 per cent. Scandinavian.

As a result, the character of the American people was visibly altered in the nineteenth century. It was less exclusively British, and more German and Irish; and as the latter included many Catholics, it was no longer entirely Protestant. The Germans contributed not only a certain seriousness, but also their pompousness, their stolidity, and their belief in system and authority. The Irish, on the contrary, swarmed in the cities, where they supplied their spirit of unrest, injecting that element of devilry and charm so typical of the Celt. Without their love of amusement, mischief, and disorder, the American atmosphere might have been too heavy to breathe. It was this America, still fundamentally English though tinged with German and Irish, that many of us knew in our youth.

After 1880, and especially after 1890, an entirely different immigration took place. Between 1880 and 1914 a veritable tidal wave carried over to America almost 22 million immigrants, of whom more than nine-tenths were Europeans. In 1907, 1,285,000 arrived, and over 1,200,000 in 1914. The important point is that their origin was almost entirely different from that of the earlier settlers. It was the Latin and Slav countries and not northern Europe (Germany, Scandinavia, and Great Britain) that now contributed, as is strikingly illustrated in the following table:

IMMIGRATION

	Per Cent. Nordic [1]	Latin-Slav [2]
1860–70	98.4	1.6
1870–80	91.6	8.4
1880–90	80.2	19.8
1890–1900	48.4	51.6
1900–10	23.3	76.7
1910–20	22.8	77.2

The total immigration in the decade 1900–10 was only 10.6 per cent. British and 4.2 per cent. German, while Austria-Hungary accounted for 26.3 per cent., Italy 25.1 per cent., and Russia 19.6 per cent. It was a fantastic medley of peoples: Africans, Armenians, Bohemians and Moravians, Cubans, Dalmatians, Bosnians and Herzogovinians, Dutch and Flemish, Hindus, English, Finnish, French, Ger-

[1] United Kingdom, Germany, France, Belgium, Holland, Switzerland, Denmark, Sweden, and Norway.
[2] Austria-Hungary, Russia (including Finland and Poland), Balkan and Mediterranean countries, and Portugal.

mans, Hebrews, Irish, southern and northern Italians, Japanese, Koreans, Lithuanians, Magyars, Mexicans, natives of the East and West Indies, Poles, Portuguese, Rumanians, Russians, Ruthenians, Scandinavians, Scotch, Slovaks, Spaniards, Syrians, Turks, and Welsh—and those who are set down in the statistics as "other peoples."

Without considering the natural and often brilliant abilities of these many races, we must admit that from the American point of view the new immigrants were not the equal of their predecessors. The early settlers had come to exploit a virgin soil and had borne all the risks and toil of a creative work. They were the real pioneers. The newcomers, recruited in their very homes by the immigration agents, were attracted by a wage level that seemed high in comparison with the mediocre standard of living of southeastern Europe. Instead of heading for the great open spaces of the West, they now congregated in the Atlantic ports or in the industrial and mining centres of the East— truly a bewildered and inarticulate crew existing on the margin of the original civilization!

From the religious point of view the change was even more striking, for the majority of the immigrants were no longer Protestant. There were Jews from Russia or Poland, and Catholics from Italy and the Slav countries; and altogether their material and moral assimilation was slow and difficult. They formed solid indigestible blocks in the lower quarters of the big cities, and even when by the second generation they had acquired an American veneer, they were out of sympathy with the spirit of the country and the Protestant and Anglo-Saxon traditions laid down by the Fathers of Independence. Thus in the first years of the twentieth century the problem of the melting pot was becoming acute.

The census of 1920 even more than that of 1910 clearly illustrates this lack of homogeneity, for which possibly there is no remedy. Of the total population of 105½ millions, the whites numbered 95 millions (90 per cent.) and the negroes 10½ millions (10 per cent.). Of the 95 million whites, only 58 millions were born in the United States of American parents, while 36½ millions were directly or indirectly of foreign origin, 13½ millions were born abroad, and 15½ millions had both parents of foreign birth. Thus the real Americans, or "100 per cent. Americans" as they call themselves, amounted to only 61 per cent. of the whites and to 55 per cent. of the total.

These statistics indicate a very serious problem. Undoubtedly the influx of immigrants can be stopped. In fact it has been stopped since the War by drastic legislation. And yet that cannot alter the fact that they have 10 million blacks and 36 million foreigners already within the country. As long as they can be absorbed both physically and morally, well and good; but if they have only acquired a very thin veneer, or if under the social uniformity of modern America they still preserve their foreign mentality, what is the country coming to?

In the first place we must definitely consider the negro element as unsuitable for assimilation. If it were even partially absorbed, a serious alteration in the physique and the personality of the white race would inevitably result. Among the whites the new foreign-born population is inherently less adaptable to the original traditions of the United States than was the immigration of fifty years ago. In 1880 some 83 per cent. came from Germany, Scandinavia, and the United Kingdom, but in 1920 only 40 per cent. On the other hand, the proportion from Latin and Slav Europe increased between these dates from 4 per cent. to 46 per cent. This raises two questions—bitter questions for the American of the old school:

    1. Can the white race be absolutely sure of maintaining its integrity in the future, while it has 10 million ne-

groes in its midst, and with sexual intercourse more common than people care to admit?

2. With fifty years' inundation of Latin-Slav Catholics and Oriental Jews remaining undissolved like a layer of silt, is there any hope of preserving intact the Protestant spirit and British traditions from which the moral and political character of the country evolved during the seventeenth and eighteenth centuries?

This latent uneasiness was crystallized by the War, when with an instinct of self-preservation the old-type Americans rallied together and closed their ranks. The change in the atmosphere during the past twenty years has been startling, for there has been a complete reversal of ethnic, social, and political thought. During the hundred years from the end of the Napoleonic wars up to the Great War, the United States welcomed the foreigner with open arms. The classical conception of America as the Melting Pot of races was widespread, and it was generally believed that the New World could assimilate, more or less slowly but completely, an indefinite number of immigrants. America proudly assumed the *rôle* of asylum for all who wished to begin their lives over again. The idea that ten races could contribute to the development of the American people did not shock public opinion in the least. While some boasted of their pure British and Dutch descent, others prided themselves no less on their composite origin. The following quotation from Sinclair Lewis, written ironically in 1925, would not have been considered a subject for sarcasm twenty years earlier:

Martin Arrowsmith was, like most inhabitants of Elk Mills before the Slavo-Italian immigration, a Typical Pure-bred Anglo-Saxon American, which means that he was a union of German, French, Scotch, Irish, perhaps a little Spanish, conceivably a little of the strains lumped together as "Jewish," and a great deal of English, which is itself a combination of Primitive Britain, Celt, Phœnician, Roman, German, Dane, and Swede.

Up to the end of the nineteenth century the Melting Pot had been successful, in appearance at any rate. It had worked rapidly enough, and had transformed the Nordic races of Europe into Americans. So long as the immigrants were Protestants, the operation was carried out with extreme ease. The Latin-Slav Catholics and Jews also appeared to be assimilated, though with considerably more trouble. Sometimes the foreigners seemed almost to have been born again. With their beards shaved off and decked out in ready-made American suits, they appeared to have forgotten the past like a bad dream. They realized that the work of their hands henceforth would give them independence and respectability. If for a while they clung to their language and customs, it was not because they wished to do so, but rather because the overworked Melting Pot necessarily required a certain amount of time. In any case there was no alternative to Americanization, which imposed the strictly Anglo-Saxon outlook to an extent that will probably not continue in the future. The immigrants were bound to adopt not only the customs and standard of living of the New World, but also Anglo-Saxon ethics in the social, moral, and even religious fields.

Between 1880 and 1890, when the second wave of Germano-British immigration was being assimilated, the results appeared more or less satisfactory. The regular American type was being evolved. On a British foundation were superimposed layers of Germans, Scandinavians, and Irish and a sprinkling of Jews. The whole mass was strongly impregnated with Protestantism, for even the Catholics and Jews seemed to adapt their religions to the Protestant outlook.   In their boundless optimism, the Americans were confident that all this composite humanity would finally be absorbed, physically and morally, without leaving any appreciable or dangerous residue.   Those were the days when environment was believed to be more powerful than heredity.

About 1910, at the high tide of the Latin-Slav influx, there began to be doubts as to the efficacy of the Melting Pot.   The War brought the matter quickly and decisively to a head, and the lack of national unity came as a startling revelation to thinking Americans.   They had believed themselves detached from Europe, but now they suddenly discovered innumerable bonds, intimate and entangling, that still united them to the Old World.   It was a case of being convinced not by theories, but rather by clearly defined object-lessons.

I was in New York on August 4, 1914, and I saw it all with my own eyes.   Here are some of my notes:

"An amusing but significant detail: All the hotel kitchens are disorganized, for the chefs and their assistants are invariably French.   For several days they have given only the most distracted attention to their pots and pans, and today they abandoned them altogether.   They left in a body, having either volunteered or been mobilized.

"A more serious matter and one which gives food for anxious thought: Today there were processions of the various nationalities in the chief avenues of the city.   The French gathered in groups in front of their consulate and at the office of the Compagnie Générale Transatlantique.   They are silent and calm (I like this absence of hysteria and bravado).   A hundred yards away a noisy mob of Germans are thronging in front of the North German Lloyd building.   Farther off is a band of Austro-Hungarians who have evidently been scarcely denationalized by their stay in America, for the passion and violence of their native land has suddenly been reawakened in them.   Those who are anxious about the unity of this country cannot help thinking of Sinbad's ship in the *Arabian Nights* which sailed so close to a magnetic mountain that it had all its nails suddenly drawn out of it."

The outbreak of the War thus disclosed the fact that hundreds of thousands—even millions—of foreigners were still unabsorbed, although the Americans had been flattering themselves that they had completely assimilated them. It may be necessary, they said, to let them preserve some of their picturesque customs for the time being, but when in the event of a European war their reaction turns out to be German, Austrian, Hungarian, Serbian, or French, and not American, then there is something decidedly wrong. With such "citizens" the United States became a sort of ethnic mosaic and ran the risk of being no longer a nation. It was not for this that these immigrants had been admitted originally. Not that their defection—rarely more than sentimental—was at all dissentious or in any way imperilled the safety of the state. But there was trouble enough already when so many Americans did not reason as true Americans, but voted from an alien point of view. For example the Italian-Americans during the Fiume controversy, and the German-Americans during the presidential campaign of La Follette, remained fundamentally Italian and German.

The original American—in so far as the term still means anything—submits with growing impatience to this disloyalty, and is now exasperated by political ideas which formerly he tolerated good-naturedly. As in such earlier manifestations as the "Know Nothing" movement or the anti-Catholic "American Protective Association," he is particularly irritated by the fact that whole sections of the population remain impervious to Protestant thought, and to the social and political conceptions that proceed from it. We find this instinctive protest in the Prohibition quarrel, in

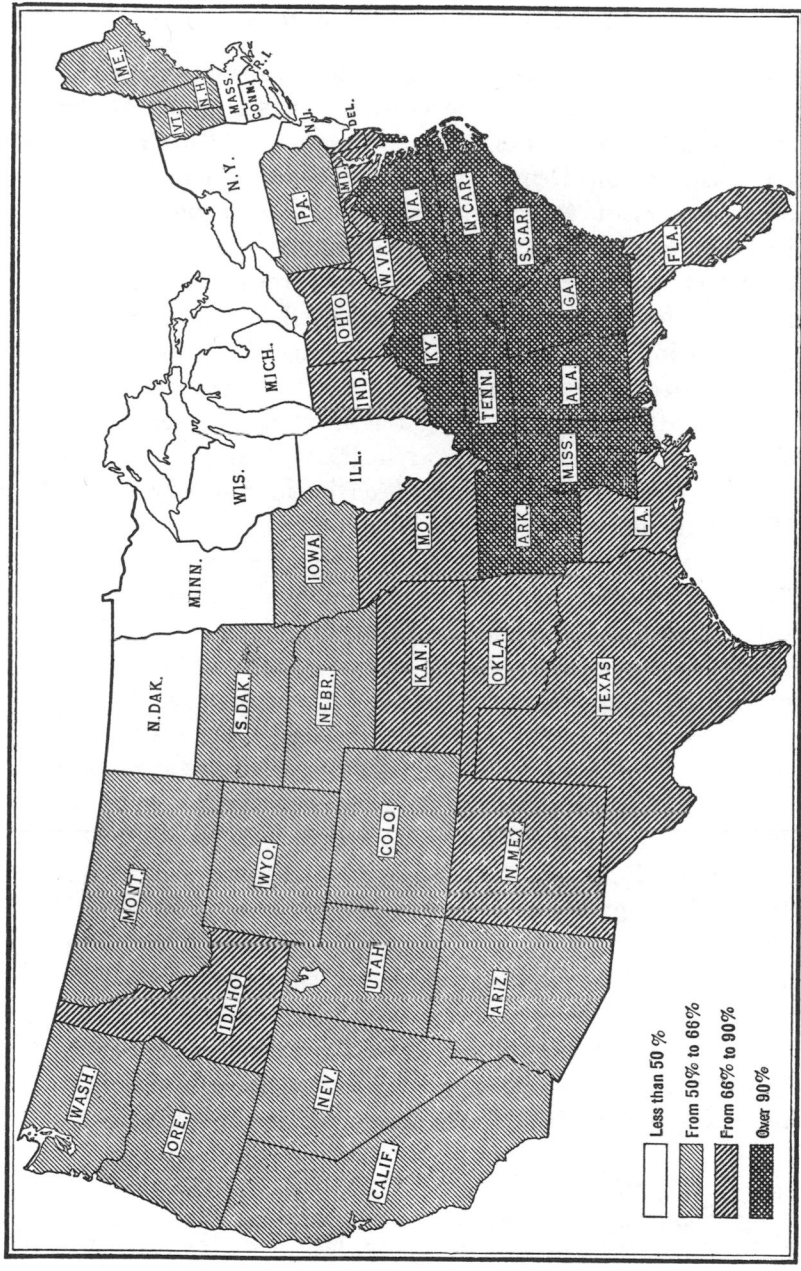

FIG. I.—NATIVE-BORN WHITE AMERICANS HAVING BOTH PARENTS AMERICAN-BORN. PERCENTAGE OF THE TOTAL POPULATION BY STATES.

Less than 50 %
From 50% to 66%
From 66% to 90%
Over 90%

the public school controversy, and in the dispute over the teaching of the doctrine of evolution.   It is also one of the main factors in the difficulties between the Democrats of the East and the Democrats of the South, and in a dozen other aspects of American life at the present time.   This irritation has resolved itself into a new nationalism, narrow and sectarian, which one meets with wherever the old-fashioned Protestant American had awakened to the menace of the alien influences that are springing up about him.

To understand the geographic aspect of this reaction we must keep constantly in mind the chart of the regions in which the original race has remained relatively pure, as compared with those that have been invaded by foreigners. Protestantism still incontestably dominates the first group of States, whereas in the second a strong influx of Catholics has flowed through the breach.   Our conception of the whole social and political aspect of the United States will be clarified by a knowledge of the psychology of the different parts of the country as indicated by this map.

A cursory inspection reveals three zones.   The South, and the States bordering it on the north and west, are at present the most homogeneous and also the most truly American and Protestant—provided, of course, we do not class the negroes as foreigners, for they really are true Americans. It is this group of twenty States that comes to the fore whenever it is a question of Protestant nationalism or anti-foreign reaction.   In some of the old slave States the proportion of the white population that was born of American parents in the United States is over 90 per cent.,[3] whereas in the rest of the South and the intermediate States bordering on it, the proportion is everywhere over two-thirds.[4]

[3] Virginia, North and South Carolina, Kentucky, Tennessee, Georgia, Alabama, and Mississppi.

[4] Louisiana, Arkansas, Florida, Delaware, Maryland, West Virginia, Ohio, southern Indiana, Missouri, Kansas, Oklahoma, Texas, and New Mexico.

The second zone, in which the original inhabitants account for one-half to two-thirds of the white population, comprises northern New England, a semi-rural district which has not yet been overrun by foreigners, Pennsylvania, Iowa, Nebraska, and all the far western and Pacific Coast States.

In the third zone the majority of the population is of foreign origin, either foreign-born or with one or both parents foreign. Under this classification come the industrial districts of the Atlantic Coast and the Great Lakes [5] and also the northwestern agricultural districts, which are German and Scandinavian.[6] In the three States around Boston, and in Michigan, Wisconsin, Minnesota, and North Dakota, less than a third of the population is of American origin.

We must, however, study the nationalities of these foreigners, for on this depends their adaptability. The Germano-Scandinavian immigration was largely agricultural, but the Irish, and especially the last wave of Latin-Slavs and Jews, settled in the cities. The urban population still amounts to only 51½ per cent. of the total, but 75 per cent. of it is foreign-born, which proves that three-quarters of the newcomers did not go on to the land. Thus the agricultural immigration of the past was mainly Protestant, while the present urban immigration is to a great extent Jewish and Catholic. This is a decisive factor which we must bear in mind.

The foreign element in the United States revolves around two centres. The focus of the Germano-Scandinavians (mainly Lutheran and Protestant, though partly Catholic) lies in the States of Wisconsin, Minnesota, and North Dakota. Out of 486,000 foreign-born whites in Minnesota, there were, in 1920, 219,000 Scandinavians, 75,000 Germans, and 29,000 Finns. On the other hand, the centre of

[5] Massachusetts, Rhode Island, Connecticut, New York, New Jersey, Michigan, and Illinois.
[6] Wisconsin, Minnesota, North and South Dakota.

the Latin-Slav immigration (Jewish and Catholic) lies in Boston, New York, Chicago, and generally in the larger cities of the East and centre. Out of 1,078,000 foreign-born whites in Massachusetts, 183,000 were Irish, 117,000 Italian, 109,000 French-Canadian, 92,000 Russian Jews, 69,000 Polish, 28,000 Portuguese, 21,000 Lithuanian, and 20,000 Greek. The three largest cities are thus tending to become more and more foreign. In 1910 the Germans were the dominant foreign race, but in 1920, except for Cincinnati, Milwaukee, and St. Louis, where they still retain first place, they have been overtaken by the Russian Jews, the Poles, and the Italians. The Irish, who are very numerous everywhere, hold first rank in Boston, second in Jersey City, Philadelphia, and Washington, and third in New York, where, however, their influence is preponderant.

In New York, the statistics to remember are that out of 1,992,000 foreign-born whites, or 36 per cent. of the total, the 1920 census shows 480,000 Russian Jews, 391,000 Italians, 203,000 Irish, 194,000 Germans, 146,000 Poles, 127,000 Austrians, 71,000 English, and 64,000 Hungarians, quite apart from the 161,000 negroes, whose number has since then increased to 200,000. New York is the greatest Jewish city in the world, with a million and a half Jews, and one of the greatest, if not the greatest, of Catholic cities. It is certainly not a Protestant city. Today it is hardly an occidental city. When the offices down town close at night, and one is crammed into the subway along with countless stenographers with swarthy complexions, hook noses, and a flavour of the ghetto, or when from the narrow streets of the East Side pours out a hurried mass of brown Levantines and bearded Semites, the impression is distinctly oriental.

Though statistics cannot give us complete information, they do help to locate the centres where Americanism is building up moral barriers against the pressure from outside. First we have the South in its entirety and the South-west as the citadel of traditional Protestant orthodoxy, with an innate horror of anything foreign. In the country districts and the small towns of the States along the north bank of the Ohio River (Ohio, Indiana, Illinois), the anti-foreign and anti-Catholic reaction is hardly less violent, and the same applies up-state from New York and Boston.

The great moral and financial forces which control the life of the nation have stubbornly survived even in the heart of the big cities, although there they are half submerged by the flood of foreigners. Intellectually and socially New York is swamped by a fantastic cosmopolitanism, but in Boston, Philadelphia, Baltimore, and even Chicago, the original forces have survived in undiminished vitality and are still in control. It is not, however, in the East that they are the strongest, but in the West, where the descendants of the New England Puritans, who quitted the Atlantic States in the nineteenth century, swarmed across the Continent and formed a social *élite,* in the literal sense of the word, in their new surroundings.

These American migrants went west in two parallel currents, one from New England and the other from Virginia and the South. Generally speaking, the Ohio Basin is the dividing-line between the two zones. New England colonized Michigan and the northern part of Ohio, Indiana, Illinois, and also Iowa, Nebraska, and Kansas, while the Southerners went to Missouri and Arkansas and the southern districts of Ohio and Indiana. The two migrations took with them different conceptions of government, the one scattering the seeds of Republicanism, the other of future Democrats, but both were imbued with Puritan ideals which have flourished in the new country. Just as the whole of a conquered territory can be controlled by a few garrisons, so the West has been dominated by this implanted Puritanism.

Beyond the Mississippi these original currents linked up and crossed each other: one from St. Louis followed the upper reaches of the Missouri toward Montana and Oregon; another from the plains of the centre went to Salt Lake and the Pacific; and a third from the lower Mississippi, to Southern California by way of Texas and the Santa Fé Trail. A more recent migration has emptied certain sections of Kansas, Iowa, and Nebraska of their wealthy farmers, who have gone on to the sunny slopes of Southern California, to make of Los Angeles, by a singular paradox, another centre of Puritanism. Modern historians are making a detailed survey of these migrations of the old race elect, and when completed, their charts will indicate the moral strongholds of Anglo-Saxon Protestantism and will provide us with a valuable clue to the anomalies of American politics. Boston, the old Puritan fortress, is today half conquered by foreigners, but her spirit survives in fifty cities of the West and on the Pacific. In fact, "Rome is no longer at Rome."

From the beginning of our study we have found a fundamental opposition between the two camps, between tradition and cosmopolitanism. In view of the gravity of the problem, which affects the very soul of the nation, can we wonder at the existence of its vigorous nationalism! No other country is so difficult to understand or so complex in its moral structure. Not that the psychology of the typical American is at all complicated superficially. Assimilation, like a steam-roller, ruthlessly crushes the finest flowers of the older civilizations, and as a rule only allows to survive an æstheticism that is sadly childish and implacably standardized. The immigrant arrives old with centuries of inherited experience, but America makes him young and boyish again. So many and such varied elements have been drawn on to produce this people! These broken stalks torn from the old roots of European culture, after being precariously transplanted, continue to produce new sprouts as well as the fruits of unexpected throwbacks and the mysterious vagaries of heredity. Hence the past still means much more than a forgotten dream.

Theoretically it is quite possible to trace all the different races that have contributed to the formation of the American nation; in fact, official statistics give the exact proportions due to each race. But I cannot but feel that it would be impossible for any one man to possess such varied knowledge that he would be able to sympathize with the innermost aspirations of all the races that have been cast into the Melting Pot. He would have to have a combination of heredity and personal experience which the study of books cannot, and which life does not, grant to any one individual.

The first essential would be a heritage of English Protestantism. No one can possibly understand the United States without a profound, almost innate appreciation of their Puritanism, with its self-satisfaction, and its privileged relationship with God. Just as in England a Catholic is always more or less a foreigner, so one must have, in order to understand America, one of Cromwell's Roundheads as an ancestor, or at least an early disciple of Wesley. Then you are one of the family! These are fine distinctions. Of course you could substitute a pious Lutheran from Germany as a great-uncle, or an old aunt from the Canton of Neuchâtel, both pillars of the orthodox church, full of missionary zeal towards the heathen, vulnerable to the follies of a Welsh revival, willing to be psychoanalyzed by Freud, and suspicious of French "frivolity." Such forbears would give you an insight into the problem.

On the other hand, French Catholicism in one's ancestry is quite useless. The cousin from the Sarthe, baptized but yet sceptic, will give you no clue, nor will the village priest, pacing his proverbial and charming garden, but indifferent alike to anti-alcoholism and the attractions of moral uplift.

Above all, no help need be expected from that college friend, the Radical-Socialist from the provinces. As an introduction to American Catholicism, you should have a working knowledge of an Irish extremist and the atmosphere of fanaticism and conspiracy of Dublin, Cork, or Galway. Hunt up an Irish Father with a blue chin like an Italian bishop, or a local politician from a stormy county of Connaught, and either of them will make plain many things in Boston, New York, or San Francisco.

Also it is well to have a little Teutonic blood in one's veins, and with it, traditions handed down from some disciplined German Herr Professor solidly ensconced in his systems and unshakable in his faith in statistics, in orthodox science, and in police regulations, until they regulate his very thoughts. Again I repeat, no French in this collection of ancestors, except possibly a gay dog from Montmartre or a Bohemian from Montparnasse to give you an insight into Greenwich Village. The individualism of the Gaul and the intellectual realism of our Latin culture will only lead you astray. France is at the opposite pole from the gregarious nation that is America.

We have more than exhausted our potential ancestors, and yet we have not provided that which is absolutely indispensable, an insight into the soul of the Jew and of the Orient. Surely you can lay claim to some Israelite uncle from London or Frankfort. He is sure to turn up again in New York! Or even better, can you not unearth some Alsatian Jew, a "kike" from Breslau, a "sheeny" from Lemberg or Salonika, or even—and I do not exaggerate—some Hebrew from Asia, with goat eyes and patriarchal beard? We must beware of falling into the error that it is only the Wall Street Jew that must be studied. If you are to appreciate the United States, the synagogue Jew, just escaped from the ghetto, is equally important.

So we keep coming back to our religious origins—Luther,

Calvin, Cromwell, Wesley, and the prophets of Israel—not to mention the Catholicism of the New World, a Catholicism subdivided by racial jealousies far more extreme than ours, and yet less actually Roman than Irish, German, or French-Canadian.

But even now we are far from the end of the list! You must still find among your ancestors an Italian macaroni-eater, a Slav from the lower Danube, a Greek with his devotion to his clan, and finally a cringing, insinuating Armenian. Penetrating still farther into the mysterious past, we must have had personal experience in order to understand the modern spirit of the Hungarians and the Bulgars, in whose veins still ferments the indomitable blood of Attila. And then unless we turn back to the taciturn Fins of northern Europe, how can we possibly comprehend the Finnish lumbermen of Oregon, isolated, anarchistic, and obstinate?

But I have not finished yet. We still need a nigger mammy, some typical Aunt Jemima, to instil in us the poetry of the southern night, the wailing melodies of the negro slaves, and all the confused legends of the Congo that persist in the mind of the sentimental African. Then, on the Mexican frontier, we must be able to penetrate the soul of the Spanish and combine it with the haughty reserve of the Indian. And if the yellow races mean nothing more to us than a grinning mask, can we ever react fully to the bitterness of the race question in California, that furthermost boundary of the Occident?

CHAPTER II

THE MELTING POT

In the American Melting Pot, the temperature at which fusion takes place varies with the different races. In certain cases it occurs at a very low degree, being practically automatic. In others, however, a high temperature is needed, and then even after prolonged heating an insoluble residue is liable to remain. This is particularly true of the Jewish race, for although their transformation at first seems to take place easily and quickly, the operation later proves to have been incomplete. The difference in these reactions to the Melting Pot is of utmost importance; in fact, since the War the Americans have made it the key-note of their immigration policy.

A century of experience has proved that Protestants of Nordic origin are readily assimilated, and Calvinists particularly so. There is almost no question of Americanizing an Englishman or a Scotchman, for they are hardly foreigners and feel quite at home for many reasons that go far deeper than the mere similarity of the language. The Dutch, the Germans, the Scandinavians, and the German Swiss all have low melting-points, though if they are Lutherans or Catholics they are less easily assimilated, as we shall see when we analyze the political conceptions of Lutheranism and Calvinism. Though the Germans frequently retain their identity for several generations, it is less owing to a difference in their customs than to their political outlook, and to the fact that they are always conscious that behind them in Europe lies an organized government, powerful and ambitious. The result of these low melting-points is that wherever the foreign population is mainly German or Scandinavian, there is really no problem of assimilation. In Wisconsin, which might almost be described as a German principality, there is something very comfortable, well kept, and old-fashioned about the country-side, a feeling of German *Gemüthlichkeit*. Yet it does not strike one as being foreign. In the Viking States of Minnesota and North Dakota, the men occupying the various government posts give the impression of being vigorous Scotchmen, although actually they are Scandinavians. In many of these western capitals overlooking their oceans of wheat, both the attorney-general and the governor are probably Norwegian. They were born in Bergen or Christiania, they will tell you, for you would hardly have guessed it from their accent, which is slightly harsh, but nothing more. Young-looking and fair-haired, they seem to rise from the very pages of Ibsen. Solness indeed might have been a contractor in Dakota, a thorough-going American who causes no anxiety to the purists of the Americanization movement.

Assimilation only begins to be troublesome with the Catholics, even German and Anglo-Saxon Catholics, and it is a question whether it is not civilizations rather than races that resist. The Irish Catholic, who speaks English and whose mode of living is perfectly normal, does not assimilate in the true sense of the word; for after two or even three generations we find him and his priest as distinctive as ever. Although one would never think of referring to either the English or Scotch as foreigners, the Irish, on the other hand, have remained apart in the large American cities, forming their own communities, with their own tendencies and individuality and even an Irish patriotism. In the same way, largely because they are Catholics, the French-Canadians group themselves around their priest and live isolated in the cotton-manufacturing towns of New England. In every case the resistance to assimilation comes from the

Church, which scarcely conceals its hostility to the efforts of the Puritans to change the mode of living of the country by means of the law.

When we come to the Slavs and the Latins, we must ascertain whether religion is the real obstacle to a rapid Americanization, or whether it is not the inevitable resistance of a civilization that differs fundamentally in its conception of the individual, the family, and the clan. People with a strong sense of blood-ties like the Italians or the Greeks are absorbed only with difficulty. They continue to lead their frugal lives, un-American in their thrift, and haunted by the thought of their home country and of the relatives to whom they send their savings.

As for the races that are individualists in their work— the Frenchman who insists on thinking for himself and by himself; the Mediterranean with his genius for gardening and love of the soil; the Finnish lumberman and the Mexican navvy—they all aggressively assert their individuality as if they could not fit into the American machine. Thus the really obstinate elements are in the last analysis the Latins, the French, the Finns, and the Mexicans, who all resist for the same reason, because they are anti-social at heart. Americanization tends to destroy the family and to reduce the originality of the individual. The instinctive resistance to it may arise from a longing for social conditions that possibly are incompatible with modern developments and mass production. The new immigration policy in its turn may simply express the antagonism of the dominant group to this individualistic revolt.

Our argument applies with particular force to the Jews. They appear to assimilate at the lowest melting-point, but even after three generations one finds them still with their national traits unaffected. As there are three millions of them in the country, a million and a half in New York alone, the problem is important, more especially as they include Jews of every class of society, from the aristocratic banker of London or Frankfort to verminous refugees from the ghettos of the Ukraine and Poland.

The Jew gives the impression at first of being very quickly Americanized, for no other foreigner has his easy adaptability. In any case, the American atmosphere offers him every attraction. He respects money, success, and worldliness; he is restless and ambitious, and his eagerness to succeed is not without a certain vengefulness for centuries of hatred and oppression. In moral origin, he is closely allied to the Puritan—the same biblical tradition, the same belief that his is the chosen race, the same easy step from religious mysticism to the conquest of power and riches.

The Jew passes through the first phase of his Americanization with disconcerting rapidity—there is something suspicious about his excessive zeal. If the Stars and Stripes is waved at a jingo demonstration in New York, you may be sure that it is a Jew who holds the standard, while the 100 per cent. American whose great-great-grandfather was a friend of Washington stands aside disgusted. Caught suddenly into the rhythm of the New World, he is soon more American than the Americans themselves. He seems at first to throw off his own traditions gaily. He changes his name, and Schönberg becomes Belmont, Jonas becomes Jones. He "passes," as the negroes say; that is, he moves among the Christians without being remarked. Thus in the shortest possible period, like the law student who crams a three-year curriculum into three months, the bearded Jew from a far-off European ghetto is Americanized until no trace of the alien remains. He even makes light of his religious tradition, for although in the first generation the immigrant remains faithful to his Sabbath, in the second he is content with half-way measures. He joins societies for the promotion of ethical culture, where he mixes with broad-minded Protestants anxious about their duty to society. The number of Jews who disappear in this way in the ocean of America must be considerable.

Of course there are orthodox Jews who remain faithful to their synagogue, and who are always on the alert to reclaim their lost brethren. Also, not only in the foreign quarters of the large cities but even in the well-to-do districts, it must be admitted that the Jews keep more or less apart in spite of themselves, bound to each other less by their religion than by racial ties. Socially they are only too anxious to attach themselves to the Christians. Surreptitiously they have invaded their hotels until they have crowded the Gentiles out. They have wormed their way into the clubs in spite of the ostracism and insults designed to exclude them. With their brilliant intellects, they have firmly established themselves in the universities, where the mediocre element tries instinctively to oust them. So this pseudo-American ferments at the bottom of the Melting Pot, unassimilated to the end.

The fact remains that notwithstanding its material adaptation, the original traits of the race persist and leave their indelible mark on every thought and action. Though they may be willing to sacrifice everything, even their mysticism, and be ready to adopt that dreary social pragmatism which is the real religion of modern America, yet these children of Abraham cannot escape the spirit of their ancestors, for they are infinitely more religious than the Americans. Their outlook may have coincided for a moment with Protestantism, but the soul of their religion has survived untouched. During the last twenty years of the nineteenth century, when the great influx of Russian Jews was commencing, there were already in America many distinguished Israelites who had adapted themselves to American culture; but many of them who had thrown off their religion were now brought back into the fold. Today the mystical traditions of orthodoxy have been reimposed in

modern form on those Jews whose religion had become
bitter and dry through the taint of their contact with the
Christians. Even in the lowest grades of society we come
across these irreconcilables, who attempted to become a part
of western civilization only to repudiate it in the end.

The knowledge that the Americans have encountered
something which they cannot assimilate has long stirred up
an anti-Semitic feeling which accounts for the aloofness
of the Jew in his American environment. First, the Gentile
fears, and with reason, the competition of the Jew in business, and despises him as a matter of course, although
regularly at the end of every month the balance-sheet shows
that the Jew has outstripped him again. This is doubtless
the result of his commercial astuteness, but it is due also
to his insatiable ambition and to his business activity, which
at times amounts to frenzy. The Americans, especially in
New York—that new Jerusalem—have a grudge against
him, because he forces them to keep up with his feverish
pace.

If the pace set by the Wandering Jew is killing in business, in intellectual circles it is far worse, for there the
American is decidedly not at his best. Left to himself, the
100 per center is not given to brain-work. In the universities he prefers to go in for sport and flirtations, and in
the libraries all he wants is light reading. Now the Jew, on
the contrary, in the same universities and the same libraries,
is deep in some serious book on science, sociology, or
philosophy—it isn't a fair fight, they protest!

Just what use does he make of his alert intellect, this
descendant of the prophets, who according to Péguy has
never stopped reading for two thousand years? He has a
mind that can neither be tamed nor disciplined, for he questions everything for his own particular ends. This is just
what the Americans do not want. They require a type of
mind that can be dealt with collectively and fitted into an

organization in which the individual is asked to make his own personality subservient to the common good. The Jew on the contrary is an intellectual revolutionary to the point of suspicion, and therefore in spite of their apparent similarity when they first come in contact, the Protestant and the Jew soon diverge. In spite of the great value of Jewish collaboration, the Protestant American has adopted a hostile attitude which has developed into an anti-Semitic movement.

In this brief review of the thirty millions of foreigners who have settled in the United States in the past century, we have presented the problem in its simplest aspect. In actual practice their assimilation is a process of extreme complexity which extends over several generations and involves a whole series of stages. The rate at which the different races advance varies according to their ethnic temperaments and their adaptability, so that they lie strung out along the route like the seeds thrown by the runners in the legend of the Horatii and Curiatii. If this upward movement were not continuous, or if it were blocked at any point by events or legislation (as in the case of the coloured races), the American social system would be more closely allied to the castes of India than to the civilization of Western Europe, where ethnic equality is the rule.

The movement of adaptation is continuous, however, varying only in intensity and speed, so that the relationships of the different ethnic groups are in a constant state of flux. The last to arrive must do all the dirty work and be content with squalid houses in the poor quarters of the large cities. One finds them huddled miserably together in the slums of New York, Boston, and Chicago. In the second generation the children of these immigrants go to the public schools, speak fluent English, and so advance a step in the social scale. They master new trades and obtain positions vacated by others who have also moved up. At the same time with their increased wage they improve their standard of living, and migrating into other sections of the city, they install themselves in homes that their parents could never have afforded. They are soon unrecognizable under their American veneer, and frequently they even modify their names to obliterate all traces of their origin. So the French-Canadian Boulanger becomes Baker, and the Italian Canelli is changed surreptitiously into Connolly.

I have often thought that the best way to describe this social evolution would be to write a novel of the type that was popular during the last century. I would call it *The History of a House,* and I would make an old house in New York or Philadelphia tell the story of the extraordinary guests it had sheltered, with their foreign languages, their strange customs, their family ceremonies, and the intimate dramas of their transplanting from the Old World. What a fantastic procession it would be—Irish in 1840, Germans in 1850, Italians in 1880, Austrians, Hungarians, Russians, Poles, and Syrians in 1900, and negroes in 1920!

Although we have traced it fairly closely over three-quarters of a century, the psychology and physiology of this process of Americanization seems more baffling than ever. To describe its outward and visible form is easy enough, but can we discover what is really going on in the subconscious minds of these people, and how far there is any real absorption? How much is only the mingling of the newcomers with the original inhabitants?

Apart from the majority of Protestants and many Scandinavians who adapt themselves at once, as well as the more enthusiastic of the Jews, the generation that debarks is hardly Americanized at all. Yet such sudden wholesale transplanting is not accomplished without serious dislocation. Although the old ethnic stem still sprouts a few leaves, it has been severed from its roots; for traditions are sacrificed that cannot be revived. This explains the extraordinary rebirth of these immigrants who cross the Atlantic and from the American point of view it is a sign of progress; for daily habits do not survive this grafting and the newcomer slips into his place like an article made by mass production. It is also the cause of the serious psychological troubles that are now confronting the educational experts. The children, either born in America or brought over as infants, literally breathe in from the first the atmosphere of the New World; and in spite of their home influences, they nearly always refuse to speak the language of their parents. At heart and sometimes even openly, they despise their parents for their old-fashioned clothes, for the ridiculous way they wear their hair, and for their language, which the young folks soon no longer understand. They simply must conform to the average standard with that reverence for uniformity that is common to Americans and children. It is almost a tragedy, this rupture of moral contact between parents and children, where the younger generation despises the culture of the old.

What is the moral value of this second generation? As a rule the first has given no trouble, for the immigrant is submissive; he respects the law and brings with him a discipline ripened by centuries. As for his children, we soon see what they have learned—the manners of the New World, a passion for material independence, and a standard of living that leads them utterly to despise worn-out old Europe. The danger lies in the fact that they have absorbed the boundless ambition of the Americans, without acquiring at the same time the traditional stolid restraint of the Puritan conscience.

The third generation, they will tell you, is thoroughly Americanized, and as a matter of fact it is scarcely distinguishable. Yes, but its Americanism is morally shrunk in comparison with the vigour of the pioneers and is sadly lacking in tradition. The immigrants and their sons have lost the rich heritage of magnificent civilizations, and the amputation has been clean and merciless. As the immigrants are usually of the lower classes, one might say they had little to lose. In fact, this is the opinion of the Americanizers, and most of the Americanized as well. Both despise old types of culture, and are ready to erase them without remorse in the conviction that they are working for progress. The conception held by many of these races, that the family is the responsible social unit, means nothing in America. Nor are they impressed with the philosophy of life that arises from prolonged and intimate contact with the soil, and produces such a personality as the French farmer, with centuries of experience and ironic wisdom behind him. Such things carry little weight, for without the slightest trace of conscious imperialism, the American acts from an honest conviction that the Protestant's is the better civilization, and that it is his duty to impose it on the foreigners for their own good.

The result of this cleavage with the past is a leaning toward Nietzsche-ism without the balance of Anglo-Saxon civic virtue. An increasing quantity of human material is being produced that lacks alike the sturdy morality of the early Americans and the European tradition of brilliant achievements. From this we can trace three different reactions which mark the different stages of the racial crisis: First, when the immigrants, by sheer weight of the numbers that are not amenable to assimilation, change the old American atmosphere until the early inhabitant feels he is literally turned out of his home, as has been the bitter experience of the New Englander. Secondly, when the foreigner is absorbed superficially, but by reason of Catholicism or heredity retains at heart his own moral and political ideas; and as a result, the old nationalist community reacts instinctively, because these new citizens do not reflect their ideas. Finally, when the foreigner on the strength of his naturalization papers insists that he is absolutely American, although he is fully conscious of his origin, and is not willing to give up his religion or intellectual and artistic traditions.   Then the real American wonders uneasily if the inspiration of the United States is really no longer Protestant, but is instead Catholic, Jew, Latin, Slav, and Heaven knows what besides!

Here we have a people who feel themselves betrayed from within, trying to refresh themselves at the well-springs of their moral and national vitality.   I propose to study the principal aspects of their resistance to foreign domination, which corresponds to a phase—temporary, possibly, but significant—in the history of the United States.

CHAPTER III

IF we wish to understand the real sources of American inspiration, we must go back to the English Puritanism of the seventeenth century, for the civilization of the United States is essentially Protestant. Those who prefer other systems, such as Catholicism, for example, are considered bad Americans and are sure to be frowned on by the purists. Protestantism is the only national religion, and to ignore that fact is to view the country from a false angle.

We must go even further, and realize that America is not only Protestant in her religious and social development, but essentially Calvinistic. In spite of the influence of the German immigration, the attitude of the country is the very antithesis of Lutheranism. According to Luther all worldly laws are bad, and nature is given over to injustice and evil. In worldly matters in which the state operates, force is the only law; and therefore the New Testament cannot be applied literally. The saints must live in the world as best they can and must carefully protect the purity of their spiritual lives. In earthly matters it is the prince who has received from God the right to wield the sword and to conduct the affairs of state in accordance with the rules of Providence, which, however, have nothing to do with the moral law. The Christian is able to serve the state in temporal matters, and yet retain the freedom of his soul. This conception is one of religious mysticism and political cynicism.

The Anglo-Saxon of Calvinist leanings regards such political morals as nothing short of scandalous. Calvin looked upon doctrines as a means to an end, and taught that

33

the duty of the individual was not to concentrate upon himself, but rather to co-operate in furthering the will of God in this world. Born anew through grace, the Calvinist has a mission to carry out; namely, to purify the life of the community and to uplift the state. He cannot admit two separate spheres of action, for he believes that the influence of Christ should dominate every aspect of life. He considers it of utmost importance that the virtuous should take their place in the life of the community as active Christians, whereas in former times they withdrew from the world in order to remain pure. What an amazing change from the quasi-mediævalism of Luther to the practical idealism of the American!

From this arises the feeling of social obligation that is so typically Anglo-Saxon. The idea that his personality is being constantly suppressed is almost painful to a Latin. He cannot comprehend the Calvinist point of view that the group and not the individual is the social unit and the foundation of the religious structure. On the other hand, in America those who follow lone trails are heartily disliked, for the weight of numbers, propriety, and all social forces compel submission to the community. Under such conditions liberty no longer seems to be the unquestioned right of man, and it only exists hemmed in by a network of moral regulations. It is not a question of liberty resisting authority, but rather of liberty undertaking to support authority—being first satisfied, of course, that the state is working for the Protestant conception of the Kingdom of Heaven on earth.

A Puritan democracy has duties as well as rights, and this is the essential difference between it and our Latin democracies, which are individualist and negative. A second difference which is not less important is the conception of the *élite*, taken in the etymological sense of the word; that is to say, of the moral aristocracy. Every one cannot be called to grace by predestination, for that is reserved for

the salt of the earth.   Judging from their sense of duty
toward society, the American Protestants are imbued with
a missionary spirit that is typically Anglo-Saxon.   Not only
do they believe that they have been called to uplift the outside world—a duty toward savages, negroes, and Frenchmen—but they also feel the need of home missions to
evangelize their own community through and through.   As
in England, it is this missionary spirit which animates the
crusades against cigarettes, alcohol, and the slums, and such
movements as feminism, pacifism, anti-vivisection, Americanization of immigrants, and even the gospel of eugenics
and birth control.   In fact, were it not for England, America
would have a monopoly of the passion for reform and uplift.
Every American is at heart an evangelist, be he a Wilson, a
Bryan, or a Rockefeller.   He cannot leave people alone, and
he constantly feels the urge to preach.   His good faith may
be incontestable and his efforts often magnificent, but one
is always aware of a certain moral superiority which is the
most unsympathetic of Anglo-Saxon traits.   His self-satisfaction as a member of God's elect is almost insufferable,
and so is the idea that his duty toward his neighbour
is to convert, purify, and raise him to his own moral
heights.

One of the results of this leaning toward social service
is that the Americans have lost all sincere convictions con-
cerning the equality of all men, for they undoubtedly despise
the blacks, the Mediterraneans, and many other races.
Though they insist that they believe in mankind from the
religious point of view, yet if you press the question, their
definition of mankind is very restricted.   Contrary to first
appearances, Protestantism seen from this angle is less
democratic than Catholicism, which in the United States,
at least, is inherently more human.   Indeed the ideas of
Calvin are fundamentally opposed to the Catholic doctrine
of the redemption of mankind, according to which Jesus
Christ did not die to save the chosen few, but for the sake

of the whole world. The universality of Catholicism is thus in marked contrast to the ethnic beliefs of these American Pharisees.

Luther instructed his followers to descend into the arena and dedicate their physical strength to the service of the state, but he did not stipulate that they should also bring their souls into the struggle. This reservation was important, for it did not allow the faithful to enjoy worldly goods and power with a clear conscience. Calvin, however, united religion and daily life for the first time since the days of the ancients, for, according to his creed, the better the faithful performed their daily task, the more they worked for the glory of God. Though the Catholic Church has always allied itself to riches, it has never held up wealth as a symbol of godliness, believing that the poor man can retain his nobility of soul, and possibly be even nearer to God. The Puritan on the contrary regards his wealth as an honour, and when he hoards up his profits, he says smugly that Providence has been kind. In his eyes and in the eyes of his neighbours, his riches become the visible sign of divine approbation, and in the end he cannot tell when he is acting from a sense of duty, and when from self-interest. In fact he has no wish to make any distinction, for he is accustomed to regard as a duty everything that is most useful to his own advancement. As a result of this more or less deliberate lack of psychological penetration, he does not even rise to the level of a hypocrite. This same confusion of thought is also found among nearly all English Protestants, and it is difficult to say whether it is astuteness or simply naïveté.

Under these conditions it is hard to distinguish between religious aspirations and the pursuit of wealth. In fact ever since the commencement of the splendid colonization which has created the United States of today, those virtues were magnified which best furthered physical endurance and material achievements, whereas those which led to calm mysticism were apt to be considered useless and even harmful. Thus religion came to be partially materialized, and the church grew accustomed to expending her forces for the benefit of production, although the vocabulary of the mystic still survived, along with the habit of attacking all problems from a religious point of view. Money thus became not only the symbol of creative power, but a sort of moral justification. Efficiency was looked upon as a Christian virtue, and one could no longer separate what had been accomplished for God from what had been contributed to the development of the country. The idea of service, which has become so popular in America, springs from the Puritanical idea of wealth sanctified by labour.

All the original Puritan characteristics still survive after three centuries among the Protestants, the lineal descendants of the Puritans, among most of the social reformers, and even among the Christian Scientists. But we must classify separately, as representing an entirely different tradition, the Lutherans, the Anglicans, and especially the Roman Catholics. Unfortunately it is impossible to give exact statistics to indicate the respective influence of the various groups; for though the frontiers of the Catholic Church are clearly defined, those of Protestantism are not.[1]

[1] The principal Protestant denominations in order of the number of their communicants are approximately as follows:

Methodists	8,433,000
Baptists	8,189,000
Presbyterians	2,509,000
Lutherans	2,466,000
Disciples	1,383,000
Anglicans (Episcopalians)	1,129,000
Congregationalists	858,000
Others	3,399,000
	28,366,000

There are many Christian Scientists in the wealthy districts of the big cities, but they have systematically kept apart, and do not publish any statistics of their membership.

According to the *Year Book of Churches, 1924–25,* there were, in the year 1923, 18,261,000 Catholic communicants and 28,366,000 Protestants, though the latter figure would be increased to almost 80,000,000 if we took account of the innumerable adherents who are in sympathy with Protestant ideals, though not officially registered as communicants.

The Methodists are numerous in the East, in the South, and in the Middle West, especially the Ohio Valley; the Baptists in the South and Southwest; the Presbyterians in the East and the eastern border of the Middle West, particularly in western Pennsylvania; the Lutherans in the German and Scandinavian districts of the Northwest; the Congregationalists in New England; the Anglicans in the East; the Disciples in Ohio and generally throughout the Middle West, and the Quakers in Pennsylvania, New Jersey, New England, and the Middle West. In general Protestantism dominates the South, the West, and the Far West, but less completely the Middle West and the northwest prairies. The Catholics, on the other hand, are numerous and powerful wherever foreign immigrants have accumulated as in the cities of the Northeast and the Middle West, and also in Louisiana, Wisconsin, Montana, California, and along the Mexican frontier.

In general, the Anglicans belong to the wealthy upper classes, while the Methodists are the well-to-do tradespeople whom God has been pleased to bless in business. The Baptists are smaller folk, without prestige, who live in the third-rate towns; the Presbyterians and Congregationalists are the descendants of the New England intellectuals of fifty years ago; the Lutherans, the timid and suspicious Germans; the Quakers, the solid bourgeois with money-bags and scrupulous consciences; and finally the Catholics are foreigners 'inferior' in race and class, and accordingly despised by the Anglo-Saxon Pharisees.

In order to appreciate the influence of Protestantism in

this confusion of sects, we must not look at it as a group of organized churches, for its strength lies in the fact that its spirit is national. To make lists of communicants and clergy means very little, for the true Protestant does not admit in their strictest sense either the sacrament, the priesthood, the ritual, or the dogma of ecclesiastical authority— in a word, he cannot tolerate priestcraft. As an institution, American Protestantism is lax, extraordinarily tolerant and never jealous; but as a moral and missionary force, on the contrary, many of its characteristics are the very opposite of our French Protestantism in that it is the religion of the majority, a national religion, and is subject accordingly to the classic temptations of all state churches.

Protestant thought in the United States is divided into two schools, Fundamentalist and Modernist, which correspond more or less to the orthodox and liberal divisions of the French Reformed Church. This controversy between the letter and the spirit is not new, but dates back in both the New and Old World to the middle of the nineteenth century. On the American side of the Atlantic, however, the Modernists have been so active since the War, that the Fundamentalists have had to defend themselves with an ardour that cannot be imputed altogether to religious motives. This in fact is the very heart of the American religious problem.

American Modernism has freed itself to a remarkable degree from dogma, ritual, and the literal interpretation of the Scriptures; in fact, from all formalities extraneous to purely religious thought. It is no exaggeration to say that those who come under its influence soon abandon the the last shreds of belief in dogma or in direct revelations from God. This phenomenon is all the more surprising on the part of a people whose churches are so closely associated with their daily lives. Modernism is, however, strictly in line with Puritan traditions, for its chief preoccupation is moral sincerity and social welfare. It insists

that Christianity should come first all through life, and that
it should adapt itself to the conditions of the time, in order
to fill its appointed *rôle* as guiding factor of the community.
They contend that if religion does not occupy itself with
morals or even politics, it cannot possibly justify itself to
the conscientious, and surely this is more important than
formal belief in hidebound doctrines! Personally I think
that it is owing to this penetration of religious thought into
every-day life that America feels she is superior to the
Orient.

This supremacy of the conscience is the essence of religion
in its purest form. Nevertheless Modernism conceals certain dangers from which the Puritan Fathers were not
exempt, in that it emphasizes the confusion of spirituality
and worldliness. The American is entirely at ease only
in practical matters, for he is completely out of his element
when he is not active, and Pragmatism expresses his possibilities and his limitations to perfection. Simply to exist
is not enough; he must always express himself in some
tangible way. In the study of science he values laboratory
equipment rather than research, and in religious matters
he is more interested in the bricks with which he builds his
church than in prayers and meditation within it. The
inevitable association between religion and his other activities ends by Christianizing his daily life, but it also runs
the risk of bringing materialism into the church. After
two weeks in the United States one is already aware of this
collaboration, which permits a certain type of Modernism
to dominate religion. One often hears it said that a good
Christian makes the best citizen, as he is more efficient in
the office and the factory. From this it is only a step to
the thought that in order to produce more the country must
become more Christian, and after all this is really the doctrine of "big business."

Whenever a conflict arises between conscience and practical necessities, American optimism side-steps it, not by hypocrisy, but by admitting that it is normal and desirable that religion should be a factor in social progress and economic developments. Such conflicts do arise, when tender consciences question the motives of the powerful interests, but bitterness is generally avoided. When the spiritual *élite* take it upon themselves to face social or ethnic problems, to denounce scandals, or to insist that a solution must be in conformity with Christianity, obviously they cannot please everybody. The rich, for example, overwhelm the churches and the welfare organizations with their generosity; but later they claim the right to dictate their political activities. Social uplift naturally pleases the Christian capitalists only as long as they control it. They do not hesitate to reprove the religious leaders if they ever attempt to put in practice the more revolutionary doctrines of the New Testament, for they maintain that the church should not meddle with problems which it does not understand and is not equipped to solve; and immediately no more money is forthcoming! In America social reforms cannot be accomplished without funds; so we cannot logically conceive of a church which obeyed the dictates of Christianity without coming up against the ill will of Money. We can picture scrupulous souls in the near future undergoing the equivalent of the temptations of Christ. The Devil, a banker naturally, will conduct them to the top of a skyscraper, where he will spread out beneath their feet all the immense riches they can acquire to construct churches, schools, clubs, and hospitals—"All that I will give to you," Mephistopheles will say, "to use to the best of your ability for the benefit of social uplift; but only on the condition that you bow down and worship me." And if the good souls really wish to carry out their programs, they will bow down. But if they prefer to keep their spiritual liberty intact they will have to refuse, and then grapple with the fact that they must carry on in poverty.

Active Modernism finds its chief recruits in the eastern States among the vigorous rich manufacturers. To this attempt to attach the churches to the chariot of production, the South and West have replied by a revival of Fundamentalism, which is of course a reaction against other things as well. They are faithful to the literal interpretations of the Scriptures, which they venerate almost more than God himself; for, like their fathers, they try to believe everything the Bible contains. They swallow without reserve the divinity of Christ, his miraculous birth, the perfect holiness of His life, His physical resurrection, His ascension into Heaven in a materialistic sense, His promise to return to earth again in the flesh, and for good measure they also accept the most impossible miracles of the Old Testament. They question nothing, for if they once began, where would they end? During the Dayton trial William Jennings Bryan, whose authority as the popular leader of the Fundamentalist movement was boundless, replied as follows to the ironical questions put to him by counsel:

Q. "Do you claim that everything in the Bible should be literally interpreted?"

A. "I believe that everything in the Bible should be accepted as it is given there."

Q. "But when you read that Jonah swallowed the whale— or that the whale swallowed Jonah—excuse me, please, how do you literally interpret it? . . . You believe that God made such a fish, and that it was big enough to swallow Jonah?"

A. "Yes, sir. Let me add, one miracle is as easy to believe as another."

Q. "Perfectly easy to believe that Jonah swallowed the whale?"

A. "If the Bible said so."

There were ten newspaper columns in this strain. The sceptical lawyer thought that he was holding Bryan up to ridicule, whereas he was only giving him a martyr's halo in the eyes of millions of admirers. They might laugh at the Fundamentalists in the East, and caricature them, but in the South he was taken seriously.

These Fundamentalists come exclusively from the Protestant sects, in particular from the Baptists of the country districts and the little towns which have been peopled for generations by the old type of Americans. In the South, where they have been soured by fifty years' fear of the negro, they are especially numerous, and also in the Puritan colonies of the West. This does not mean that the western States are backward from the economic point of view, on the contrary, life there is very energetic, for the days of the pioneers are only just over, and initiative and progress are sought after and admired there more than anywhere else. But unfortunately the pioneer has no leisure to think, although he manages to read his fifty-page newspaper! All his energies are concentrated on material accomplishments, but in spiritual matters he is conservative. Though superficially free, he is mentally bound; hence the peculiar paradox that, though he sincerely believes that he is leading the world into the future, in reality he belongs to the past.

The actual form of the Fundamentalist movement is interesting. From the religious point of view it is essentially a reaction against the growing influence of new thought imported from abroad, such as the scientific scepticism of Europe. Popery, and also any philosophies which sow doubt among the younger generation, are looked upon as a danger to the integrity of Protestant traditions. Confronted with these abominations, they turn back to the Bible, the Holy Book of their ancestors, which is still the rallying-point of the nation. From the moral point of view Fundamentalism preaches a similar reaction against the customs of the present

century, which, dangerous in themselves, become doubly so
if they are imported from abroad.   In their struggle to
preserve the old moral tone, the bigotry and zeal of the
ministers, especially the Baptist and Methodist, know no
bounds.   They give vent to furious diatribes against the
modern Babylons of New York and Paris, and with rage
they lay their curse on wine, dancing, and cigarettes.   In
the last analysis their following comes from the lower
middle class in the South and the West, who are generally
Baptists or Methodists, sometimes Presbyterians or Congregationalists.   They are the people who are opposed to
the eastern cities and the financial domination they stand
for.

The Fundamentalists are the spiritual descendants of
Cromwell, and they have remained faithful to his inflexible
religious bigotry, until morally they are more insular than
the English themselves.   European visitors rarely encounter
them, for they stand aloof, obstinate and suspicious.   The
Ku Klux Klan expresses both their prejudices and their
fears.   They are instinctively hostile to the broader conceptions of social welfare, for they are hypnotized by the literal
preservation of dogma, by the defence of old-fashioned customs against those of today, and by a vague fear of an intrusion into the negro question of the conscientious scruples
of the North.   In their objection to the socialization of the
church, the Fundamentalists of the South and the East are
in sympathy.   The latter, though less numerous, actually
comprise two hundred of the most bigoted millionaires in
New England, who prefer that religion should not meddle
with business.   Though for different reasons, they both
desire that the Protestant Church should not drift toward
the engrossing preoccupation of social problems.   There are
always certain questions that they feel should not be tackled.

What with the ice-bound faith of the Fundamentalist
and the nebulous beliefs of the Modernist, it is difficult to

know where to look for the true spirit of American Protestantism. Can we even legitimately express it in the singular?
In spite of all these contradictions, an essentially American
view-point on religion does exist. The seventeenth century English Puritans brought with them the pessimistic
doctrine of original sin, and although the Fundamentalist
ministers still preach it, it obviously no longer harmonizes
with the general atmosphere. A hundred years of achievement crowned by magnificent material victories have inclined
the Americans to believe in man, though less in his original
virtue than in his power.

The mysticism of success is perhaps their genuine religion,
and with it is combined a certain guileless optimism, as
well as the utilitarian outlook of Bentham. Being perpetually in need of movement and progress, they unconsciously worship energy and life. For a century values
have steadily risen about them; so they believe naturally in
infinite progress and devote to its service all those homely
virtues which were bequeathed to them along with the moral
pessimism of the Puritans. Take for example the jargon
of the Rotary Club, those sanctuaries of "service." We
have *pep, punch, go, vigour, enterprise, red blood, he-man,
go-getter, high-powered*—expressions which invariably
exalt the vitality of the individual, in order to place it at
the service of the community, without, however, distinguish-
ing it from self-interest or personal profit. It is a strictly
utilitarian outlook, but it satisfies the naïve idealism of
the nation. It has been personified in the immortal Babbitt,
the Rotarian, who believed with all his soul that he was
serving the good of humanity by lining his pockets with
comfortable dollars.

Even their conception of Christ Himself has had to be
adapted to fit the scheme of things. The American Christ
is not the sentimental mystic of tradition, nor yet an apostle
of non-resistance as in Russia, nor—perish the thought!—a

revolutionary. He is a leader, a sort of superman. For some time it has been common to represent Him as the perfect type of useful citizen, an efficient producer, almost as a successful and honest business man. Some even look upon Him as a *booster*,[2] an amazing transformation, compared with the old Protestant dogma. He is no longer a Christ of sacrifices, but rather of moral energy, and the road to Heaven now lies less through redemption than through work—we might almost say social welfare!

This concentration on action is excellently demonstrated by the type of minister that is desired by the faithful. In the first place he must be young, and secondly a live wire, as the expression goes—a drawing-card to attract the crowd; not too proud, a *good mixer,* and able to break the ice. A mystic would be unappreciated, except possibly in a rich community tinged with Anglican snobbishness, where he would be installed in an elegant temple, if possible rather out of the ordinary. But in general they prefer their pastor to be a good practical man, efficient at raising money, in close contact with life, and even a little over-effusive in his cordiality.

The worldliness of this Protestantism and its pretensions to being a national religion reserved for the privileged few have antagonized many of its followers as well as its adversaries. They feel that something is lacking, almost the spirit of religion itself; for the cult has been reduced until it embraces little more than ethics. Others, and especially foreigners, look in vain for sympathy or pity in this intolerant code of morals, which leaves its mark on everything, right down to civic virtue. The Protestant churches are always complaining of the indifference of the masses; yet the mysticism of the faith healer makes numerous converts among these credulous people so lacking in critical faculty.

[2] A "booster" may be defined as an enthusiastic and optimistic citizen who believes in and works for the sensational development of his own favourite projects.

On the border-line of Puritanism and Protestantism are three churches notable for their resistance to the general tendency. First we have the Lutherans, owing to their timid doctrines, but more especially because their members are recruited from a race that is foreign to both British and Calvinistic traditions. The majority of these Lutherans co-operate with the other denominations only with considerable reluctance. The Modernists terrify them by the vagueness of their teachings, and they find the idea of a social church most unsympathetic, for they prefer not to mix politics and religion.

Secondly we have the Anglican church, which holds itself even more aloof, largely because its inspiration is not strictly Protestant. Its belief in the sacraments and the apostolic succession gives it a Catholic tinge, which is further emphasized by its ecclesiastical hierarchy. As in England, its right wing is at present distinctly intrigued by ritualism. In keeping with the desire for adoration, its churches are left open constantly for private prayer and meditation. Its leaders are artists whose appreciation of grandeur and solemnity leads to a combination of architectural beauty and impressive religious music. But the atmosphere is hardly American, for many British influences still persist. Out of three Anglican rectors in the United States, we can count on one being an Englishman, one a Canadian, and only one an American. London is the source of inspiration for this aristocratic clergy, who are often British in their traditions, their culture, and even in their physique. Their secret desire is to meet the Archbishop of Canterbury, and the greatest honour they can have conferred upon them is to be asked to preach at Westminster.

Yet in spite of all these traits which savour so much of the *ancien régime,* the Anglican cult has a singular attraction for the Americans. Ritual and vestments enjoy great prestige in this unpretentious community, just as religious poetry is most seductive in an atmosphere steeped with prosaic moralism. They are also attracted by the elegance and social status of the Episcopal Church, and its membership is frequently used as a stepping-stone to social success. It is interesting to note that the Methodists are leaning toward ritualism in certain directions, though the Baptists still maintain their harsh Fundamentalism unadulterated.

The Catholic Church, however, is the chief opposition to American Protestantism, for, besides its powerful vitality, which no doubt leads to excessive ambitions, it also has great religious prestige. There are many who still believe that the priest possesses mystic powers in spite of the efforts of a materialistic civilization to banish such ideas. In *Main Street,* Sinclair Lewis describes the railroad as the only romance of the drab inhabitants of the little prairie town, their only mystery besides mass at the Catholic church. What a significant remark! The Baptist ministers may detest such mysteries, but there are many religious sentimentalists in America who are still swept away by them; for it is quite possible for spiritual ecstasy to exist among those who are not seeking social advancement only. In this desert, what an oasis for the soul in search of relaxation!

From still another point of view, which is more difficult for Europeans to understand, Catholicism is a sort of refuge, because more than any other it is the church of the foreigner. This is because it is not regarded as the exclusive sanctuary of the *élite,* but much more humanly as a haven with a welcome for all. Even in spite of sincere protestations to the contrary, American Protestantism is still the religion of the Anglo-Saxon or the "superior" race. When it receives a foreigner into the fold it does not accept him as an absolute equal, and until he has been thoroughly Americanized he is never quite at ease among the privileged "brethren." The Catholic Church, on the other hand, ex-

presses without apparent ulterior motive the invocation of
Christ, "Come unto me, all ye who are weary and heavy
laden, and I will give you rest." It is no respecter of races
or persons. There is something extraordinarily human,
broad and unassuming about this great institution, where
the humblest, the sinner, and even the negro (almost!) can
communicate together. When one compares it with the
Protestant churches, one realizes how profoundly true is its
title, the Universal Church.

We are struck by the same repose when we consider the
attitude of the Catholic Church toward moral problems.
The solicitude of the priest is entirely concentrated on the
family, and through it on the education of the young; for
he champions the rights of the family against both the
state and the community. Any campaign against licence
or immorality is sure of his co-operation, providing it is a
question of protecting the home; but on the whole he is
immune from the urge for moral uplift. He adopts instead
an attitude of reserve that is akin to scepticism, for he is
indulgent toward the human weaknesses which he realizes
he cannot correct. In their attitudes toward moral perfection in the individual, the difference between the priest and
the minister is very interesting. The latter shows himself
to be a poor psychologist by his fanatic zeal for reforming
existing customs, and he denies the limitations of mankind
as obstinately as if he could not even see them. His childish
attitude is very far removed from the subtlety of the Jesuit
or the French moralist of the *Grand Siècle*.

In comparison with the naïveté of the reformer, the
Catholic priest seems to be endowed with years of secular
experience. He does not ask too much of frail humanity,
nor does he use up his reserve energy in demanding the impossible; for he knows beforehand just how much to expect,
and good opportunist that he is, he accepts the world as he
finds it. From the moral point of view there is nothing

noble in his attitude, and in this respect, he may even be
inferior in dignity to the Protestant; yet from the psychological point of view the priest is undoubtedly the more
civilized. It is also curious to note that his complete submission to an august and universal authority gives him a
certain poise, which troubled consciences deny to the
Fundamentalist ministers. Although Bryan believed that
the world was created in the year 4004 B.C.—or, in his
more liberal moments, in the year 15,000 B.C.—there are
many priests who admit quite frankly that they are evolu-
tionists. Also, they are nearly all against prohibition, and
in favour of a popular Sunday. In this they show that
they are realists, and furthermore, good politicians. The
pity for human weakness which results from their indul-
gence and scepticism is a trump card in a country where
the poor immigrants are looked upon as second-class citizens.

The Catholic Church is, therefore, the natural rallying-
point of those who are being jostled by Americanization,
and whose customs are being trodden under foot. In
championing them the Church runs the risk of going to
extremes in opposition to the genuinely humane spirit of
Americanization, and also of sharing the exclusiveness of
the races it is trying to protect, such as the Irish, the Germans, the Italians, the Poles, and the French-Canadians.
Thirty years ago that great statesman, Cardinal Gibbons,
steered the Catholic Church into a very different path. He
wished it to take its place among the national institutions
of the country, not as an Irish or German influence, but as
simply and essentially American. In the face of bitter
resistance he set out to break up the nationalist groups
within the Church itself, but since his death, Catholicism
has reverted to its previous type, and again become the religion of the foreigner. It is still divided into national
groups whose religious forms are often exotic or primitive.
The influence of the Irish together with the Germans pre-

dominates once more; for out of every five priests, at least three are of these two nationalities. Though the Catholic Church may be the champion of international liberalism elsewhere, in the United States it is linked up with the most fervid nationalist movements, such as the Irish. In the great cities of the East and Middle West, and even in the Far West, this traditional alliance between the Irish and the Catholic priests gives the religion a mediæval aspect which is both primitive and pathetic.

The faithful are astonishingly devout, but they are ruled by the fear of hell fire and by the priest, whom they endow with superhuman powers. One can scarcely say that he is venerated, but he is undoubtedly loved and obeyed implicitly; for his flock shut their eyes to his defects as a man. They shower the "poor father" with gifts, and he can ask for anything for his church or his political party. Similar traits are to be found among the other Catholic communities, German, Italian, or Polish, all of which are still close to the religious institutions of the past. Hence the foreign note which permeates the Catholic Church in the New World, where all its old political and religious roots are piously preserved. Boston is now a Catholic city, and when an Irish cardinal appears surrounded by his Celtic bishops who kiss his ring while the immense cosmopolitan crowd kneels along the route, the old-time Protestants look on uneasily as at some mysterious mediæval ceremony which they cannot understand. They had this same feeling of uneasiness during the lengthy and grandiose ceremonies of the Eucharistic Congress in Chicago in June, 1926; for in Protestant America these Roman customs absolutely cannot be assimilated either morally or socially.

The Catholic Church is thus a thing apart in the heart of the American body politic. It collaborates in its own time and in its own way, but in the long run it remains distinct and does not fuse. Further, it maintains a much stronger contact with Europe than does Protestantism. In France a pastor is generally better informed on foreign affairs than the average *curé;* but in the United States it is the reverse, for the ordinary minister, especially in the South and the West, is very provincial in his knowledge and experience. Even when he has travelled he is astonishingly ignorant of the Old World; indeed, of the outside world in general. Now the priest is quite different. He often speaks several languages, he goes to Rome at least once in his life and sometimes frequently, and he looks upon Europe as a centre of interest and attraction. He would have brilliant possibilities if unfortunately he did not have the soul of a politician and if his footsteps were not forever dogged by materialism.

For materialism in America is the real power that aids assimilation. The priest who tries to save his congregation from over-rapid Americanization is himself a complete American in his outlook on life and in his daily habits. He is a business man who administers his church on the same lines as the most practical Modernists. Not only in his parish but also in his religious institutions, he is accustomed to a degree of comfort which he does not intend to abandon. He insists on having central heating, baths, and Pullmans whenever he travels; and worse still, he has reached the point of despising his European colleagues for their poverty. "Poor fellow," he says, when he thinks of a country *curé* in France, "I am sorry for him!" With what disdain he compares the modest French presbytery with his own comfortable, well-ordered house, and his magnificent seminaries with all their modern luxuries which flaunt opulence at every turn. Like all good Americans, he believes that the intensity of religious life is measured by the cubic contents of church buildings, and meditation and mystical repose seem to him little better than morbid manifestations.

Thus, no matter where we turn, every-day materialism is

tending to encroach on spiritual life. Neither Protestantism nor Catholicism is threatened from without by aggressive disbelief, for the agnostics, though numerous, maintain the Protestant vocabulary and the Protestant outlook
on moral problems. They like its background and are not
hostile in any way. Neither is Catholicism likely to capture
the country in spite of its undeniable vigour, for it would
be prevented by secular traditions. In America the dominant
force that is threatening to carry everything before it,
Protestant, Catholic, and Jew, is the obsession for tangible
and material accomplishments. At times it seems as if the
object of religion were no longer to kindle mysticism in
the soul and spirit, but to enlist them and organize their
energies. In this it is the most powerful lever for production that the world has ever known.

CHAPTER IV

PURITAN RESISTANCE TO FREEDOM OF THOUGHT

THE future of American civilization would work out quite differently if the Lutheran or the Catholic conception of the state were to become more powerful than the Calvinist. The recent revival of Calvinism is a sign of its struggle to retain supremacy in order to safeguard the national customs from foreign influence. Countless crusades of every description are undertaken to convert the unbeliever and impose by force the conditions of life advocated by the majority. The minority, they say, have no right to complain, for it is being done for their good. In anything that touches the life of the community, the American is in reality a sort of "collectivist." He is as intolerant as a convert, especially since in religious matters he is an absolutist.

The opposition to this program comes either from scattered groups or from the business interests that are unable to fall in with the plans of the moralists, for business will not agree unless it either profits by these campaigns or guides them.

The Lutheran is out of sympathy partly owing to his hereditary respect for the state, and partly because he is determined to keep his German customs. The Catholic, and even at times the Anglican ritualist, is indignant that the state should submit to the dictates of individual consciences instead of to the church, for both prefer ecclesiastical authority and family traditions. The Irish colonies of the great cities have imported an original viewpoint of their own with regard to methods of government, and their half-Catholic, half-cynical outlook has become Americanized.

54

The English idea of government by disinterested gentlemen devoting themselves to the general good, which existed in America before the wave of Irish immigration of 1840, has not been entirely stamped out. The Irish newcomers, however, looked upon the state as the property of the people and especially as a means of obtaining the greatest possible advantages for themselves and their friends. A clash was inevitable between the ideals of the Puritan democracy and that extraordinary *pot-pourri* of farce, intrigue, hurly-burly, and whimsicality that goes to make up Irish politics, and which we must admit has, with all its faults, saved America from becoming as dreary as a prayer-meeting!

The reformers have had to reckon with still another power. In America as elsewhere business competition follows the natural laws of the struggle for existence. It does not conform to the standards of brotherly love, and all the "service" in the world cannot change it. Therefore nothing can be done against the wishes of the manufacturing interests, especially since they have been amalgamated and disciplined by the evolution of modern industry. When the religious *élite* wish to modify the national customs or preserve those that are dying out, they are accordingly careful not to antagonize the business world. Whenever the self-interest of the capitalist coincides with the idealism of the apostle, the "urge" for moral uplift becomes irresistible; for in America the wealthy are Christians, and nothing forbids Christians to be wealthy. In such an alliance lies the vital force of this community. Though it receives its inspiration from Puritan mysticism, it really expresses itself in material wealth, and it is not at all concerned with the liberty of the individual.

It is essential to realize that the liberalism of the eighteenth century philosophers counts for little among these social forces. It is sometimes held that American political thought is based on the Constitution, which was largely

drawn up by Jefferson and is very French in its disregard
of religion.   In actual fact, however, as may be seen by
the renaissance of Puritanism and the extraordinary irrup-
tion of the Ku Klux Klan, the political thought of the
Protestant masses is very different from that of Franklin,
Paine, Jefferson, or Washington.   Instead of going back
to these great liberals who were so close to secular thought,
we must turn rather to the narrow fervour of the Crom-
wellian Roundheads, who were totally opposed to such ideas.
If we overlook this, we are bound to be shocked when we
find in America certain intolerant aspects of Protestantism
which in Western Europe are now supposed to belong to the
past.

It is generally believed that the First Amendment to the
American Constitution in 1791 [1] assured complete religious
equality, and the Americans were free to choose God, Je-
hovah, or Buddha as they pleased, or even to maintain that
there was no God at all.   This, however, is not the case,
though it is true that there is no established church.   It
is nevertheless understood that America is a Christian nation and that Protestantism is the national religion.   This
distinction seems perfectly plausible to the Protestants, for
though their idea of a church is attenuated, their religious
zeal is vigorous in the extreme.   A Catholic who is not
used to separating religion from the church is apt to find
the distinction too subtle.   President Wilson in 1917 had
printed on the title page of the New Testament that was
distributed to the soldiers, "The Bible is the word of God.
I request you to read it," and the public did not feel that
he had exceeded in the least his *rôle* as head of a Christian
government.

In many States of the Union, Protestantism was the
established religion in the eighteenth century; for in those

[1] "Congress shall make no law respecting an establishment of religion,
or prohibiting the free exercise thereof."

days a nation without a religion was an anomaly. Jews, atheists, and in certain cases even Catholics did not enjoy the full rights of citizenship. Under these conditions the First Amendment did not really secularize the state, but aimed more at holding the balance between the numerous Protestant sects. What the American liberals desired both at that time and since was to divorce the state from the churches, but not to separate it from the Christian religion, and certainly not from Protestantism. The official indifference to religious matters which characterizes French secular thought seems scandalous even today to most Americans.

Even after a century of progress, laws protecting religion still exist in many States. To work on Sunday is everywhere an offence, and the unfortunate Jew, after having observed Saturday as his own Sabbath is obliged by the Christians to respect the next day as well. In North Carolina the law forbids the sale of gasoline during church hours. In Maryland it is a crime to utter impious words about our Lord. In New Hampshire it is heresy to deny the existence of God. In several States—Maryland, Arkansas, and South Carolina—Jews have not, for a long time, been accorded the same legal status as Christians. In Massachusetts in 1921 a Finnish lecturer who had mocked the Bible was condemned as follows under the Blasphemy Act:

"The religion of Christ is the prevailing religion of this country and this State. . . . Congress and the State legislature open their sessions with prayer addressed to the God of the Christian religion. . . . Shall we say that any word or deed which would expose the God of the Christian religion or the holy scriptures to contempt and ridicule would be protected by a constitutional religious freedom? We register a most emphatic negative."

It is wrong, therefore, to speak of religious liberty or equality as traditionally American.

Christianity in its Protestant form is so closely woven into the whole fabric of society that it is impossible to conceive of a separation, even suppose it were desired. The recent passage of a law in the State of Tennessee, forbidding the teaching of evolution in the public schools, and the famous trial which resulted in 1925 from the violation of this law are not isolated and interesting facts, but are quite in line with the traditions of secular legislation. The intolerance thus denoted is not simply a relic of the past, but a reflection of present-day sentiments and of a type of nationalism that cannot distinguish between patriotism and religion.

In the stubbornly insular State of Tennessee on the western slope of the Alleghanies are some of the most backward people in the South. Its population consists of honest, frugal farmers of pure Anglo-Saxon origin who have preserved their Protestant faith on ice. Dayton, where the trial took place, is little more than a village, having at most a few thousand inhabitants, all eminently respectable. Their ideas of the world are narrow, for they are not intellectual; neither have they travelled. On the other hand they are anything but fools. They are the prototype of millions of other Americans in the Mississippi valley who live in hundreds of other Daytons, and whom we of the Old World can never hope to meet. One point, however, must be noted: in Dayton there are no Catholics, no Jews, and no Anglicans. Every one belongs to the Protestant churches, of which two are Methodist, two Baptist, one Presbyterian, and one Christian Brotherhood. All the social life of the town is centred around these churches, and nine-tenths of the population turns to them for recreation and distraction, for the poetic relaxation of which every one feels the need, and indeed for all that art, music, and conversation can give in such an atmosphere.

What a light the trial sheds on this reservoir of Methodist emotions, preserved intact in this far-off county a hundred and fifty years after the death of Wesley! Under the direction of the Fundamentalist ministers, who preached mediæval dogmas with the fervour of the Inquisition, the little community obstinately shielded itself behind the Bible to avoid the contamination of modern ideas and foreign influences. The eastern States, with their Catholics, Jews, and foreigners, were almost as abominable in their eyes as decadent Europe; and they felt that they must at all costs avoid contagion. We can easily see how the people of Tennessee have remained impervious to outside influence. They believe themselves to be legally masters in their own house, and they intend to worship God in their own way without advice. Both the Federal and their own local State Constitution forbid favouritism in the schools toward any one church to the detriment of the others; so no genuine religious teaching can be given by the State, although the majority undoubtedly wish to legalize their own faith.

Now at long last they hear tell in Tennessee of the doctrine of evolution, and they consider it dangerous to their faith. Darwin's works are publicly burned in the Mississippi valley by Baptist ministers assisted by enthusiastic crowds. Evolution is considered scandalous and is cursed by ministers who preach the physical resurrection of the body, the reality of hell fire, and literal belief in the book of Genesis. The South has been converted to such orthodox views for reasons of its own, which touch it very closely. If the monkey can become a man, may the negro not hope to become white? The Southerners prefer to believe that the various species have been fixed once and for all, by divine wisdom, at the level that Providence has decreed.

As the Fundamentalist sects control the Tennessee legislature, it was only natural that they should profit by the fact to forbid legally any teaching in the public schools of theories contradicting their particular interpretation of the

Scriptures. Under their influence the following text was adopted:

"Be it enacted by the general Assembly of the State of Tennessee, That it shall be unlawful for any teacher in any of the universities, normal and other public schools of the State, which are supported in whole or in part by the public school funds of the State, to teach any theory that denies the story of the Divine creation of man as taught in the Bible, and to teach instead that man has descended from a lower order of animals."

In the newspapers of the time we find John Washington Butler, the proposer of this law, described as a man of "solid physical stature, slow in movement and in words, burnt as brown as an Indian by working in the fields, and above all full of self-confidence." And the paragraph concludes: "These people, who fear God, do not doubt themselves." When he brought in his bill, Butler simply hoped to defend his faith, nothing more. "I know nothing of evolution," he said, "but I have read in the papers that boys and girls have come home from school and told their parents that all that is contained in the Bible is nonsense. For myself I think that all right-minded people believe in the Bible."

John Thomas Scopes, professor of biology in the Thea County High School at Dayton, was guilty of teaching his pupils that man was evolved from a lower species of animal. He thus came under the displeasure of the law, and the State of Tennessee initiated the prosecution. It was upheld by the great popular champion of Fundamentalism, William Jennings Bryan, former candidate for the presidency of the Republic, and Secretary of State under President Wilson. The trial was like a regular circus performance and was attended by fervent crowds. To it came celebrated lawyers, countless experts, scientists who had been dragged from their laboratories for the purpose, and witnesses from every corner of the country. To improve matters it was July, and in the South the weather was as hot as an oven. With the exception of two, the jurymen were all farmers of the old type. According to the papers, the majority of them wore belts; for suspenders, that hallmark of the European intellectual, upheld the trousers of only a small minority—no doubt about this, for every one was in shirt-sleeves, including the lawyers, the jury, the judge himself, and even the ministers who inaugurated each session by prayer. He may be narrow as regards dogma, but the God of the Americans is certainly liberal in matters of style! A delighted America saw herself portrayed to the life in the naïve discussion in which the *vox populi* was called upon to pronounce in defence of the faith.

When we study the opposing theses of this extraordinary trial, we are at the very heart of the struggle that is perpetually recurring between the tyrannical ambitions of the majority and the liberal attitude of the minority in defence of their rights. The desire of the churches to obtain the sanction of civil authority for their dogmas is as old as the hills, and when the Fundamentalist Bible was installed as the official fountain of truth in the public schools, it was after all exactly what local public opinion and the authors of this law desired. If one reads the declarations of Bryan, that religious demagogue who throughout the trial was the faithful interpreter of these ideals, it is obviously hopeless to look there for any separation of church and state.

"Power in this country," he declared, "comes from the people; and if the majority of the people believe that evolution breaks down religious faith and threatens Christianity, they have the right to demand that it be suppressed or at least confined to the little group of research men, who may study it as a theory not yet proven. The only morality comes from the

Bible, all our institutions and our social life are founded on an implicit belief in it, and without that belief there is no ground on which moral teaching may be founded."

Far from being a dispute over dead constitutions, texts protecting minorities, or the philosophic liberalism of the eighteenth century, this was a burning question to these simple folk who dreaded lest their faith might be contaminated by agnosticism. The great Fundamentalist leader stirred them to the core when, with arms extended as on the cross, his eyes raised to Heaven, he cried pathetically, "Would they have me believe that I was once a worm and writhed in the dust? Will they take from me my hope of a hereafter? I want to go beyond this world, to where there is eternal happiness for me and others!"

The Attorney General, who had been elected by the people, went him one better, but he fully represented them when he said: "When science treads upon holy ground, then science should invade no further. . . . They say it is a battle between religion and science. If it is, I want to serve notice now, in the name of the great God, that I am on the side of religion."

Advertisements plastered all over the walls of Dayton during the trial tersely summed up the popular point of view: "Shall we tax ourselves to damn our children?" The defence hadn't a hope in the world.

They began by contesting the use of public authority for sectarian ends, maintaining that it was a breach of the principle of the separation of church and state. They argued that no legal authority, no matter what it might be, had the right to impose religious conditions on the exercise of a public function. To consecrate a dogma or even an interpretation of the Bible by means of legislation was not in accordance with the Constitution of Tennessee, as established in 1790 for which the Jefferson Constitution of

Virginia had been used as model.   At first the defence maintained this thesis brilliantly.   Soon, however, unable to resist the insidious atmosphere of the trial, they allowed themselves to be drawn into religious controversy.   Using all their skill to prove that evolution was not contrary to the Bible, they pleaded that their client had not violated the law. Although their best plan would have been to contest the bigotry and intolerance of the law as being unconstitutional and anti-American, in the end they practically accepted it by trying to exonerate him on the ground that he had not violated it.

When the discussion drifted into theology, the real character of the trial was shown to be religious rather than judicial.   In order to succeed or obtain a hearing in such an atmosphere of blind faith, every one had to prove himself a true believer.   Even the Court, although a State institution, was not neutral in this respect.   Every session began with prayer, and its impartiality consisted in asking first a Fundamentalist minister and then a Modernist to invoke the Almighty, each side officiating according to a sort of proportional representation.   When one of the lawyers began to be a bit bored by the length of these insidious and demagogic prayers, which in truth were addressed more to the jury than to the Creator, he proposed that they should be suppressed.   He was firmly put in his place by the Attorney General: "I find it necessary to advise you, in order to govern your conduct, that this is a God-fearing country."

The crowd that filled the room was sulky and excitable, and it kept close watch on the infidels from New York.   A free-thought propagandist who was let in by mistake was conducted to the police station, but was released on condition that he would keep quiet.   Judge Raulston, who presided, was a genuine product of the Tennessee mountains. This lay preacher lost no opportunity of affirming, with the full authority of the bench, his respect for the Bible and

the faith.   Before such a tribunal the position of an atheist
would indeed have been enviable!   Though Europe may
have laughed and the Atlantic States made sheepish excuses
for this outburst of fanaticism, the impression caused in
the South and West was tremendous.   When Bryan died,
struck down in the middle of the trial by a cerebral hem-
orrhage, it was as a saint and martyr that they conducted
him to the tomb.

In the end Scopes was found guilty, and so he should
have been; for he had undoubtedly broken the law.   The
real problem is whether the law in question is constitutional.
That has yet to be decided by the Supreme Court of Tennessee, and finally by the Supreme Court of the United
States.   Following in the wake of Tennessee, Mississippi
passed a law forbidding the teaching of evolution, and a
similar resolution was adopted by the Florida legislature,
while other States show tendencies to work in the same
direction.   If this current of opinion becomes general,
will it not threaten all freedom of thought?   The rampart
which protects such freedom is simply a text in the Constitution, drawn up over a century ago, and though it is
scarcely probable that it will be abrogated or amended, who
knows how judges may not interpret it under the pressure
of heated public opinion?

If it can be made a crime today to teach evolution in the
public schools, why should such an interdiction not be extended to private institutions tomorrow?   Will not the very
existence of free schools be threatened by sectarian majorities intent on moral unity and impatient of any deviation
from it?   A law in the State of Oregon, passed in 1922
but later declared unconstitutional by the Supreme Court,
shows the menace clearly.   It also exposes the existence at
the other end of the country of the same intolerance as in
Tennessee.   Oregon represents the centre of Anglo-Saxon
Puritanism in the Northwest.   In contrast to the persistent

Liberalism of the exotic and charming San Francisco, the nationalism of Portland and Los Angeles is very extreme. The revivals of Billy Sunday, the evangelist, not to mention prohibition, find a fertile soil in both cities. Two Puritan migrations from the Mississippi valley made for these points, one in the second half of the nineteenth century going to Oregon, and one in the beginning of the twentieth century toward Southern California. Though in appearance more modern than the people of the Alleghanies, we find here the same bias, the same fears, and the same religious intolerance.

By popular initiative Oregon passed a law in 1922 declaring that all children between the ages of eight and thirteen years had to be educated in the public schools, although it meant the suppression of private elementary education. The inspiration of this measure appears to be astonishingly like those of the anti-evolutionists of Tennessee. In Oregon they wish to use the public schools, which are controlled by the Protestant majority, to protect from Catholic, Jewish, and even Lutheran influence that portion of the younger generation which for religious or ethnic reasons has not been assimilated with sufficient rapidity. A pamphlet published at the time of the vote by the initiators of this law gives their reasons without beating about the bush:

"Our public schools . . . are the creators of true citizens by common education, which teaches those ideals and standards upon which our government rests. Our nation supports the public school for the sole purpose of self-preservation. The assimilation and education of our foreign-born citizens in the principles of our government, the hopes and inspiration of our people, are best secured by and through attendance of all children in our public schools. We must now halt those coming to our country from forming groups, establishing schools, and thereby bringing up their children in an environment often antagonistic to the principles of our government. Mix the children of the foreign-born with the native-born, and the rich with the poor. Mix those with prejudices in the public school melting pot for a few years while their minds are plastic, and finally bring out the finished product—a true American."

This is the classic argument against allowing two types of youth to develop. It is with growing impatience that the true Americans tolerate the separate point of view that is being systematically encouraged by the Catholic Church, through the family and its own schools. Ranged against this determination to remain distinct though loyal is the full force of the free masons, the Protestant masses, and the Ku Klux Klan. If it were not for out-of-date constitutions upheld by the authority of the Courts, the organized majority would have demonstrated ere now as it did in Tennessee that unity comes before liberty.

The anti-liberal legislation of Oregon, Tennessee, and Mississippi is at once less dangerous legally and more dangerous actually than it appears at first sight to be. These bigoted outbursts are still scattered, and if it is finally decided that they are unconstitutional they will not survive, although of course similar laws may be enacted elsewhere, and judges under the pressure of public opinion may further weaken their timid resistance to such innovations. The real peril is that instruction of every kind will be constantly under suspicious supervision. It would not be so bad if education were superintended by professional inspectors whose competence and impartiality were assured. The supervision is more likely to be exercised by a hysterical public, extraordinarily lacking in critical sense, and always likely to be inflamed by some eloquent evangelist.

In the Fundamentalist States and in all the Protestant States generally, the schoolmaster is given very little rope, and even the universities do not escape pressure. In the case of State universities supported by public funds, the budget is at the mercy of the legislature; that is to say, of universal suffrage; and any unorthodox course of lectures runs the danger of being suppressed. In the independent universities there are always the trustees to be considered, and although these controllers of the purse-strings are generally well disposed, they have no marked leanings toward extreme ideas.

Under these conditions a liberally-minded professor who is anxious to teach what he believes to be the truth runs the risk of raising a scandal either in the local press or in the university itself, and so losing his appointment. In 1924, to take one example out of hundreds, the professor of biology at the University of Minnesota discussed the Fundamentalist theory of creation in his class and refuted it. The effect was immediate. Mr. Bryan hurried to the scene, and before a vast assembly of over 8,000 people in the largest auditorium in Minneapolis, he fulminated against the iniquitous doctrines of evolution and the godless professor who taught them. The newspapers, knowing their public, reproduced his speech *in extenso,* and so spread the message from one end of the country to the other. With the danger of such a campaign of indignation always imminent, the professors' hands are bound. They soon realize, not only from the atmosphere in which they live, but also from their immediate chiefs, that they are expected to be as conventional as possible. A good professor in the West or the South does not flaunt his independence of thought, and utters nothing that might offend the susceptibilities of the trustees of the university, the important manufacturers and bankers of the town, the ministers of the leading denominations, or the local Congressman.

Of course this may only be a passing phase in the history of the United States, but there is no doubt that at the present time the great Protestant majority is clinging to the old, old belief that has been disputed by philosophers throughout the ages, namely, that there is only one social truth, and unless every one accepts it the unity of the nation is imperilled. We thus have the extraordinary paradox of the descendants of English and Scotch Nonconformists being changed into the narrowest of conformists, and the United States becoming a country where a man who does not fall in line socially and morally runs the risk of not being allowed to express himself freely. In a word, a transformation of the rights of the individual is taking place under our very eyes. The principles of the freedom of speech, of the press, and of association, the inviolability of the individual and of the home, the right to be judged by a jury according to regular procedure, are all solemnly guaranteed by the Constitution, and were handed down to America as part of the sacred heritage of British freedom. Now, however, a new doctrine, vigorous but undefined, is trying to undermine them by teaching that the rights of the community are almost unlimited, if it is defending itself against alien ideas, or against a germ of dissolution threatening its integrity. For the past thirty years, and especially since the War, it is not only the liberty of speech and the press that has been dangerously censored, but even the liberty to unite and the elementary rights of the citizens against an arbitrary police.

The American Constitution still survives, however, without essential alteration, and its revered text upholds in writing the rights of the individual against the State. We must admit that the present tendency of public opinion is out of harmony with it on many points; for, aroused by the menace of foreign ideas, the people are preoccupied with the problem of assimilation and moral standardization. The letter of the law which restrains them was written at an earlier date, and it is doubtful whether the Constitution would be drawn up in the same spirit if it had to be done over again today.   Jefferson, that great liberal aristocrat whose vague theism has since been denounced as atheistic by generations of rural ministers, is less popular in the West at present than the Fundamentalist demagogue of Dayton.   If any relic of the Jeffersonian tradition still survives, it is to be found, strange to relate, in the democratic centres of the great eastern cities, for ethnic or religious minorities are always in favour of liberty although they may be without doctrinal convictions.   But what are we to think of a country of British origin where liberalism has to seek its champions among foreigners and Catholics?   The reason is clear enough.   In its pursuit of wealth and power, America has abandoned the ideal of liberty to follow that of prosperity.

CHAPTER V

PROHIBITION belongs to the same type of legislation as the law against the teaching of evolution, for both are measures of national moralization. Machiavelli says that a foreign population can easily be governed so long as no attempt is made to alter its customs, but in their dealings with people who differ from them, the true Americans admit of no such opportunism. They feel that their vocation is to "save" their neighbour, and that it is their special duty to impose Anglo-Saxon customs on foreigners; for they look upon assimilation almost as a form of conversion.

Every race establishes its own particular list of sins. In the United States the supreme abomination for years was sexual intercourse outside of marriage, while cigarettes, billiards, dancing, and drunkenness followed after in the maledictions of the Methodist and Baptist ministers, not to mention, of course, lying and stealing. Since the War, however, intemperance seems to have risen to first place among the anathema. The prohibition movement thus originated in the holy of holies. Hence its enormous force.

If, as Renan says, truth can only be expressed in the form of a dialogue, can we hope to do better than study the hysterical controversy going on between the Wets and the Drys? In its present form as a Federal law, prohibition is a result of the War, but under normal circumstances it is probable that it would have progressed to more rigid enforcement by means of local action without, however, arriving at total suppression all over the country. The new feature in the prohibition amendment is that the majority, having freely accepted it on their own account, decided to impose it upon unwilling minorities. The vote on the Eighteenth Amendment was in fact only the crowning act in a long series of preparatory victories, for, before attacking the Federal Constitution, the Prohibitionists had patiently besieged first the village, then the county and the city, and finally the State.

When the United States Congress voted in December, 1917, that prohibition should be extended to the whole territory, it had already been rigidly applied in twenty-seven States. Nine pioneer States had even adopted it prior to 1914. These were:

Maine   *Rural New England Puritans*
Kansas   *The heart of western Puritanism*
North Dakota   *Norwegian farmers*
North Carolina ⎫
Georgia   ⎪
Tennessee   ⎬ *Southerners who feared drunkenness among the negroes; also largely composed of Fundamentalists*
Mississippi   ⎪
Oklahoma   ⎪
West Virginia ⎭

Between 1914 and 1917 eighteen other States followed their example:

New Hampshire	Utah	Nebraska
Michigan	Washington	South Dakota
Indiana	Arkansas	Montana
Iowa	Alabama	Oregon
Idaho	South Carolina	Arizona
Colorado	Virginia	New Mexico

Between 1917 and 1920 the following associated themselves with the movement:

Ohio
Kentucky
Wyoming
Nevada
Texas
Florida

Thus by 1920, when the Eighteenth Amendment came
into force, thirty-three States had already gone dry on their
own initiative. They made up practically the whole of the
South and West, except for California and the German
region west of Chicago, covering in a general way the entire area under the old-time American and Protestant influence.

The states in which either the majority or part of the
population remained under a wet régime were only fifteen
in number:

Massachusetts ⎤ *Industrial New England, overrun with Irish,*
Connecticut   ⎬   *French Canadians, Latins, and Slavs*
Rhode Island ⎦

New York   ⎤
New Jersey   ⎥
Pennsylvania ⎬ *Catholic and Jewish aliens of all races*
Illinois   ⎦

Missouri   ⎤
Minnesota ⎬ *Germans and Scandinavians*
Wisconsin ⎦

California   *Cosmopolitan and Catholic influence*
Louisiana   *French Creoles*
Maryland   *Catholic*

Vermont   ⎤   *Almost dry already*
Delaware ⎦

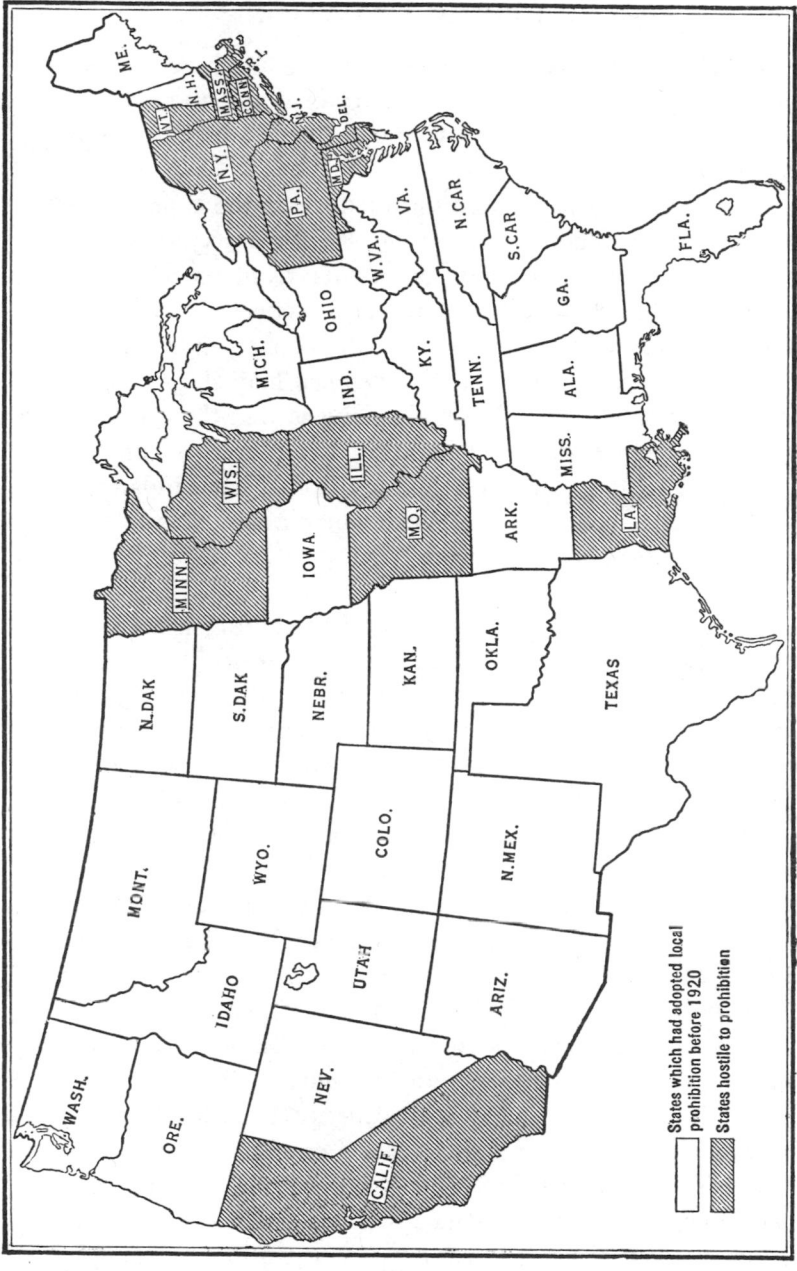

FIG. II.—LOCAL PROHIBITION BEFORE THE ENFORCEMENT OF THE EIGHTEENTH AMENDMENT (1920).

States which had adopted local
prohibition before 1920

States hostile to prohibition

Except for the last two States these regions have all been invaded by foreigners, and the Puritan domination of the masses has been replaced by Catholic, Jewish, and Lutheran influences.

This chart of the prohibition territory at the time of the inception of the new régime is most instructive, in that it emphasizes how far prohibition results from the clash between the old inhabitants and the new, between Protestants and Catholics, and finally between the country-side and the cities (as would be apparent on a detailed map showing prohibition by counties). The main thing is that the centre of gravity of aggressive Protestantism has moved during the latter part of the nineteenth century from New England to the great open spaces of the West, where a new "God's own people" carries on the severe traditions of their Boston ancestors.

To account for the fervour of the Prohibitionists we must of course realize what drunkenness means in the United States. The climate, though wearing in the long run, is dry and stimulating, and therefore permits no liberties to be taken with alcohol. The humid and oppressive atmosphere of the British Isles requires a daily pick-me-up in order to keep the people up to a normal level of vitality. In America, however, there is not a shadow of excuse to add a coefficient to the already high-pitched atmosphere. True, the American is perpetually thirsty, and he rushes at a glass of ice-water like a dog into a brook. When he feels worn out with the active life that the climate forces him to lead and to which possibly his race is not completely adapted, it is refreshment, not stimulant, that he needs. Now the British imported into America the same attitude toward alcohol that one finds in the everlasting drizzle of Lancashire or the Clyde. The Americans have carried the habit to extremes in accordance with one of the most typical traits in their character; namely, exaggeration of thought and action. How many of them can restrain themselves in the use of alcoholic drinks? Little by little the American bar or saloon became a public scandal, a degrading centre of drunkenness, vice, and the lowest forms of political activity. It was largely owing to the saloon that the saner elements of the population looked upon alcoholism as a cancer which had to be removed at all costs.

Three separate groups worked for prohibition, and their united efforts were necessary in order to achieve success. First of all there was the essential factor of Protestantism— "Protestant" rather than "religious" in the broad sense of the word, for the Catholic Church did not take an important part in the campaign. Either through lack of interest, or in deference to the beer- and wine-drinking element in her congregation, she generally maintained an attitude of reserve, scepticism, and even discreet disapproval. The American priest, like the French *curé,* cannot see that he is committing a crime when he offers a visitor a glass of wine. The same suspicious reserve was shown by the Lutherans. It was the Calvinists and the Anglicans (with certain exceptions) who were the true militants of the prohibition movement. It is no exaggeration to say that they approached the question with passionate fanaticism, and in their zeal to save souls they preached abstinence in the belief that drinking was a sin. They also realized that alcohol is injurious to the health and stunts the race, but such arguments are only a secondary consideration. There is thus a certain amount of Protestant moral uplift in the prohibition movement.

Alongside these militants we find the important employers of labour, the manufacturers of the East, and the farmers of the West and the South. They have thrown their immense weight into the balance, for though they do not approach the question as missionaries, they have learned from experience that the drunkard is a poor workman

With the development of industry it becomes plainly dangerous to trust delicate and costly machinery to an intemperate mechanic. The farmer who must reap his wheat today and not tomorrow runs the risk of heavy loss if drink should deprive him of the hired men on whom he is counting. How could he be other than a Prohibitionist? Add to these arguments the ever-present terror of a drink-crazed negro, and naturally the South also goes solid for prohibition.

Finally, in certain influential classes of society, notably among the rich Protestants of the East, the Fundamentalists of the South, and especially among the middle classes of the farming districts and small towns of the West, public opinion has now come to favour anti-alcoholic measures of the most drastic character. The West of today is anything but a fantastic land of adventurous pioneers, where the descendants of the gold-seekers are as free in spirit as they are in custom. Instead it is populated by respectable bourgeois who are morally timid, who think like their neighbours, never miss church, go to bed early, and in short are as boring as the Garde Nationale of Louis Philippe! They are first cousins to the English Pharisees of the Victorian era, with all their pretension and love of etiquette; and in America at the present time nothing can be done against them or without them. They want prohibition in order to cleanse public morals, and if we look at the map we realize that wherever they are numerous they have succeeded.

This fine unity between the various advocates of prohibition does not exist in the opposite camp. The latter contains a large army, no less convinced and equally susceptible to violent outbursts; but it is a mixed lot and only shows real vigour in limited areas which are far from impressive from the point of view of square miles. Hostility to prohibition is found above all in the cities, first in the upper strata of society (except for the pillars of the church), then in the middle class in general, and finally among the lower-class foreigners. We must, however, beware of the fallacy that all true Americans are dry by conviction; for if so, how can we explain the extraordinary attraction that alcohol has for so many of them? In the best clubs and the smart set, the efforts of the extremists excite only sarcasm and anger, and conversation inevitably drifts back to the Eighteenth Amendment, nine times out of ten to condemn it.

Among the foreigners it is chiefly a question of customs, for they wish to live their own lives without interference from the law. The Italian wants his Chianti, the German his beer, and the Irishman his whisky. They are quite impervious to the arguments of the Prohibitionists, and only ask to be left alone. Their priests, who naturally are in no hurry to see them welded into the Anglo-Saxon uniformity, do nothing to abet this particular form of assimilation. The demand for this "home rule for foreign customs" is one of the most popular planks of the Democratic program in the great eastern cities. For the same reason the German population of Illinois, Wisconsin, and Minnesota are still hostile to prohibition even in the country districts. As Catholics and Lutherans they offer an unrelenting opposition, and it is unlikely that they will ever be brought to look upon beer-drinking as a crime.

It is difficult to say whether there was a majority for prohibition at the time that America came into the War. It is scarcely probable, for to its avowed adversaries we must add the millions who were indifferent, and who, though now incapable of opposing an accomplished fact, would never have aided its attainment voluntarily. If a majority did exist, it was chiefly against the saloons, which all right-minded people wished to see swept away; and it was probably only to suppress them that so many resigned themselves to prohibition at all. Also it is unlikely that either group could have carried away public opinion except under unusual circumstances. The War imposed a rigid collective discipline on the whole nation and strengthened the Messiah-like suggestion that in such extraordinary times moral regeneration was essential. This made it possible to pass a Federal law even when it was decidedly against the expressed wishes of several States. It must also be added that four million soldiers were temporarily unable to vote, whereas the Prohibitionist organizations were marvellously equipped and ready for every conceivable form of wire-pulling.

What the Prohibitionist missionaries had not been able to accomplish alone became possible as soon as the manufacturing interests lent a hand. Ever since 1914 these interests had been concentrating on intensive production, and their final unanswerable argument was that Prohibition was essential on account of the War. Conditions were undoubtedly abnormal, and the opposition have a certain amount of justification when they say that the measure was suddenly sprung upon them during a period of war hysteria. It does not necessarily follow, however, that America could easily go back on what was done in 1917.

The anti-alcoholic movement dates back a century. The campaign to amend the Federal Constitution in favour of prohibition dates back only to a meeting of the Anti-Saloon League held at Columbus, Ohio, in 1913. At that time, as we have seen, most of the States were on the point of being convinced, and the chief obstacles were a few clearly-defined centres. For example, there were fewer saloons in all the country south of the Mason and Dixon Line than in New York City alone. What a temptation to disregard the autonomy of the States and consider the nation as a single unit, and so to apply the will of the majority in all its crudeness! All the prohibition societies followed the lead of the Anti-Saloon League and the W.C.T.U. (Women's Christian Temperance Union), and concentrated on this single aim.

A two-thirds majority in Congress was necessary to pass a resolution submitting to the States the proposed amendment to the Constitution, and by the autumn of 1913 this majority had been obtained, although it took the War to carry it through. On August 1, 1917, the Senate voted by 65 to 20; on December 17 the House of Representatives voted 282 to 128; and finally on December 18, by a combined vote of the two assemblies, the resolution was carried by a two-thirds majority of Congress. Thirteen months later, on January 16, 1919, it obtained the necessary ratification of three-quarters of the States, and became legally the Eighteenth Amendment to the Constitution of the United States.[1]

As the Constitution only gave an outline of the principle, special laws had to be drawn up to deal with its enforcement. Even at that time prohibition was to a great extent an accomplished fact, for when the United States went into the War in 1917, very severe restrictive measures had been taken by the Government. Later, on July 1, 1919, a law entitled the "War-Time Prohibition Act," which had been prepared while America was at war, had decreed the immediate closing of all distilleries, breweries, and saloons. Permanent legislation was required, and this was taken care of by the Volstead Act which was passed on October 28, 1919, and the Campbell-Willis Act on November 23, 1921.

[1] The actual text of the Eighteenth Amendment is as follows:

"Section 1: After one year of the ratification of this article the manufacture, sale, or transportation of intoxicating liquors within, the importation thereof into, or the exportation thereof from the U. S. and all territory subject to the jurisdiction thereof for beverage purposes is hereby prohibited.

"Section 2: The Congress and the several States shall have concurrent power to enforce this article by appropriate legislation.

"Section 3: This article shall be inoperative unless it shall have been ratified as an amendment to the Constitution by the legislatures of the several States, as provided by the Constitution, within seven years of the date of the submission hereof to the States by the Congress."

These texts are essential, because they define intoxicating beverages and also lay down the method by which the law is to be applied. According to the Volstead Act any beverage is considered intoxicating if it contains more than half of 1 per cent. of alcohol, which means that beer, cider, and wine are forbidden as well as spirits. According to the Campbell-Willis Act the use of beer for medicinal purposes is prohibited, and the importation of wines and spirits for surgery or the preparation of medicines is strictly limited. The principle of prohibition has thus been embodied in an amendment to the Constitution which it would be extremely difficult to revise on account of the extraordinarily complicated procedure necessary. On the other hand the practice of prohibition, that is to say, the strict interpretation of the amendment forbidding wine and beer, is the result of a simple vote of Congress, and can be annulled by a contrary vote without requiring a two-thirds majority. Therefore it is around the Volstead Act that the battle is now being waged between the Wets and the Drys, for in order to admit beer, cider, and wine only a slight increase in the permissible percentage of alcohol is necessary. It is a question of appreciation in which politics means more than doctor's orders, and this brings us to the extent to which public opinion has really ratified prohibition.

We must first distinguish between the votes of the elected and the real desires of the masses. In the House of Representatives deputations from forty-two states declared themselves in favour of the Eighteenth Amendment either unanimously or by a majority. Only six States (New York, New Jersey, Connecticut, Rhode Island, Maryland, and Nevada) voted partially or totally against it. There can thus be no doubt about the attitude of Congress, especially as the vote was not on party lines, with 141 Democrats and 137 Republicans in favour, and 64 Democrats and 62 Republicans against. It is, however, openly admitted that

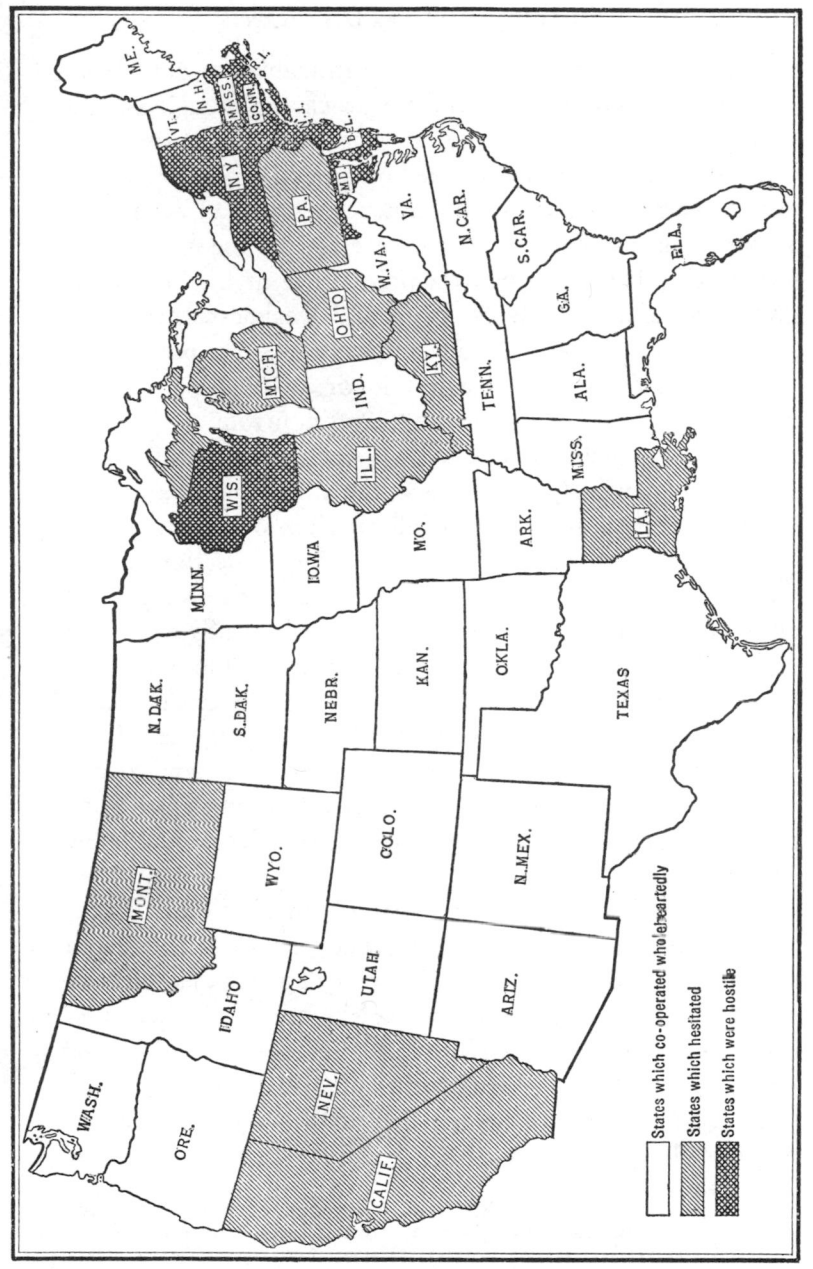

FIG. III.—THE ENFORCEMENT OF FEDERAL PROHIBITION.

☐ States which co-operated wholeheartedly

▨ States which hesitated

▩ States which were hostile

Congress voted under direct and formidable pressure from the Anti-Saloon League, which was clever enough to impose its own wording of the law and to obtain most of its demands. Its agents had carried on an ambitious and vigorous campaign in different constituencies, and had even gone as far as blackmail. In some cases, with the aid of detectives they had unearthed the private life of the local Congressman, noting his debts, his moral weaknesses, and any stains on his reputation. Then they were in a position to order him to vote as he was told or be exposed. In all probability Congress was much more in favour of prohibition than the public, especially as the war enthusiasm of 1917 had artificially surcharged the atmosphere, and had deprived the opposite party of all freedom of action.

We must now decide the value of the ratification by the various States. In every case, except that of Connecticut and Rhode Island, the Amendment was confirmed and often unanimously by a vote of the legislature.[2] On the other hand we must not overlook the fact that in certain cases States which were notoriously hostile or at any rate lukewarm, ratified it, partly through indifference and partly through the hopelessness of resisting an accomplished fact. Such, for example, was the case of New York and New Jersey.

The attitude of the different States toward the enforcement of prohibition is most instructive. The Eighteenth Amendment relies on their aid in carrying out the Volstead Act by means of appropriate legislation, the police, and penalties. We can classify the States into three groups which will give us the clue to the whole situation.

In the first group we have the States which by conviction aided the enactment of Federal prohibition. They

---

[2] This point is of considerable importance, and especially when the vote was unanimous, as in Delaware, Michigan, Kansas, Nebraska, Utah, Colorado, Idaho, Wyoming, Oregon, Washington, New Mexico, Arizona, Arkansas, Tennessee, West Virginia, Florida, and Delaware.

passed laws which at times equalled or even passed the Volstead and Campbell-Willis Acts in severity. These States are the real stronghold of the Prohibitionist movement.[3]

In the next group we have the hostile States which either resolutely refused to co-operate, as in the case of New York, New Jersey, Maryland, and Rhode Island, or else as in Connecticut, Massachusetts, and Wisconsin, where the laws passed lacked severity in spite of the terms of the Federal legislation. In the third group [4] come the hesitating States, many of which decided to fall in line with the Federal legislation only after long delay; some even went back on their original good intentions, while in others the opposition was strong enough to paralyze all action.

This survey gives us a rough idea of public opinion. The Prohibitionists are in the majority in the country districts, especially in the South and West and possibly even in the up-State districts of the Atlantic seaboard. The big cities, New York, Boston, Philadelphia, Baltimore, Chicago, St. Louis, New Orleans, San Francisco, and many others, are openly hostile. This hostility is based on a fundamentally different conception of religion, customs, and society. A

---

[3] Severe local legislation was passed in the following States:

South	West	East and Centre
Virginia	Iowa	Indiana
North Carolina	Missouri	Virginia
South Carolina	Minnesota	Delaware
Georgia	Kansas	Vermont
Florida	Nebraska	New Hampshire
Alabama	North Dakota	Maine
Mississippi	South Dakota	
Texas	New Mexico	
Oklahoma	Arizona	
Arkansas	Colorado	
Tennessee	Utah	
	Wyoming	
	Idaho	
	Oregon	
	Washington	

[4] In this group are Kentucky, Illinois, Ohio, Pennsylvania, Michigan, Louisiana, Montana, Nevada, and California.

Catholic foreigner is no more in favour of drunkenness than an American, but he clings to his wine and beer; and his religious education does not incline him to moral austerity. Above all, he does not want to be interfered with. Now the old-time Protestant concentrates on a clean social life, for he is full of moral aspirations and takes little stock in liberal arguments which would restrain him from imposing his will on others, especially when he considers it his duty to do so. He is all the more unwilling to consent to a compromise because he is not fond of wine, and because he realizes that if beer were again allowed to flow in the saloons, the average American would be incapable of self-restraint. Once he starts to drink he is done for, and therefore (to the Prohibitionists), the common-sense solution of forbidding spirits but allowing wine and beer seems not merely dangerous but criminal. It is a question of conscience, and there can be no trafficking with the devil. Add to this certain vague nationalistic feelings, for beer is the drink of the Germans, and wine of the immoral Frenchmen. Surely neither one can be seriously recommended!

The best example of this psychology is the attitude of the people of California. After many negative votes a law was finally approved by a referendum in 1922, with 445,000 votes in favour and 411,000 against. It gave the State of California the authority to apply prohibition. Now California was a great wine-producing State. Can we possibly imagine the Gironde having a plebiscite to forbid the use of wine? Yet California did it. The secret of this paradox lies in the different elements which go to make up the population and also in their geographic distribution. In central California, with its easy-going, sceptical cosmopolitanism inherited from the early gold-seekers, a compact block of counties voted against prohibition in the referendum. San Francisco, a more or less Catholic and Latin city, registered 91,000 votes against and 32,000 for. Simi-

larly Sacramento went 15,000 against and 10,000 in favour.
This was the territory of the Wets, but all Southern California went to the opposition. The country is the same,
with the same Andalusian atmosphere, but the people are
very different. Los Angeles shelters tens of thousands of
those wealthy and retired farmers from Iowa, Nebraska,
and Kansas who are too Puritanical to tolerate wine, gaiety,
or immorality. In the referendum this great urban population gave 143,000 votes for the Drys against 84,000 for
the Wets. Thus all the south of the State voted dry, as
well as certain counties at the extreme north that had been
penetrated by Puritanism from Oregon. The geographic
division of the two parties was striking. But what about
the wine-growers? It was of course understood that they
should not suffer too heavily, and in many counties—Fresno,
for example—they even voted for prohibition themselves.
The reason is that as soon as wine was forbidden they sold
their grapes at increased prices to the thousands of people
who now make their own wine illicitly at home.

In the last analysis the extent to which Federal prohibition is applied depends on local public opinion. In many of
the States which adhered to the law of their own accord
and even forestalled it, the application is more or less satisfactory, always provided, of course, that there is no great
city, frontier, coast-line, or mountain-range to aid the local
bootleggers. Conditions are the reverse wherever the new
régime was imposed from outside and contrary to the desire of the population; for here the local authorities take
no interest in the matter, and sometimes even oppose it with
ill-concealed hostility. We could hardly expect, for example,
the New York police, who are largely recruited from the
Irish, to show any particular zeal in tracking down bootleggers, or that judges elected by the Wets should be excessively severe with their penalties. Inertia was all that
was needed to block the system, and the Federal agents

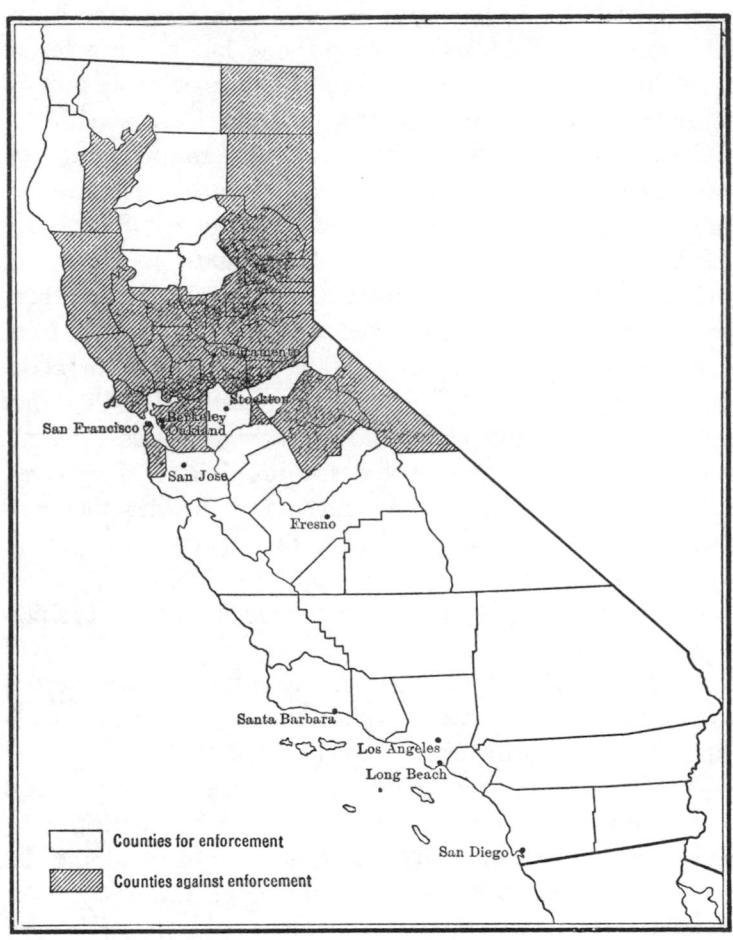

Counties for enforcement

Counties against enforcement

FIG. IV.—CALIFORNIA REFERENDUM OF NOVEMBER 7, 1922, ON
THE ENFORCEMENT OF FEDERAL PROHIBITION BY LOCAL
LEGISLATION.

and judges on whom the duty fell were soon overwhelmed. Rum-runners, bootleggers, and illicit distillers of every sort flourish, not to mention the lonely mountaineers of the northern Alleghanies, whose individualistic and savage resistance reminds one of the attitude of the Vendée toward the edicts of the central government.

We can quite appreciate that the central government was tempted to resort to force, for it was nettled by failure and could never escape from the vigilance of the grand inquisitors of the Methodist and Baptist Churches. Finally in April, 1925, a military man was appointed to take charge of the prohibition branch of the Treasury Department, and he concentrated under his authority all the services connected with its application. He organized a regular Ministry of War, with its own army, navy, air force, police, and secret service, at a cost of some $20,000,000 a year. In spite of the unexampled patience of the American people toward high-handed police measures, meddlesome regulations, and wholesale spying, one may well ask if such an undertaking is not beyond the strength of any government!

In view of the extreme bias of all reports, it is difficult to say just how far the life of the community has been affected to date by the Eighteenth Amendment. Any generalization is still premature, though several facts are beginning to emerge. It is only too evident that an enormous number of people continue to drink intoxicating liquors, and it is even a question whether many do not drink far more than before. In the clubs, the universities, and the colleges, and even in the country clubs where women are numerous, liquor is not merely fashionable but socially indispensable. At a dance, a picnic, or a bridge party, the guest who does not bring his hip-flask is likely to be considered a bore even by the women and young girls. Alcohol has become extremely dear, as its price must include not only the profits of the rum-runners, but bribes to the police and a share to all sorts of other intermediaries. So the poor classes have to fall back on adulterated products, which are usually injurious and often fatal. As the poor people bitterly remark, any one who has enough money can defy the law. (It is interesting to note that this point of view is otherwise quite exceptional in America.) This spectacle of the law thus openly flouted and the prevalent atmosphere of low intrigue is bound to have a demoralizing effect on the population.

There is nothing astonishing, therefore, in the serious moral disorder that has been revealed by statistics, especially since 1920. A survey made in 1925 by the Federal Council of the Federation of Churches of Christ showed that the young people were drinking more than before, and the respect for law and order had diminished. Statistics published by the World League Against Alcoholism also showed that the number of arrests for drunkenness, which had fallen from an index of 119 in 1913 to 43 in 1920, had risen again to 67 in 1924. In Chicago the figures are positively terrifying; arrests for felonies rose from 15,273 in 1920 to 16,516 in 1924, whereas those for misdemeanours rose from 79,180 to 239,829. In New York deaths from alcohol, which dropped to a low figure after 1917, have started to rise again. The establishment of Federal prohibition appears to have coincided with a recrudescence of immorality. Doubtless 1920 is a bad year from which to start our comparisons, for between 1917 and 1920 wartime prohibition had been established by a strong central authority and had produced undeniable results which have not since been maintained. To say that the new régime caused the present moral relaxation would be unjust; still, it certainly did not prevent it.

Personally I was chiefly impressed by the fact that the masses of the people undoubtedly drink less than before, partly because alcohol is dear and hard to get, and partly

because the occasion does not present itself. The illicit
traffic is there, but it is hidden; and one can go through
whole regions without seeing any liquor or meeting a single drunkard. Drinking has come to be a privilege from
which the less fortunate are excluded, not to mention those
who dislike intrigue and unnecessary trouble. Under the
new conditions the psychology of temptation has been reversed, and the great mass of the people—those whom one
does not know personally—are undoubtedly benefiting in
health, standard of living, working efficiency, and increased
wages. As the output of a sober workman is greater, the
employers have been able to increase labour's share of
profits without adding to the cost of production; also, that
portion of wages which formerly was spent in the saloons
now goes into Fords, tires, gasoline, radios, houses, and
even into savings banks. The Eighteenth Amendment has
done its share in raising the standard of living of the American workman to the highest level that the world has ever
seen. The leaders of industry, who realize that this increase in the purchasing power of the people amounts to millions of dollars a year, will never voluntarily accept a return
to the old ways.

If it were merely a question of hygiene with no religious
and political complications, prohibition would never have
stirred up such a bitter dispute. To dictate the habits of a
people in the name of ethics and religion is an intolerable
interference with the private life of the individual. It
might be possible in the case of a homogeneous nation living in a restricted territory, for then it would not give the
impression of being imposed from without. There was no
prohibition crisis so long as the matter remained in the
hands of the various States; that is to say, while the wishes
of the minorities were respected. The real trouble began
when the zealots for national morality tried to force a general ruling on States which were ethnically and geograph-

ically distinct, and which accordingly refused to accept it. In spite of the clearly worded amendments which were inscribed in the Federal Constitution after the Civil War, the North has never been able to impose its solution of the negro question on the South, and in the same way it is far from certain that the South and West will be any more successful in imposing their prohibition point of view on the East.

CHAPTER VI

THE COLOUR PROBLEM

THE Americans have inherited from the English a horror of intermarriage between white and coloured people that is little less than fanatic, and therefore the existence of ten and a half million blacks within the country creates an insoluble problem before which even the stoutest must quail. After the Civil War the victorious Northerners imagined that they could solve the negro question by suppressing slavery, but the race hatred that has since resulted is much worse. Slavery in a sense was a solution, for it established a definite hierarchy, in contrast to the present brutal domination of one race over the other, which is maintained by a system of intimidation without any regard to the law. The North may have thought that it had imposed its point of view, but the South has undoubtedly had the last word.[1]

During the saturnalia of the reconstruction period after the Civil War, the blacks, with the aid of northern politicians, obtained political control in several southern States, with such lasting effects that they are still felt today. The dread of a return of those frightful years explains many things, or at any rate serves as a pretext. The old slave-owners were ruined, and as if this were not enough, they

[1] The South comprises the States of Maryland (southern section), Virginia (eastern), North Carolina (eastern), South Carolina, Georgia, Alabama, Florida, Mississippi, Louisiana, Texas (eastern), Arkansas, Oklahoma (eastern), Missouri (southern), Kentucky (western), and Tennessee (western). The Allegheny region, where there are no blacks, does not belong, properly speaking, to the South.

South Carolina and Mississippi are over 50 per cent. negro; Louisiana, Alabama, and Georgia 37½ per cent; Arkansas, Florida, North Carolina, and Virginia between 25 per cent. and 37½ per cent.; Texas, Tennessee, Delaware, and Maryland between 12½ per cent. and 25 per cent.

were asked to endure the supreme humiliation of being ruled by their own slaves. The birth of the Ku Klux Klan in 1866 was the first attempt at liberation. Gradually the whites regained control of the local governments and by arbitrary legislation deprived the blacks of the advantages that had been won for them in the war and which had been guaranteed by an amendment to the Federal Constitution. They were again relegated to a state of semi-slavery, and ever since, the Southerners have concentrated all their efforts on re-establishing conditions as if the war had not taken place. After 1890 the North no longer tried to resist this tendency.

If we are to believe the Southerners, the whole question has been settled, and there is no longer a negro problem—or at any rate, if there is one it is entirely a local matter which they are capable of managing without interference from the rest of the country. The negro, they say, is acknowledged to be of an inferior race that has been degraded by slavery and is not susceptible to education. He must be ruthlessly kept at the bottom of the ladder as God intended, and it is absolutely impious to try to alter him. It is only at this level that he can be useful to the community, and so long as he is content to remain there forever without trying to rise, they will admit that they are very fond of him individually and that he has great charm. Through years of living side by side they have learned to understand him. They know how to talk to him, how to make him work, how to joke with him and yet keep him in his place. He is a child, and they treat him as such and protect him because it is their duty. Properly handled, he is easy to manage, but give him authority and he becomes a dangerous brute that must be crushed. It is not a question of sentiment—and this is important—nor yet of ethics and morals, but of prestige, and even of the very existence of the white race. The South has always been a white man's country, and they intend to keep it so; if necessary, at the point of the sword. Busy-bodies in the North who stir up the darkies by talking to them of their dignity and their rights neither know them nor like them—"so for heaven's sake," they say, "leave us alone, for we know what we are doing."

This argument, which is repeated again and again, throws a clear light on the undercurrent of thought in the southern mind. Their selfish good humour is mixed with the paternalism of the master who will never admit that the servant can become his equal and is ferociously jealous lest the latter should try to improve his position. They will resort to anything to keep him in his place—violence, massacre, and even torture.

At present the blacks are crushed under the heel. In the first place, all political rights are denied them. According to the Fifteenth Amendment to the Constitution, ratified on March 30, 1870, "the right of the citizens of the United States to vote shall not be denied or abridged by the United States, or by any State, on account of race, colour, or previous condition of servitude." The southern States refused to ratify it, but the measure went through in spite of them. After 1890 laws were passed in all the southern States which, without actually designating the blacks, excluded them from the suffrage. Sometimes it is done by establishing electoral lists; sometimes the applicants are asked to give a "reasonable interpretation" of the Constitution, and naturally a negro never succeeds. A clause called "the Grandfather Act" automatically allows the whites, even though poor and illiterate, to vote without this examination, provided they are ex-soldiers or the descendants of those who voted in 1867. The fraud is evident and is contrary to the spirit of the Constitution, but the North winks at it; for to interfere would mean another war. If by chance a negro were to slip through the meshes of the net, he would not dare present himself at the polling booth; for he would be beaten off with clubs, and his very life would be in danger. In the eastern border States of Virginia and North Carolina this severity has been somewhat relaxed, but in the South as a whole practically all the negroes are treated as pariahs. No negro has ever been appointed or elected to a public position, although in certain rare exceptions, the Customs for example, they have been employed, owing entirely to Federal influence. Otherwise the whites maintain a united front without a single break. There is no doubt that southern politics are based not on equality, but on force.

The amendments to the Federal Constitution voted after the Civil War did not aim at suppressing the distinctions between the races, but were simply intended to avoid the injustice of differential treatment. Southern legislation, however, has definitely maintained the latter.

By the "Jim Crow laws," which are rigidly applied, the southern negroes are ordered to travel in separate coaches, and to sit only in the back of the trams. These laws go even further and reserve certain quarters of the towns for the whites, and forbid the blacks either to rent or buy houses there. There are whole counties which the blacks may not enter, and they cannot even leave the trains passing through. Such legislation is almost superfluous, since the whites take it on themselves to apply these rules whether they are legal or not. A negro was once lynched by a furious mob in a theatre, because he dared to sit down in the part reserved for the whites. A complete "sanitary cordon" has been established, which even includes the churches. In the South the majority of both races are Baptists or Methodists, but their churches are always separate; so they do not even pray together. Humiliation extends to the most trivial details of daily life. No matter who he may be, the negro must go into a house by the back door; for no white

servant would allow him to enter otherwise. He is never
addressed as "Mister," be he a bishop or a doctor, but simply as John or Joseph. Sometimes, if they wish to be
especially polite, they call him "Professor," an appellation
to which a certain amount of irony is attached in English,
I have noticed.

Against such oppression, which at times amounts to persecution, the black man is helpless. He has no political
representation and has no way of airing his grievances.
Also it is difficult for him to obtain justice, for the two
races are by no means on an equal footing in the courts.
The statements of the whites are always accepted until they
are proved to be false, but a coloured man must produce
ten times as much evidence. The southern administration
makes no attempt to conceal such injustices. In the matter
of education, for example, the black population is deliberately kept in a state of inferiority. In South Carolina
the negroes number 51 per cent. of the population, but their
share of the education funds amounts to only 11 per cent.
The whites do not wish them to progress, for they need
them to supply the lowest type of manual labour.

We find the same injustice in municipal administration,
for the blacks are relegated to the unhealthy and badly-kept
parts of the towns; and all the money is spent on the quarters reserved for the whites. In the part that belongs to
the privileged race the streets are swept; there are pave-
ments, gutters, and arc lights; but two hundred yards away
the negroes live in hovels with cesspools instead of sewers,
and total darkness in their streets at night. In 1922 the
death rate in the southern cities was 12.1 per 1,000 whites,
but 20.5 among the blacks. How often have I heard these
figures commented upon with a grim smile—"Tuberculosis
and pneumonia may perhaps be the solution of the problem, and may save us from being overrun by these crea-
tures."

The Southerners can exploit these illiterate masses with complete impunity, since there is no court of appeal where they can receive justice. Only a short while ago it was quite common for them to take advantage of the small coloured farmer in the country districts. They deceived him about the exact area of his farm, and when he had to pay his rent in kind, they gave him very little say as to what he had produced, even dictating the amount of his payment to him. His final reckoning was indefinitely delayed, and in the end he was forced to accept it, whether correct or otherwise. Such conditions no longer exist to the same extent, for war-time prosperity has even reached the small black proprietors, and in addition the wholesale immigration of the negroes to the northern cities has at last made the southern employers reflect. But the economic contest between the races is not carried on with equal weapons, for not only must the negro win the good will of the employers, but what is far more difficult, he must also overcome the ferocious jealousy of the "poor white" class, who are the bitterest enemies of his race.

In a colony of "planters," a white planter controls coloured labour. This is an accepted system of production. In a colony of "settlers," however, where the population is homogeneous, the presence of a negro *bloc* is bound to be unhealthy. Owing to competition with a race of more modest needs, the white worker must reduce his standard of living down to that of his competitor. One of the residues of slavery is the "poor white," who on the one hand is unable through lack of land, to raise himself to the level of the employer class and on the other is menaced by the presence of servile labour. In spite of their purely Anglo-Saxon descent they are a mediocre lot, often living in squalor. As a result of the climate, malaria, parasites, etc., they are physically feeble; and being perpetually in debt, they constitute a reserve of cheap labour from which the employers can go on drawing indefinitely.

In the South they will tell you that all the unskilled labour is reserved for the negro, and that the skilled work is done by the superior race. If this were always so, contact between the two races would be limited and rivalry greatly diminished. In point of fact, however, there are many whites who are ready to do the lowest type of manual work, while an increasing number of negroes are attempting occupations which require considerable technique. The employers naturally do not raise any objections to such ambitions; for not only is the coloured labourer paid less, but he is more obedient. The white labourer, however, is left on the frontier between the two races, in constant fear of being dragged down and merged with the inferior one. In the wealthy families some of the old-time sentimentality still survives from the slave days, but the "poor white" sees in the negro nothing but a brutal competitor who is trying to rob him of his job. His hatred is unrelenting, merciless, and mingled with fear. To understand the South, we must realize that the lower we descend in the social scale, the more violent is the hatred of the negro.

The ruling classes have profited by it, for they deprived the negro of his vote (with the help of the "poor whites"), and then by means of the economic menace of the blacks they in their turn have dominated the "poor whites." A strike is almost impossible, for there can be no question of labour uniting in mixed trade unions. It is all very well for the American Federation of Labor to recommend such tactics from Washington, but the local trade unions in the South will never adopt them. Thus a gang of potential strikebreakers is always at hand. As above everything else the white workman fears being ousted by the despised inferior, he is bound body and soul to the fortunes of his race, which appear more important to him than any other considerations.

Though the wage scale is lower than in the North, and in the factories he is less well protected by social legislation, at least he has the satisfaction of feeling that he is a member of the aristocratic race.

In spite of the complexity of its causes, the race hatred in the last analysis is always concentrated on the physical protection of the race; for this is really at the root of the matter. Any discussion of the problem reveals the widespread existence of a sexual apprehension that cannot be quieted, and which penetrates every thought and act. This vague physical terror of the black population is especially evident in the small villages where the blacks, being in the majority, are positively overwhelming. It is a haunting fear of those instincts of barbarity and bestiality that the blacks have inherited, and which may suddenly break forth in an attempt at rape. If a man goes out at night leaving a woman alone in the house he never feels entirely at ease, and this anxiety, having become an obsession far stronger than reason, leads to the worst horrors of hysterical fury.

One can easily understand that in such an atmosphere of repression, justice soon gives way to passionate vengeance whenever a rape takes place, or if there is the slightest suspicion of its even being contemplated. They feel that at all costs they must make an example of some one at once, and the mob which collects is never content until it has drawn blood, often with the most frightful refinements of cruelty. The best elements of the community often take part—society people, high officials, and even judges. Not only do they approve, but they make no attempt to hide their presence—they have told me this themselves! This explains the tragic undercurrent of anxiety and ferocity that is always present in this land of romance. The cordial, polished gentleman with whom you are talking is possibly a murderer who has gone into the wood at night to kill a man outnumbered a hundred to one; and thousands of

others, your friends among them, may have been his ac-
complices. Outwardly, Texas, Georgia, and South Carolina are civilized States of the twentieth century, but in
reality they should be classed along with the countries still
guilty of pogroms.

"We are only defending the frontiers of the white race,"
they will tell you in the South. All efforts are concentrated
on the prevention of mixed marriages and above all on the
defence of the white woman. In all the southern States
and in several others as well, miscegenation is prohibited
by law. If either of the parties to a marriage has a black
grandparent, he is legally classed as a negro, and the law is
enforced. A union without marriage between the races is
almost impossible, for though it is no longer the affair of
the district attorney or the police, the Ku Klux Klan or some
other secret organization takes it in hand and soon informs
the couple that they must either separate or leave the country, as otherwise their lives will be in peril and their assas-
sins will go unpunished.

The white woman may be successfully defended, but the
case of the negress is very different. If we wish to prove
that intermingling of the two races is going on, we have
only to compare the colour of the primitive Africans with
that of the civilized negroes of America. The former are
black in contrast to the diluted colour of quite a third of
the latter. In the old plantation days the masters used to
take mistresses from among their slaves, and even today
there are many middle-class men who keep a coloured
woman and have children by her. Therefore, although the
whites declare that the negro is physically repulsive to them,
you know that it simply is not true. On the contrary, one
of the most complex aspects of life in the South is this in-
describable attraction of the black woman. It is a mystery
which alarms and humiliates thoughtful Americans on account of the biological and moral perils to which it leads.

The South is unable to shake off this shirt of Nessus, and it pays a terrible price for its régime of violence and hatred. Materially the disastrous effects of the Civil War are over and forgotten with the return of prosperity, but intellectually and morally how barren! Everything is poisoned, even religion. The old rights of the master over his slaves are still present, and a black woman is defenceless against the whims of the white man, who need take no responsibility for the results of their union. The victims probably do not always resist, but at any rate the best class of coloured woman is subjected to insulting advances in the streets and the shops, and their husbands defend them at the risk of their lives. Where the colour question is concerned, the white race has lost all sense of justice. Everything is permissible, even crime. Religion has no restraining influence, for the churches are divided into black and white; and the conscience of the Christian no longer suggests that he is doing wrong in maltreating the inferior race.

In the South, at any rate, the negroes have passively resigned themselves to existing conditions. Their attitude is that of parasites, gravitating around the whites, whom they consider their patrons. The title "Boss," which they often use for the whites, reflects their instinctive recognition of their ethnic position, and when they classify themselves into their own social categories, their viewpoint is much the same. To be the descendant of a slave is humiliating. At Charleston, Richmond, etc., certain groups from the West Indies whose ancestors were free are regarded as superior, and therefore they do not mix with the others. By much the same snobbery that we find among the domestics of old British families, it is considered the thing to be descended from the slaves who belonged to one of the first families of Virginia. Therefore it is not astonishing that a relatively fair skin is appreciated by the negroes themselves.

They distinguish all sorts of shades of colour which escape
us—black, brown, deep brown, yellow, reddish brown, deep
yellow, dark brown, chocolate, gingerbread, fair, light
brown, red, pink, tan, olive, copper colour, blue, cream,
pale black, dead black, bronze, banana. . . . Pale complexions, which are more common among the educated negroes, are more frequently met with in North Carolina and
Virginia than in the extreme South. It is interesting to
note that in the smart negro churches the best pews are reserved for the palest of the faithful. On the contrary,
among the lower classes of negro the really black man inspires greater confidence, an observation which applies, for
example, to the minister of a low-class Baptist community,
whose colour renders disloyalty to his race impossible. Coloured people actually exist whose tint is so pale that they
can be mistaken for whites. They can "pass" (a sacred expression among the negroes) ; that is to say, they move un-
detected into the superior race, where they are lost.

With the possible exception of a small *élite,* humility is
the dominant trait of the southern negroes. They are docile, passive, and accept their subjugation without a murmur.
A Spartacist revolt is the last thing to be feared, for their
efforts are directed rather toward adaptation. Circumstances have developed in them an extraordinary instinct
for judging people and knowing what they can get out of
them. They have a keen perception for social differences
among the whites. With the rich they quickly adopt a flattering attitude, but they utterly despise the "poor whites."
So long as they keep their place and are willing to sign,
as it were, a declaration of everlasting inferiority, the South
will admit that they are part of the family, and indeed more
truly American than the New York Jew or the Boston
Italian. But let them try to climb socially, and they are
looked on as dangerous beasts. In reality the South fears
their progress even more than their brutality.

If the black zone could be surrounded by an impenetrable "sanitary cordon," the problem would be at a standstill in this enclosed space. Instead, however, a factor of enormous importance has entered into the situation with the recent migration to the North of part of the negro population. In 1917, when industry was short of labour owing to war mobilization, the blacks deserted their native States *en masse,* attracted by higher salaries and the better social treatment which they hoped to find in the North. Also they were profoundly discouraged by their prospects in the South. The more or less cultured negroes of the Atlantic States made their way to Philadelphia, New York, and Boston, while a primitive type went from Mississippi toward St. Louis, Chicago, and the great manufacturing cities of the Middle West. The two chief waves, one between 1916 and 1920 and the other from 1922 to 1924, involved some six or seven hundred thousand negroes or more. There are now in the northern States almost a million and a half blacks, of whom a quarter of a million live in Harlem (New York) and 150,000 in Chicago. The frugal workman who earned from $1 to $3 a day on a plantation in Mississippi often gets $8 to $10 now in the industrial region of the Great Lakes. But his material prosperity does not help solve the race problem.

Having emancipated the negro, the Northerners have always affected a kindly attitude toward him, partly on principle, but largely because they were never in direct contact. His sudden arrival in great hordes was bound to produce a serious crisis. Let us take for example what has happened in Chicago. First there was the housing problem. The newcomers camped down on arrival in the districts already occupied by coloured folk, and from there they spread to the neighbouring quarters. The invasion was peaceful but effective, and houses belonging to whites were soon entirely hemmed in by blacks. The occupants were disgusted, and gave way rather than struggle. Today an immense quarter stretching from the stock-yards to Lake Michigan is entirely coloured. Certain streets are 90 per cent. negro, as is very evident to the passer-by. In the slums, in comfortable residences, and even in the former palaces of the newly rich, you see blacks at every door, at every window, and on every veranda. They swarm like flies.

The same thing occurred in the factories, and when the soldiers returned from Europe they found that in many cases their places had been taken by the intruders. The employers who saw in the negro a useful strike-breaker took him on, not only for inferior positions, but even for skilled jobs. Trouble started with the jealousy of the foremen, who systematically relegated the negro to the lowest positions. It was among the workmen themselves, however, that the resentment was most violent, and especially among those of foreign origin. The coalition against the black was tacit and spontaneous, and he was boycotted in the trade unions. Thus the whole life of the worker was jeopardized, for his trade-union solidarity was weakened to the advantage of the employer.

The atmosphere rapidly degenerated into a race war. In 1919 a chance incident, the murder of a black by a white and the refusal of the police to arrest the murderer, brought matters to a head. For several days there was an absolute reign of terror while the infuriated mob massacred the negroes in a veritable pogrom. Peace was finally restored superficially, but daily intimidation still continues. Outrages are common, and the menace of a fresh crisis is latent. The poisonous virus of the South has penetrated only too well, and the danger is all the greater since the northern States have accorded civil equality to the negroes. They are allowed to vote, their representatives sit in the local assemblies, their children go with the whites to the public schools, and mixed marriages are not forbidden by law.

What remains to be done to solve the problem? Legally very little, but socially almost everything; for a pitiless ostracism excludes the coloured man from all social contact. We must admit that the new experience in the North has only retarded the hope of a solution. Although theoretically well disposed, the Northerners are beginning to lose their old tolerance; for instead of merely giving free advice to others, they are now coping themselves with the difficulties of intimate contact. The negro on his side endures this ostracism with growing impatience. As he becomes more civilized by city life his hostility takes on a bitterness and a hardness which the South never had to contend with, for in the North there are no hereditary sentiments to relieve the tension.

In the great cities of the North the negroes are no longer the "good niggers" of legend, for they are neither humble nor deferential. In the economic struggle they have not fared so badly. In the factories they get good wages, they have their own newspapers, banks, and theatres, and among their *élite* are to be found lawyers, doctors, writers, and artists—a living proof of the fact that the race is able to rise. What more do they want? Their grandparents never dreamed of such progress, but at the bottom of their hearts they are longing not merely for civil equality but for social equality, or at least the theoretic possibility of social equality; and the tragedy is that they do not realize that it is impossible. "Are we not men?" the best of them will ask. "We are conscious of our merits. Why should we be treated as infectious pariahs? Or even worse, as if we did not exist?" Just as the South has always feared, they are basing their pretentions on rights, or a semblance of rights.

There are now two negro questions, one in the South and one in the North; but the second reacts on the first. The coloured man who has lived in New York, and particularly if he has been to Europe in the army, frets under the traditional suppression. This opens up a new phase.

Booker T. Washington made the first great effort toward uplift when he founded Tuskegee Institute at the end of the last century and with the aid of certain rich Easterners tried to give professional education to his people. This policy is being continued in the South by a sort of negro *élite* consisting of their Methodist bishops, their schoolmasters, and the remarkable executives at Tuskegee. However, the more ardent elements of their *intelligentsia,* especially in the North, are no longer content with such pacific collaboration. By means of the "Urban League" and the *Messenger* they have united to defend the material interests of their brothers who have migrated to the cities. In their reviews, too, *The Crisis* and *The Opportunity,* they exalt their race consciousness and their artistic and intellectual achievements, which are vehemently opposed by those who wish to keep them under the yoke. W. E. Burghardt Du Bois, that penetrating coloured writer who maintains that the blacks can equal the whites in everything, demands uncompromised social equality.

Though we must not take too seriously the Messiah-like movement for a return to Africa inspired by the agitator Garvey, on the other hand we must not ignore the fact that this American *élite* is strengthening the unity of the black race all over the world. Among these people a negro who "passes" is a traitor, and a woman who marries a white is criticized, and if she becomes a white man's mistress she loses all caste. New York is the centre of this advanced negro thought, but the South is also evolving toward it, either through outside influence or natural development. The wealthy negro of the Cotton Belt, whose credit is better than the "poor white's" with the local banks, is a new factor in the evolution; but exactly how the Baptist and Methodist ministers will react is still a matter of conjecture. They are born leaders, however, and even when illiterate and undeserving they have great influence with the masses. There is a great gulf between the civilized negro of Harlem and the husky brute of the Mississippi plantation, and obviously the solution of the problem cannot be the same in both cases.

The whites have reacted differently in each case. In the North where the negro is not hated, they wished him well of his freedom; for they hardly ever saw him until quite recently and looked on the whole question as missionary work to be conducted far away in the South. Since then, however, he has come so much closer that the problem is seen from a different angle, and it has taken much courage for the Protestant churches to look it squarely in the face. The leaders of the Y.M.C.A., the Federation of Churches of Christ, and so forth, adopted the Christian viewpoint without hesitation or reserve. It was a generous attempt and free from ulterior motive, but in practice they were obliged to yield to a thousand compromises. It is all very well to say that all men are brothers, but contact is impossible in the same clubs, the same universities, and the same swimming pools. In point of fact the negro is received scarcely more freely in New York than in New Orleans, though certain daring spirits do frequent intellectual black circles; and a few Mediterraneans, who are severely frowned on, continue to associate with the common negroes. Meanwhile, the great majority is inclined to take the attitude of the South; so the separation of the races, though it may be slightly less insulting, is just as real.

The South remains firm in its resistance, though interesting experiments are being carried out. As the negroes have no elected representatives capable of speaking for them officially, various substitutes have come forward spontaneously. In several cities, the local Chamber of Commerce has appointed a commission to bring the two races into contact.

and in a similar spirit the Commission on Inter-Racial Relations originated in religious circles in Atlanta in 1906. In more than 800 counties sub-committees were created to establish permanent personal contact between the better elements, in order to arrive at a mutual understanding on the practical difficulties of daily life. In the end the indirect effect of the migration to the North was very similar. At first the Southerners tried to retain the negroes by force, for naturally they were furious at losing their labour supply; but later on in the country west of the Mississippi they began to replace them with Mexicans. Finally the more sensible among them saw that if they were to hold the blacks, the only reasonable way was to treat them better. All this, however, is only a drop in an ocean of hatred, for the South really has not changed; in fact, its influence is spreading to the rest of the country.

An unprejudiced observer is forced to a painful conclusion. In the old days the whites may have been able to keep ten million men of another race under their yoke, but it is now very difficult and will probably be impossible in the future. What then are the avenues of escape? A return to Africa? The idea cannot be seriously entertained. The destruction of the race? Equally impossible. Fusion? This is occurring to a certain extent, but one hardly dares suggest it as a solution.

The only answer is that the whites must learn to live side by side with a race that they cannot possibly assimilate. However, they can comfort themselves with the knowledge that the percentage of blacks is diminishing. In 1920 there were 10,463,000 blacks out of a total population of 105,711,000, or some 9.9 per cent., whereas in 1860 they comprised 14.1 per cent. The reason is that though their birth rate is greater than the whites' (25.3 per 1,000 in 1922 as against 22.2), their death rate is also much greater (16.3 as compared to 11.6). They die like flies in the cities into which they are pouring more and more rapidly. No doubt their death rate could be diminished by hygienic measures, but the southern whites look on such efforts with apprehension.   On the other hand, if the negro standard of living were improved, we must not forget that the birth rate would decrease somewhat.   The fear of an irresistible tide of blacks can therefore be set aside as chimeric.   Still, the ten million of today will be twelve or fifteen million tomorrow, and will not stop there.

Is the régime of yesterday and today to carry on?

"Yes," replies the South; "nothing else is possible."

Why not suppress the insults, recognize the negro as a man, but maintain the separation of the races?

"No!" answers the horror-stricken South.   "This very contempt is the best possible barrier, and once this line of defence had been pierced, we should have a hideous confusion."

No matter which way we turn in the North or the South, there seems to be no solution.   The colour problem is an abyss into which we can look only with terror.

CHAPTER VII

RACE CONSCIOUSNESS AND EUGENICS

UP to the beginning of the twentieth century, America believed in the theory of environment which was fashionable at that time, but when the Melting Pot began to overflow with immigrants she adopted the views of Mendel and de Gobineau. Their theories were popularized by brilliant writers who converted a large following to the thesis that, in the long run, heredity is the most important factor, and that the hierarchy of races with the Nordics in the lead is an established scientific fact. Eugenics, which in reality is a mixture of biology and politics, looked to this doctrine for a scientific basis on which to develop the future American race. This was quite in keeping with the nationalistic reaction that has taken place since the War. If you visit the United States you must not forget your Bible, but you must also take a treatise on eugenics. Armed with these two talismans, you will never get beyond your depth.

Lothrop Stoddard[1] and Madison Grant[2] have spread these ideas throughout America in their widely-read books. They have firmly implanted the theory that civilization, like a delicate flower, survives only as the result of continuous human energy; for its creative force depends on superior germ plasm. Fundamentally, therefore, it varies with the race. In our day we are no longer menaced by invasions of hordes of barbarians, but peaceable penetration by inferior human elements is an insidious danger that is equally

[1] *The Rising Tide of Color* and *The Revolt Against Civilization,* by Lothrop Stoddard. Charles Scribner's Sons.
[2] *The Passing of the Great Race,* by Madison Grant. Charles Scribner's Sons.

formidable. The backward peoples of the world are the most prolific, just as they are often the most vigorous physically. They are attracted to civilized centres by high wages and better living conditions, but their advent spells disaster, for they dislocate the established order of things and sterilize the original superior races. The mingling of the races is equally fatal, as it undermines the ethnic foundations of civilization and introduces a mongrel strain which leads to decadence. Today every one knows that acquired characteristics cannot be handed down to posterity, and as the influence of environment is strictly limited, the individual cannot pass on more than he has actually received from his ancestors. The supreme importance of heredity is the great biological discovery of modern times.

According to this theory, what can we expect from the influx of immigrants into the United States? Since 1890 they have been mostly of inferior races that do not amalgamate, and though they may have individual qualifications they also have definite limitations. History shows that the inferior races multiply on account of their vast inferiority, whereas the superior do not tend to perpetuate themselves. The aristocracy of America is thus in jeopardy, for we might almost say that the race is giving way to another that is being surreptitiously substituted for it. If we write Anglo-Saxon in place of "superior," and Slav, Latin, or Mediterranean instead of "inferior," without mentioning negroes or Asiatics, we have the political aspect of this scientific theory, in fact the doctrine of the Ku Klux Klan. Once we admit that superiority can be transmitted only through blood, we arrive at the same conclusion as the eugenists, that the character of the race must be preserved by legal measures. The Spartans were striving for the same ends when they evolved the theory that the race could be improved only by eliminating the mediocre and multiplying the best elements. It is interesting to note that the idea of

caste which has been rejected by Europe appears attractive
to certain Americans.

The attitude toward natality is bound to be entirely different in France and the United States. For political and
military reasons our great ground of anxiety is a decrease
in the total population, but this does not apply in America,
where, according to the Malthusian doctrines inherited from
England, an excess of population is regarded as an evil.
Public opinion there is alarmed by the fact that in the South
and certain parts of the West, the Anglo-Saxon stock is not
reproducing itself, whereas the birth rate among the immigrants is high. In Massachusetts, for example, the foreign-
born woman is twice as prolific as the American-born. After
a thorough investigation, Professors Ross and Baber discovered that in the middle class of the central States, which
is purely American, the families of the present generation
have decreased 38½ per cent. in size as compared with the
previous one; 13 per cent. of the marriages are childless,
and 18 per cent. have only one child. On the other hand,
among the Czecho-Slovak immigrants only 2.4 per cent. of
the homes are childless, 2.5 per cent. among the Russians,
2.6 per cent. among the Poles, 3.9 per cent. among the Germans, and 4.9 per cent. among the Italians.

In certain classes of Americans, reproduction seems
almost to have ceased. Intellectuals and university graduates
marry late and have practically no descendants. Sixty per
cent. of the women with university degrees do not marry
at all; of those who do, 36 per cent. have no children, or
in other words, three-fifths of the most cultured women
do not leave descendants. These figures have been published
and quoted all over the country. Professors Ross and Baber
come to the melancholy conclusion that the old Anglo-Saxon
element is diminishing, not merely absolutely, but also relatively, and that in a century it is probable that it will only
constitute a negligible factor in the American population

In view of these incontestable facts, the eugenists prophesy dire results. On the basis of the present ratio, 1,000 Harvard graduates, according to Dr. Davenport, will have only fifty descendants at the end of two centuries, whereas 1,000 Rumanians in Boston will have 100,000.

These sensational deductions, so dear to the New World, do not take into account the changes that are operating among the immigrants themselves. When their standard of living is raised by assimilation, they also adopt the customs of the country as regards natality. The second generation still has more children than the original inhabitants, but the fecundity of the third and fourth differs very slightly from the general level of the country. All these pessimistic calculations, though they are obvious exaggerations, favour the foreigner as against the American, the Catholic as against the Protestant. The present attitude of the 100 per cent. American, in the towns at any rate, is fatal for his race. When he has few children or none at all, he excuses himself by saying that he cannot afford more, that there would be so many difficulties about housing and servants, and he really has to buy a car; or else his wife's professional career makes a family inadvisable. Also, in many cases, marriage comes too late in life, and the sex relation therefore is only secondary. The problem is not so much depopulation as maintaining the racial equilibrium, and the danger of the present race's being replaced by another. The two chief influences reacting on American thought are the neo-Malthusian or birth-control movement on the one hand, and the Catholic Church which preaches unrestricted fecundity on the other. Morals, hygiene, and social welfare are the arguments invoked by both sides, but underneath it all lie political considerations; for it is this question that will decide the centre of gravity of the nation in the future.

As in England, the birth-control propaganda has been conducted in the spirit of a crusade, supported chiefly by the intellectuals, often from among the best people, and by a few fanatics. It is difficult to understand why they should be so vehement, for after all the average Protestant was converted long ago to voluntary birth control. Quite apart from theory, experience has taught them that nothing is more deplorable than a heavy birth rate coinciding with a heavy death rate, and that large families are apt to be a charge on the community. Anyway, the world has quite enough of the lowest classes already, certainly if a decent standard of living is to be maintained. The Malthusians accordingly concentrate their efforts on the "poor whites" of the Alleghanies and the South, and more especially on the aliens of the first and second generation, who through either their own ignorance or the influence of their priests leave nature to determine the size of their families. Good or bad, the real meaning of the propaganda is that the inferiors have many children, the superiors few, to re-establish the balance by trying to increase the fecundity of the superiors would be both undesirable and hopeless, although it is possible to slow up the reproductive speed of the inferiors. These are the ideas that are taught at the special clinics of the Birth Control League. Their activities correspond perfectly to the outlook of the responsible classes who have taken it on themselves to care for the poor. If some humorist were to propose a Conference on the International Limitation of Births, the Americans would take up the idea in a twinkling!

The eugenic movement, which was originated in England by Francis Galton, has become quite important in the United States during the past twenty years. After making due allowance for the exaggeration of the enthusiasts, we must admit that it expresses the American line of thought exactly, and therefore we should not be astonished if a new code of racial ethics and reproduction laws should be evolved from it. The eugenist lays stress on the importance of heredity in the development of the individual. He maintains that nothing can replace inborn qualities, and that it is futile to try to develop any particular traits if the character lacks the initial germ. Hence, if we wish to improve the race, we must determine which individuals should be allowed to reproduce. There is thus to be a rational selection based on biology and not on individual sentiment, for the matter is of too great consequence to be left to the caprices of irresponsible people. The program is to consist of medical, legal, and social measures designed to bring about an increase in the number of children from the superior grades of society, a decrease in the number from the inferior grades, and an absolute cessation from those below a certain mental and physical level.

The effect of such a movement is enormous. It means creating a new eugenic conscience and involves a code of morals based on reproduction, which is practically non-existent at present. The eugenists go even further and propose to legislate to reduce degeneracy and so deliberately construct a new race. The Americans love the classical Greek ideals, and in their sanctimonious way they are always ready to accept a theory if they think it is scientific. In fairness we must add that like their British cousins, thoughtful Americans possess a strong racial sense. For example, look at the way they keep the negroes and the Asiatics in their place, and even the Portuguese and Mediterraneans, if they suspect them of a touch of the tar-brush. For over a generation the idea has been growing among them that a superior race is under a moral obligation to maintain its ascendancy and produce offspring that are healthy and free from doubtful strains. This is not exactly a religious ideal, but the Protestant churches encourage it; for they consider themselves rather the *élite,* and extol anything that is considered pure. Neither is it entirely a mat-

ter of nationalism, for an American looks on reproduction
from much the same angle as a breeder of dogs.

The European individualist resents having his most intimate relations organized for the good of the community,
but the reformers of the New World hope to make short
work of "passion," for they have made such magnificent
progress that they are beginning to believe they can accomplish everything. Efficiency has such prestige on the
American side of the Atlantic that all objections are set
aside, and even the most extreme measures are approved in
its name. Eugenics in fact is part of what in the United
States is called "service."

A whole system of new legislation is being developed on
the subject. Many of the measures no doubt are not eugenic,
but simply social hygiene, such as for example the law in
Wisconsin that makes pre-nuptial examination obligatory.
Other laws are eugenic in their effect, although they were
originally adopted for very different reasons. When the
law of 1911 in Nevada orders a murderer to be sterilized
as a punishment it is simply a matter of repression, but it
is pure and simple eugenics when similar laws are applied
either to favour the reproduction of the better elements or
to prevent it among the feeble-minded. Sterilizing to improve the race is like restricting immigration to exclude
certain races. Both are distinctly eugenic.

Eugenic sterilization aims to destroy the reproductive
capacity of the individual by means of certain surgical operations which are carried out in accordance with the law,
and which are used principally in cases of degeneracy such
as lunatics and criminals. "Vasectomy" and "salpingec-
tomy," as these operations are termed, are not the same as
castration; for the patient can still have sexual intercourse,
although he cannot produce children. Since 1907, twenty-

three States have passed laws of this nature, and they were still being applied in 1926 in nineteen [3] of them.

A certain amount of confusion as to the exact objective is apparent in the declarations of various legislatures. In Nevada the intention was only to punish criminals guilty of raping girls of less than six years of age. Such vengeance against sex is undoubtedly puritanical, but when people came forward voluntarily to be sterilized it was decided that it was not always a punishment; and the courts ruled the law unconstitutional. On the other hand, the operation was considered legal when the aim was the improvement of the race rather than punishment. The legislation actually in force at the present time comes under this category, as it is applied to idiots, incurable degenerates of all kinds who are not necessarily shut up in asylums, second offenders in cases of certain crimes, and the irresponsible and vicious who, if given their liberty, would probably procreate undesirables.

The ambition of the eugenists reaches still further. When the diagnosis of depravity has been finally perfected, they hope by legal sterilization to eliminate not only idiots and degenerates, but also drunkards, tubercular persons, syphilitics, epileptics, and even the blind, the deaf, hunchbacks, and in a general way all potential parents of inadequate offspring. As in the case of vaccination, the individual will be forced to submit for the welfare of the community. But is such a program legal? Does it not violate the rights of the individual as laid down in the Constitution? In the States where such legislation has been confirmed as constitutional by the courts, it has been decided that the decision of a criminal court or of a committee of doctors from an asylum or a hospital is sufficient guarantee that

[3] Washington, California, Connecticut, Iowa, North Dakota, Kansas, Wisconsin, Michigan, Nebraska, New Hampshire, Oregon, South Dakota, Montana, Delaware, Virginia, Idaho, Minnesota, Utah and Maine. In four other States: Indiana, New York, New Jersey and Nevada, the laws have either been declared unconstitutional or repealed.

the operation is advisable. In Indiana, New Jersey, Nevada, and New York, however, these laws have been declared unconstitutional, because they do not grant to every citizen the legal recourse laid down in the Fourteenth Amendment to the Federal Constitution. The controversy goes back to fundamentals, for if a State were to assume the right to compel the individual arbitrarily, it would mean the beginning of a new epoch in human civilization.

We are far from this, however, for legal sterilization is still very restricted. Up to July 1, 1925, there had been altogether 6,244 operations, of which 4,636 were in California, 355 in Kansas, 313 in Oregon, and 262 in Nebraska. We must not overlook the fact that in future the rights of the individual will be protected less by the text of the law than by the interpretation of judges who are apt to be sensitive to the pressure of public opinion. If we enquire into what the public thinks of such extreme ideas, we discover that there has never been any popular demand for them. In order to vote a eugenic law, it is generally sufficient for it to be taken up by a few individuals, such as the director of the Board of Health, a prominent surgeon, and some university professors. The text is drawn by this handful of experts and is then quietly passed by the local legislature, always provided, of course, no organized opposition is stirred up. Hostility to such laws has generally come from the Catholic clergy, who maintain that the community has no right to prevent the birth of a human being. Doctors also have protested occasionally, and governors have even opposed their veto; but generally the public has not been aroused. The specialists tell them that the measure is for the welfare of the community, and they remind the taxpayers what it costs the budget to care for the scum of humanity. In any case, as the Americans are imbued with the spirit of progress, they are quite willing to vote a new law even if they never apply it.

In spite of these reservations, the eugenic movement is typical of present-day America, for it indicates a keen, though not necessarily intelligent, preoccupation with the future of the race. Against such considerations the rights of the individual are powerless, for by a sort of mysticism America considers the needs of the community supreme. Ever since Plato's *Republic,* this collective spirit has lain dormant, or at best has been maintained by a few dreamers. In the hands of a people who are conscious of their superiority and are ready to sterilize remorselessly negroes and Asiatics, or in fact any inferior races, eugenics may eventually relegate the "sacred rights of man" to the limbo of half-forgotten achievements.

CHAPTER VIII

IMMIGRATION

THE American immigration laws of 1917, 1921, and 1924 are the logical outcome of the instinctive fears and beliefs of the last generation. It is literally a case of political eugenics, as henceforth admission to the country is to be decided not on the personal value of the immigrant but on his heredity. Their defensive attitude proves that the American people have reached maturity. The immigration laws, indeed, are the most significant occurrence in their history since the Civil War.

The principle of unrestricted immigration predominated during the greater part of the nineteenth century, for individual selection was instituted only after 1882. By closing the door sternly to all undesirables, the 1907 law confirmed and extended certain earlier regulations and definitely announced that the country was determined to protect its population against unwelcome additions. Nevertheless, except for Chinese and Japanese, who had already been excluded by special agreements, the new law did not take racial origins into account.

Though it maintains the principle of individual selection and still further restricts admission, the new legislation also introduces the entirely new doctrine of ethnic origin. This new policy was partly initiated by the 1917 law, which absolutely forbade immigration from certain parts of the world, such as most of southern and western Asia (India, Siam, Indo-China, Afghanistan, Beluchistan, Arabia), and also the Polynesian islands. China and Japan had been previously legislated for. The object was evidently to exclude the yellow and brown races, as it was found impossible to assimilate them.

The 1921 and 1924 laws, which were drawn up on the same defensive lines, were extended to exclude certain parts of Europe also. Persons not eligible for naturalization were considered not entitled to permanent residence. This shut out all Asiatics without appeal, but other races were classified according to their geographic origin. Immigrants from Canada and from Central and South America were considered neighbours, and as such were admitted without limitation. The quota system was applied to Europe, Africa, Mediterranean, and Russian Asia; that is to say, the annual contingent of each country was not to exceed 2 per cent. of their natives residing in the United States in 1890. This was the final decision according to the law of 1924, but the law of 1921 had decreed 3 per cent. of the 1910 figures.

This differential treatment favoured the Nordic element at the expense of the Mediterranean and Slavs, for in 1890 and even in 1910 the immigrations of the latter were not so important. The result is that according to the 1924 law the annual contingent can consist of only 13.3 per cent. Latins and Slavs, as against 86.6 per cent. Nordics. Out of 165,000 allowed in each year, the Anglo-Irish can send 62,000, the Germans 51,000, but the Italians only 3,845, and the Russians only 2,248. After 1927 the figure is to be reduced permanently to 150,000 (apart from immigrants from the American continent), and the quota for each nation will be in proportion to its previous contribution to the American people.

By means of these drastic laws the country has clearly demonstrated its intention of remaining not merely for the white race but also Anglo-Saxon in character, and therefore no further mass immigration would be admitted. It is difficult to understand how such decisive measures could have been imposed without meeting with opposition from the interests that were adversely affected. Lothrop Stoddard, Madison Grant, and many brilliant eugenists had put forward the theories of Mendel and resurrected de Gobineau. There is no doubt of the sincerity of these talented men, but though they thought their ideas were purely scientific they were really partly political, and they were expressing the passions lying dormant around them. America would never have taken such a keen interest in the discussions on heredity, environment, and the superiority of the Nordic races, had the controversy not presented conditions which each town —each village, even—knew only too well. The Catholic menace, the Latin-Slav invasion, and the flood of foreigners generally, were stern realities, not the inventions of pamphleteers. When the tide of the Mediterranean and Oriental immigrations which had been dammed up by the War again reached its old level,[1] it was only natural that the idea of excluding them should have caught the public imagination, for the Americans at that time were distressed and nervous, and also jealously determined to remain masters in their own house.

Even this, however, would not have been sufficient without the extraordinary coincidence of interests opposed to a further influx of new population. The persistent introduction of labour drawn from the lowest classes was having a dampening effect on wages, and organized labour accordingly wished to restrict immigration. The interests of the employers would normally have been on the other side, for if after the Armistice they had considered only the requirements of their factories, they would certainly have preferred the free importation of an unlimited amount of labour. However, being greatly alarmed by Bolshevism at the time, they feared that if they let in "hands," they would also let

[1] *Mediterranean and Oriental Immigration*

1918	111,000
1919	141,000
1920	430,000
1921	805,000

in revolutionary brains. Thus the employers shared, for the time being at any rate, the point of view of the workers, and the coalition was irresistible.

There was, however, a certain opposition, consisting chiefly of employers determined to get labour at a discount, Jews who wished to admit other Jews, and foreign-born citizens who were anxious to have members of their family in Europe join them in the New World. Against it were also the more sentimental of advanced thinkers who were still faithful to the idea of America as an asylum for the world, and lastly the Catholic Church, always in the opposition, which with its scattered alien congregation obviously could not approve of any policy of racial exclusion. These were only minorities, however, who were out of sympathy with the general feeling of the country, and whose influence was not very great. The two political parties united and passed the various laws against immigration by heavy majorities. Out of 435 votes the opposition only succeeded in registering 58, and all these came from the representatives of the foreign populations in the large cities.

We can undoubtedly regard the new immigration policy as expressing the wishes of the whole country. It was the result of deep study and conscientious inquiry, and not the work of any one party. Even science was asked to collaborate, for Congress did not express its opinion until the eugenists had proved conclusively that Nordic Europe[2] could continue to give useful aid in the racial development of the American people, but that it would be degraded by the importation of Latins and Slavs. Weismann, Mendel, and other biologists and ethnologists were called in; but behind all this scientific apparatus it was easy to see the primitive reaction of the genuine American.

The immediate effects of this legislation were obvious enough, but the ultimate results can be only vaguely con-

[2] Nordic Europe: British Isles, Scandinavia, Germany, Belgium, Holland, Switzerland, Lombardy, and northern France.

jectured as yet. The new régime, in its restrictive sense, began to make itself felt seriously only in 1925. After several years of fairly numerous immigration, the figures descended to a very low level, where they are evidently to stay in the future.

Date	Total Immigration	Net Immigration After Deducting Emigration
1922	310,000	111,000
1923	523,000	441,000
1924	707,000	630,000
1925	294,000	201,000
1926	304,000	227,000

In 1926 the Anglo-Saxon purists attained their objective as far as immigration was concerned, for out of a total of 227,000 immigrants, Europe furnished only 94,000 and the New World 133,000. Out of all the contingents subject to quota, Nordic Europe accounted for 85.6 per cent. in 1925 and southeastern Europe only 13.3 per cent. In other words, the pre-war proportion was completely reversed, and the total allowed (165,000) was not even reached. No doubt many Europeans managed to cross the Canadian and Mexican frontiers incognito, but the immigration services will probably reduce this leakage in the future. The truth is that the Old World has ceased to play an important rôle in the peopling of the United States.

This sudden cutting off of the supply of urgently needed labour gave rise to a zealous search for substitutes. As the borders of the neighbouring countries were legally open, their citizens left en masse for the United States. The Mexicans poured into the Southwest in hundreds of thousands. According to the American Bureau of Immigration, not less than 435,000 Mexicans settled in the United States between 1912 and 1925; but this figure is only ap-

proximate, for there are today over 1,000,000, possibly
1,500,000, there. It was estimated by the Immigration
Department of California that Texas contained over
500,000 Mexicans in 1925, California 250,000, New Mexico
180,000, and Arizona and Colorado 60,000 each. They
have penetrated as far as the Northwest, where they work
in the harvests, and to the Great Lakes, where they are
employed in the iron and steel industry. It is very difficult
to keep count of them, for they are essentially nomads
and come and go across the frontier repeatedly without
being checked up. They are easy-going in their habits,
but as difficult to assimilate as the Indians. They have
undertaken all the unskilled work that the Chinese, Italians,
and Austro-Hungarians did before them; but they are the
last source of alien labour on which the employers can rely,
and after them the country will have to depend upon itself
for manual work. With them another phase in the history
of the United States will be closed.

An analogous movement occurred along the Canadian
frontier. From 1921 to 1926 the number of Canadian immigrants was given as 629,000, of whom 201,000 came in
1924, 101,000 in 1925, and 91,000 in 1926. Naturally these
were not all genuine Canadians, but included many camou-
flaged Europeans. According to the 1920 census, over
1,125,000 Canadian-born were already in the United States.
This is one of the most curious phenomena in the American
situation today. The attraction exercised by the States over
its neighbours is so strong that it continues to drain from
them an appreciable part of their people, and thus shows
that limiting immigration, although a sound measure
politically, was ahead of its time economically.

The final consequences of the immigration laws are likely
to be very serious, for when the reservoir of unskilled labour can no longer be replenished from below, manufacturers will have to rely more and more on machinery. The

whole country will be forced further along the road of standardization, and only in so far as it is able to rely on machinery instead of workmen will it be able to meet the competition of densely populated countries with low wages. This very struggle for existence, however, will maintain the American people at the high level of initiative and research which has been the cause of their economic health in the past. The new régime will prevent them from resting on the laurels of their easy prosperity.

The social effect of this evolution may possibly be far-reaching. With the final disappearance of the artisan and the substitution of a perfected organization in which each human unit is utilized as an annex to a machine, a potentially large labouring class is being created, with fingers more rapid than brains. The risk is that they may become so automatic that all initiative will be stifled. That will mean the end of the era of creative production by individual skill such as still exists in France. Circumstances have thus condemned the United States to specialize more and more in mass production and to exaggerate the industrial side of their civilization at the very time when available hands are diminishing.

The effect of this will extend far beyond the labouring class. Already with the restriction of immigration the masses have been attracted to the factories by higher wages, until it has become impossible to get domestic servants. This is a matter of extreme importance. Wealthy people can still get maids by paying fabulous wages, but the middle class find it increasingly difficult and are finally forced to do their own housework. This is speeding up social uniformity and making family life more difficult, and so reacting indirectly on the birth rate. The country has adapted itself by organizing society and standardizing even the home. The results are far from uncomfortable, but a truly individual existence is permitted only to the very few.

From this point of view America has reached a degree of social equality and democracy which no European country has ever attained. This is bound to be accentuated by the immigration régime, which will mean not only social unification, but in the end ethnic unification of the working-class as well. Differences of race, language, and customs divide up the workers at present even in the same factory, and frequently prevent them from organizing powerful trade unions. This is partially due to the extraordinary domination of the American employer, but he will not be likely to enjoy his present advantages for more than another generation—always excepting the case of the negroes, of course. The employers should foresee the approach of this new phase in the organization of labour.

In the end the most important effect of the new immigration policy will be its reaction on the total volume of the population, for from now on any increase must depend on the excess of births over deaths.

The following table shows the proportions in which net immigration (less emigration) has contributed during the last century to the numerical increase of the American people during the past 100 years.

Date	Total Increase	Net Immigration	Percentage
1820–30	3,228,000	137,000	4
1830–40	4,203,000	558,000	13
1840–50	6,122,000	1,599,000	26
1850–60	8,251,000	2,663,000	32
1860–70	8,375,000	2,356,000	28
1870–80	10,337,000	2,530,000	24
1880–90	12,792,000	4,273,000	33
1890–1900 ...	13,047,000	3,239,000	25
1900–10	15,978,000	5,558,000	35
1910–20 [3]	13,738,000	3,467,000	25
Totals	96,071,000	26,380,000	Percentage: 27.4

[3] See footnote on page 127.

Immigration has thus contributed a little over a quarter of the increase during the past century. The great influx about 1850, 1880, and 1900 is indicated by a slight increase in the percentages, but it did not seriously alter the general curve. Similarly any falling off in immigration is apparent in the results of each decade, as for example 1910-20.[4] In the long run, however, the regular excess of births over deaths remains the dominant factor. The immigration figures for the decade 1920–30, and still more after that date, will be considerably reduced, and therefore the relationship between the birth rate and the death rate will be more important than ever.

The presence of a large alien population, which up to now has been constantly renewed, certainly accounts for the great increase in the American birth rate, for 22½ births per 1,000 obviously does not reflect the normal customs of the country. The original Anglo-Saxon element in the cities is scarcely reproducing itself. This semi-sterility of the "100 percenters" dates back many years, but it has not been apparent owing to the rapid decline in the death rate, which in 1924 amounted to only 11.9 per 1,000, and also because a fairly high birth rate has been maintained in the country districts of the South and West and in the States of foreign population. The statistics suggest a normally rapid increase in population, but this is only an illusion, for with the decrease in immigration, another important source of population will dry up; namely, the exceptional fecundity of the foreigners. It is therefore improbable that the birth rate will remain above 22 per 1,000. Even if mortality is low it is not to be expected that the rate of survival, which was 10.6 per 1,000 in 1924, will continue; for in order to maintain this rate there would have to be either a return to the land, a recrudescence of immigration, or a decided change in the family customs of the people, none of which are at all likely. On the basis of a survival rate of 11 per 1,000,

---

[4] For increase of population in the United States for 1910-20, see Census Monograph 1, page 21.

the population would double itself in sixty years even without immigration. Therefore, since the survival rate, and with it the rate of increase, is bound to diminish slowly during the coming decades, it is not probable that by the end of the century the United States will have reached the 200,000,000 mark.

In 1925, with 113,000,000 inhabitants, the density of population of the United States was only 36 per square mile, whereas with the same density as France (182 inhabitants per square mile), America would have over 550,000,000. Even with a population of 200,000,000 inhabitants, which we have estimated for the end of the twentieth century, the density will only amount to 64 per square mile. Part of the country is desert, of course; but the danger of over-population is still very remote, and yet it is partly to ward off this danger that immigration is being restricted.

It is interesting to note to what an extent the Malthusian theory has become fashionable again among the Anglo-Saxons, after having been set aside by the optimism of the nineteenth century. America no longer desires great masses, which she regards as a menace to her standard of living. Her confidence in the output of the individual has convinced her that she no longer needs the immense battalions of labour who helped in the past to people her territory, build up her industries, and create her national market. Instead of the possible advantages of a large population as in Europe or China, she prefers a low human density with a high standard of living and therefore deliberately shuts herself off from the rest of the world. This is a most important decision, and it will necessitate not only the skilful organization of production, but also in the end a definite military policy. History shows that sooner or later, rich and sparsely populated territories must be defended. American public opinion is not blind to these dangers, but it has made its choice; and in spite of the objections of the employers, the restriction of immigration is so much in harmony with the wishes of the people that there is very little chance of its being seriously modified.

The danger of a numerical inundation is past, and the declining birth rate does away with any chance of over-population; yet from the point of view of the composition of the race, it is quite a question whether the measures against foreign penetration have not been taken too late, for these heterogeneous seeds will continue to grow once they have been planted. We must not exaggerate the danger, however; for it is not a real menace to civilization. All these foreigners will become Americanized, but they will not be Anglo-Saxons; for Protestant America will not assimilate them. No one can prophesy as to the future of the American type, and therefore it is only to be expected that this question should be a profound anxiety to those who are attached to traditions.

CHAPTER IX

THE KU KLUX KLAN

THE Ku Klux Klan is one of those manifestations which rage for a while and then die down and disappear. No one takes them seriously when the crisis is over, but they seem very tragic at the time. Nevertheless they reveal a latent source of trouble which may remain long after the outbreak has passed. The Ku Klux Klan is an extreme form of Protestant nationalism; in fact, we must almost consider it a fever, as otherwise we are apt to exaggerate it during the crisis and to belittle it when the temperature has fallen again.

It is more than a secret society; it is a state of mind. It is more than a whim; it is the revival of a whole series of earlier revolts against immigrants, negroes, Catholics, and "outsiders" generally. This nationalistic chauvinism dates back many years without even a change in its vocabulary. At the end of the eighteenth century we find the public on guard against "un-American" ideas. About 1830, when the Irish immigration began to be important, "native American tickets" grew up spontaneously at the elections, the idea being to keep foreigners out of elective or honorary positions. The "Know Nothing" secret society reached its climax in 1855 during the peaceful German-Irish invasion. By means of pass-words, secret ceremonies, etc., it endeavoured to combat the growing influence of Catholicism, which was making itself felt in the "ignorant foreign vote," as it was called. It is estimated that at its maximum the "Know Nothings" had some 1,250,000 members.

A generation passed, and in 1887 we see the anti-Catho-

lic American Protective Association struggling against the
Latin-Slav invasion. A false encyclical was produced to
prove that the Pope was claiming the entire American con-
tinent on the ground that Christopher Columbus was a
Catholic. Protestant America was threatened! The Middle
West and the West responded to the appeal of the A.P.A.,
and many recruits were obtained in Michigan, Ohio, Il-
linois, Iowa, Missouri, Kansas, and Nebraska. The "Know
Nothings" and the A.P.A. are the forerunners of the present
Klan in so far as the latter is directed against Catholics,
Jews, and foreigners.

The negro, however, has been the principal objective
ever since the Klan was first founded by the Southerners
in 1866 at Pulaski, Tenn. The aim of the original Klan, to
"maintain the supremacy of the white race in the old slave
States," its methods, its hierarchy, and its picturesque
language, have all been handed down intact to the present
society. When the "carpet-baggers" united with the negroes after the Civil War, the Southerners were able to
resist only by outlaw methods. They fought the "impious
domination" of the negroes in the name of their own racial
superiority, and, as Klansmen, undertook to carry out an
unwritten code which they considered to be the only just
one. Realizing that anything solemn and mysterious has
an immense effect on the ignorant and superstitious negro,
they chose as their weapon a secret society, which in any
case has a great attraction for the American mind.

Their impressive white cowls, their silent torch-light processions by night, skeleton hands clutching at the terrified
blacks, warning letters, anonymous notices, threatened pun-
ishments, horse-whippings administered to the disobedient,
and even executions, on occasion, gave them an uncanny
power. All this paraphernalia created a terrifying and
legendary prestige which was further accentuated by the
grandiloquent titles of their officers. A Grand Sorcerer

commanded the Invisible Empire.   Each kingdom had its Grand Dragon, each dominion its Grand Titan, each cave its Grand Cyclops, not to mention the Grand Monk, the Grand Turk, and the Grand Sentinel. . . . At first the Klan was composed of the better classes, but it soon attracted the worst, until finally it was dissolved in 1869 by the very people who had founded it.   Local public opinion, however, felt that by its intervention it had brought the whites safely through the crisis, and its spirit has survived in the savage determination to use force if necessary to keep the South a white man's country.

Fifty years later, in 1915, it needed only the fear of another crisis for the Klan to be revived at Atlanta, Georgia. It did not attain any importance until 1917 or 1918, when the war-time mob psychology asserted itself in the reappearance of nationalism and xenophobia.   This time the movement was founded by William Joseph Simmons—"Colonel" Simmons, rather, as he had been a volunteer in the Spanish-American War.   The Colonel is one of the many Protestant lay preachers who were impregnated with a sort of imperialistic mysticism by the War.   The secret society which he founded with the time-honoured title of the Ku Klux Klan was "consecrated as Protestant to the teaching of the Christian religion, and pledged as white men to the eternal maintenance of white supremacy."

In the South, circumstances had aroused old fears anew; for many negroes who had joined the army in 1917 had been sent to Europe, where they had often been treated as equals, and even gone about with white women.   It was essential to keep them in their place when they returned; so the Klan was to be there just as it had been in the reconstruction days after the Civil War.   Also, if alongside the negro, the Catholic foreigner should get out of hand, or the Bolshevik should preach his odious doctrines, the good Protestant citizens would have the Klan with which to keep them in order. In 1919 and 1920, the Klan probably numbered some tens of thousands, and as was the case half a century earlier, its influence took the form of spontaneous interference in the maintenance of order. There were warnings sent to bad citizens, sensational examples calculated to excite the imagination, and threatening notices, not to mention solemn processions.

The Klan's greatest period of expansion was not so much during the War, as while the peace treaties were being drawn up, for it was then that America awoke to the danger of invasion by the lowest element of the Old World. The army had come back rather anti-European in sentiment, and those who had stayed at home were bubbling over with unexpended energy. Furthermore, many demobilized soldiers found their places taken either by a negro or by some uncouth alien, and that alone was enough to excite a feeling of group animosity. "All these foreigners are banded together and organizing, with the Catholic Church in the lead," they grumbled; "we must organize too." It was at this moment that the Ku Klux Klan, which had been suffering somewhat from the blundering administration of Colonel Simmons, was reconstructed according to approved American methods, and the new directorate, in best "booster" style, made a very good thing out of it financially. Under their impulse the character of the Klan changed entirely. It was no longer simply a local southern reaction, but became the chief expression of the national instinct of defence; and accordingly its centre shifted from the South to the West and Southwest.

The *Kloran,* the ritual of the Klan, was rewritten in 1915 by Colonel Simmons to contain all the requisites of an anti-Catholic and anti-Jewish movement. The *Kloran* is a perfect handbook of 100 per cent. Americanism, for it appeals to all the prejudices of the old-time middle class, and is Protestant enough to satisfy the most out-and-out Fundamentalist. At times it reads merely like the aims of an uplift society: "To cultivate and promote a real patriotism towards our civil government; exemplify a practical benevolence; shield the sanctity of home and the chastity of womanhood, and, by a practical devotion, conserve and maintain the distinct institutions, rights and privileges, principles, traditions, and ideals of pure Americanism."

We must not misunderstand the meaning of this language. In French politics "good citizens" has a Bonaparte odour, and "honest men" are those on the side of order who can be relied upon to strike hard when necessary. In French history there are many examples of dissentious appeals and coups d'état which have relied on the aid of the "good" and the "honest." In this sense the members of the Klan are "honest men," for they are ready to take the law into their own hands should the government seem inadequate. In its outlaw methods of expressing the sentiments of the community, the Klan is Fascist in inspiration. As a secret society it has made itself the rallying-point of the movement, a sort of vigilance committee, whose duty it is to administer punishment and make examples. It is almost mob rule in favour of order, under the control of the purists of Protestant nationalism. Members must be American-born, which excludes all foreigners, and Christians, which excludes all Jews; they must acknowledge American institutions, which means nothing on the face of it, but in reality is designed to exclude Catholics, who are looked on as subjects of a foreign sovereign, the Pope.

In the South the K.K.K. reaped the harvest of a soil that had been tilled for two generations. In the Southwest and beyond the Mississippi it touched a different clientele in the small-town Americans, the descendants of the Puritan pioneers who colonized the West in the middle of the nineteenth century. Their orthodox Protestantism and old-fashioned type of Americanism has persisted unchanged beneath an impenetrable veneer of boredom. Nothing can exceed the mediocrity of these small communities, where local public opinion aggressively spies on any one suspected of being different. The Klan was never entirely successful in the big cities with their mixture of races and groups, nor yet in the isolation of the open country, but it absolutely controlled the small towns. An intellectual aristocracy scarcely exists in these shut-in communities, where even the school teacher is held on a tight leash. Society is run by a narrow-minded middle class and inspired by a Protestant clergy to whom the Invisible Empire is not without its attractions. The Baptist minister is usually in sympathy with the Klan and is often appointed Kleagle or local publicity agent. When a hooded band marches mysteriously out to offer a well-filled purse to some worthy preacher, the choice never falls on a Catholic priest or an Anglican clergyman, but always on a Baptist or a Methodist.

It is largely due to the Protestant minister, whose influence has been growing since the War, that the well-meaning but timorous middle class has been awakened to certain fears—the fear of Catholicism, atheism, and evolution; of wine and European immorality; of radicals, Bolshevists, and revolutionaries; of invasion by blacks, yellows, and Latin-Slavs; and of the mongrelizing of the race. . . . Therefore, when the K.K.K. came forward as the champion of national morality in partnership with the Fundamentalists, the Prohibitionists, and the anti-evolutionists (who are really the same people), its authority was very great. With the help of the ministers, whom the Anti-Saloon League has craftily appointed electoral agents, and the "Babbitts," those typical honest business men, the Klan is saving society. New York may laugh, but the local politicians know what they are dealing with; and they are careful to watch their step where the Klan is concerned. This accounts quite naturally for certain manifestations,

such as the anti-evolutionist law in Tennessee and the prohibition amendment, not to mention various other laws intended to purify both customs and souls. It is simply a
case of threatened Americanism taking refuge in the stronghold of conformity.

It is quite evident where K.K.K. propaganda has succeeded. Sooner or later it was bound to attract the dregs
of humanity, for they are always in favour of illegal direct
action; and the South in particular seems to have suffered
from this abuse. The program of the Klan, however, was
able to attract honest men; and the greater part of its personnel was recruited from the middle class. It also thrived
exceptionally well wherever the old-time groups remained
distinct and strong, as the geography of the Klan shows.
It is difficult to map it out accurately, partly because no
statistics are possible and also because it changes from
month to month. The Invisible Empire has no fixed
boundaries but moves like a storm across the country, with
the centre of depression changing every moment. Up to
1920 the South was the chief zone affected, but after that
the depression moved to the Southwest and West, and extended to Southern California on the one hand, and on the
other to the Northwest as far as Oregon. At the same time
it spread up the Mississippi Valley and installed itself in
full force in the old American districts of Indiana and Ohio.
Finally it penetrated to the East, principally to the small
non-industrial towns of New York State, Massachusetts,
and the northeastern part of Long Island.

This topography shows that the Ku Klux Klan is strong
wherever foreigners are not too numerous. It has never
been a power in the conglomerate cities of New York and
Boston, although in certain places which are reacting vio-
lently against foreign infiltration, it has gained great
strength. All that is needed to provoke a sudden outbreak
is a trivial incident, a scandal over some corrupt party

machine run by Irish politicians, excessive zeal on the part
of the Catholics, or the arrival of a band of negroes or
Jews. In Indiana, for example, the outburst took the form
of Americanization by intimidation; and pressure was
brought to bear on business, on elected officials, and in fact
on people generally. This difference in attitude between
the old-fashioned small towns on the one hand and the industrialized city districts with their masses of foreigners
on the other is of first importance, and explains much in
post-war American politics.

In the South the defence of the white race was the attraction; in the West the bitterness of the Anglo-Saxon
Protestants against Rome and European demoralization;
and in the Northwest it was hostility toward foreigners,
Jew or Catholic, Russian, Irish, or Mediterranean. In every
case, however, they aimed chiefly at the Catholic Church.
An anti-clerical Frenchman can understand their prejudices,
for he realizes that they are less against religion than against
the Church as a political institution led by an Italian. A
stubborn or ignorant American will never admit that a
Catholic can conform entirely to the spirit of the Constitution and at the same time serve the Church, for at any minute he may receive orders from the latter. Experience shows
that such instructions have been given, if not by the Pope,
at any rate by the priests during elections. This classic
objection is specially strong in the United States, because
the Roman Catholic Church is suspected of carrying on
religious colonization there. What was in France simply
a quarrel over doctrines is a rivalry of race in America.

The critical sense is not the most highly developed in
America, and this possibly explains the quite improbable
rumours that are continually circulating. *The American
Standard,* the fortnightly organ of the Ku Klux Klan, provides a choice collection of pearls. Here are a few quota-
tions picked out at random.

In the issue of August, 1925, we read:

"Do you know that Rome looks upon Washington as the future centre of her power and is filling our government departments with Papists? That the hierarchy for many years has been buying strategic sites in our capital? That in our Department of State at Washington, 61 per cent. of the employés are Roman Catholics? That in our Treasury Department, in which the duty of enforcing prohibition is vested, 70 per cent. of the employés are Roman Catholics?"

Or again, stronger still, in the issue of October 1, 1925:

"We again take the occasion to attack the sinister purposes and persistent efforts of the Roman Catholic hierarchy, to foist upon us the belief that Christopher Columbus was the discoverer of America, and through this fraudulent representation to lay claim to inherent rights which belong solely to Nordic Christian peoples, through the discovery of this continent by Leif Ericson in the year 1000."

A Catholic might reply that there were no Protestants in the year 1000, and therefore Leif Ericson must have been a Catholic himself. But this does not disconcert the *American Standard,* for under date of October 15 we read:

"The servile subject peoples of the Mediterranean have been willing subjects of the Vatican, but the spiritually-minded, chivalrous, and freedom-loving Nordic peoples have always been hostile to Rome."

The American Standard allows itself to be carried away by such exalted idealism; so it winds up by enunciating a program which may be coherent but would certainly be impossible in actual practice:

(1) Laws to require the reading of the Holy Bible in every American public school.

(2) Recognition of the fact that the doctrines taught by monarchical Romanism, and the principles embodied in free republican Americanism, are opposed.

(3) Recognition of the fact that since Roman Catholics give first allegiance to an alien political potentate, their claim to citizenship in this Protestant country is illegitimate.

(4) Revision of our citizenship laws, to wipe out the "alien vote."

(5) A law to destroy the alien influence of the foreign language press by requiring that the English language be used exclusively.

(6) The exclusion from America of the Jews who work against Christianity.

(7) The return of the negroes to their homeland of Africa.

(8) The voting privilege to be restricted to citizens who have spent at least four years in the American public schools.

(9) Strict adherence to the Constitution of the United States, including the prohibition amendment.

(10) The teaching of Christ Jesus, as given in the Holy Bible, the Word of God, as the standard of American conduct in public and private life.

Imperial Wizard Evans, the supreme head of the Klan, boasts that he is "the most average man" in America. In spite of their ridiculous and aggressive form, these ideas are very widespread among the more ignorant Protestants, and will likely survive the secret society which is now expressing them so vigorously. They are an inspiration to the 100 per cent. American, for they represent a tendency in which the Klan is but a picturesque and passing episode. Even the number of members, if it were published, would not tell us much, for the organization is less important than the atmosphere it expresses.

The organization, as such, has declined rapidly since 1923. In 1921, the New York *World* estimated its membership at half a million; in 1922 a Congressional committee of inquiry could not find more than 100,000; in 1923 *The World's Work* suggested the figure of 2,500,000; in 1924 Mecklin, in his excellent book on the Klan, speaks of "millions."[1] Decadence had, however, set in, first in the South and then in the Southwest. In September, 1925, the Klan was still able to fill the streets of Washington with an immense procession; but in February, 1926, an inquiry made by the New York *Times* reveals an absolute rout.

The weakness of the movement lay in the fact that when asked to carry out constructive work, it had always proved incapable. It did succeed in conquering whole States politically, such as Oklahoma and Georgia; but nothing came of it, for as soon as it came out into the open, the secret society lost its force by losing its mystery. The power of the Klan is at its best when pulling wires in the local legislatures or even in Federal politics. In 1924 it controlled at least half the Democrats at the national convention to nominate the presidential candidate, and the Republicans on their side did not dare oppose it. Now, however, the period of intimidation seems to be past, and in a few years the Klan will probably count for very little, although the prejudices it represents will survive. After all, it was a typical post-war movement. Stripped of its violence—the legacy of the South—and of its childish and grandiloquent ritual—the legacy of American Free Masonry—it still stands for a national reaction or the resentment of the old-time Americans against the alien masses.

[1] *The Ku Klux Klan, a Study of the American Mind.* Harcourt, Brace and Company.

CHAPTER X

NATIVE AMERICA VS. ALIEN IDEALS

In conclusion let us briefly review the various aspects of the present situation in the United States: the anti-evolutionist campaign, educational intolerance, prohibition, the restriction of immigration, and the fear of Catholic Europe as expressed in the Ku Klux Klan. They all spring from the same origin and can be summed up in the formula, "America for Regular Americans." At the moment American nationalism is taking the form of a cult of the native-born, but will this last?

In the nineteenth century the new contingent gladly threw open its doors to the oppressed of the world. In the United States any one could find a new fatherland and the right to call himself an American. This is now giving way to a contrary conception, according to which the country must mould its future from the one race with which its religion, moral code, and exclusive traditions are associated. The purists, who guard all the avenues of approach, contend that the country must no longer be considered as common property; for it really belongs only to those who were born into the original family. It is now a question of birth rather than adaptation.

This is the latest theory, but in practice the way had long been prepared for it by the people themselves. As always in the past, the Protestant of Anglo-Saxon stock considers himself a member of an aristocracy endowed with special privileges. In spite of the Constitution there has never been complete moral and social equality between those who were and those who were not born in the country—we might almost say between the first- and second-class citizens. Naturally this depended on the time required for assimilation and the inferiority of the newcomer in comparison with the original inhabitant. The immigrant who stammers broken English, or possibly does not speak it at all, and is unable to break away from his own peculiar habits, naturally thinks and feels different. He is bound to be regarded with suspicion by the "100 percenter" who is certain of his heredity and proud of his standard of living—so sure, indeed, of his moral superiority that he dares, according to Imperial Wizard Evans, "look God straight in the face." As assimilation gradually takes place, the distance between the two types is reduced, but any peculiarity on the part of the newcomer is unconsciously judged by the American as a sign of inferiority.

This is not to be wondered at, if we recollect that Europe has not been sending the best of her citizens across the Atlantic, during the past century at any rate. To an American child an Italian is a pedlar, a Greek a bootblack or cheap restaurant-keeper, and a Frenchman a low-class barber. It never occurs to him that other Italians and Frenchmen exist in France and Italy who are gentlemen and much more cultured than he is himself. Wise parents send their children to Europe to learn these things, but the contempt of those who have never travelled is almost unfathomable. They regard the people of the Old World as immoral and degenerate, ignorant of the most elementary rules of hygiene, dominated by a fanatic priesthood, perpetually menaced by anarchy and revolution, likely to die of hunger—this sounds like an exaggeration, but it is perfectly true!

The result of this attitude is distinctive treatment for the immigrant, and in point of fact, justice for the alien is not the same as for the real American. In all honesty a judge will believe an American witness rather than a foreigner; a doubtful case would probably go against an Italian, a

Russian, or a Greek; and of course a coloured man takes
even greater chances. If some new system of capital punishment were introduced, it would be tried out first on a Chinaman, who had already been found guilty, of course. Such
a case actually occurred in Nevada.[1] In every-day private
relations the difference between the races is even more
marked. In order to prevent foreigners from filtering into
the clubs, hotels, and homes of the old residents, a regular
system of defence is erected against them. Certain communities of pure British origin, though they are little known
to the public, have great social and political authority, simply on account of their unalloyed traditions.

This self-satisfied and ingenuous belief in the inferiority
of the rest of the world does not arise from any ill will.
The Americans are a kindly people, but they cannot understand why others do not adopt their way of thinking and
acting, with enthusiasm and gratitude. The superiority
of their civilization seems so obvious to them that to question it seems as futile as denying the existence of the sun.
A remarkable article in the *American Journal of Sociology*[2]
humorously summarizes the Americans' own idea of themselves.

"We are the greatest people on earth. Our government is
the best. In religious belief and practice we (the Protestants)
are exactly right, and we are also the best fighters in the world.
As a people we are the wisest, politically the most free, and
socially the most developed. Other nations may fail and fall;
we are safe. Our history is a narrative of the triumph of
righteousness among the people. We see these forces working
through every generation of our glorious past. Our future
growth and success are as certain as the rules of mathematics.
Providence is always on our side. The only war we Ameri-

[1] When a negro is "sterilized," are they always certain that all the
legal formalities have been observed?
[2] "The Ku Klux Klan Interpreted," by F. Bohn. *American Journal of
Sociology*, January, 1925.

cans ever lost was when one-third of us was defeated by the other two-thirds. We have been divinely selected in order to save and purify the world through our example. If other nations will only accept our religious and political principles, and our general attitude toward life, they soon will be, no doubt, as happy and prosperous as we."

In the Atlantic States and California and in a few scattered university towns, cultured circles exist where the irony of such statements as this are appreciated and where Europe is even admired at times. Still, I must admit that this quotation seems to express to the letter the attitude of the mass of Americans in the Middle West.

Their idea of Americanization is to adopt Anglo-Saxon moral, social, and religious principles. In the nineteenth century they thought that the Italian, Russian, and German immigrants would turn out to be men like themselves. It was not so much a matter of fusion, or of mixing several elements to produce a new compound, but rather the digestion by one race of all the others, until none of their individuality survived. However, when the assimilators began to see that the character of the American people was changing and that the pretended assimilation often meant only fusion or a juxtaposition, their attitude of welcome turned into hostility and exclusiveness.

They had, however, already allowed sufficient foreigners to penetrate to evolve a new American spirit in opposition to their own. As the aliens arrived in greater numbers some of them gradually began to reject the verdict that they were inferior on account of their origin, though they were just as eager to become Americans as the rest. Naturally the temperament of the Anglo-Saxon was bound to succeed better in a society based on co-operation, but the unqualified statement that the Nordic races are superior contradicts every experience. Without generalizing, one may say that when you notice a sparkling eye or a nimble mind it is often in an Italian, a Jew, or a Russian. Like uncut jewels, they had come from Europe with their traditions of brilliant civilizations, which they were asked to abandon at one fell swoop. Many, especially among the intellectuals, deliberately refused. The American-Italian who writes English with a Mediterranean flourish, the American Jew with his centuries of accumulated knowledge, and even the negro, whose music and dancing have added to the artistic patrimony of the whole human race, have all contributed to American civilization; and when they enroll themselves in the movement they insist that they should be received just as they are and with all the honours of war.

Obviously this Americanization is entirely different from what was planned by the assimilators. It is the kind of Americanization that Israel Zangwill, the Jewish writer who popularized the metaphor of the melting pot, deals with in semi-religious vein: "America is God's crucible, the great melting pot where all the races of Europe are melting and re-forming. . . . The real American has not yet arrived. He is only in the crucible. I tell you—he will be the fusion of all races, perhaps the coming superman." The Catholics cherish this idea when they maintain in all sincerity that there is no need for them to sacrifice their religion in order to become Americans. Waldo Frank makes a magnificent defence of this conception in *Our America,*[3] when he demands the right for all to collaborate in building the America of the future.

We must not underestimate the prestige and strength of this ideal, for like other types of Americanization, it attracts both firm believers and mystics. Countless immigrants have left the Old World, inspired by the liberty that they were to find in the New; and in their passionate desire for regeneration they have gladly transformed themselves, in

[3] Published by Boni and Liveright.

the belief that they were contributing to the formation of a new nation. They were filled with admiration and gratitude for their adopted country, and this very faith in a land which could revive the weary by the breath of its independence was the strongest cement of the Union. Now when the "100 percenters" maintain that the true American is not of the future but of the past, and that he alone is of the privileged few who can claim founders' rights, then the newcomer no longer recognizes the ideals of which he had dreamed.

Is it possible to contemplate a United States that is neither Protestant nor Anglo-Saxon? This is the aim of an opposition which, however, is not constructive and resists only by instinct. And yet they persist. If their policy were to become constructive and they obtained control, we might have a new America resembling in many ways the New York of today; but to the old Puritan element it would seem a shocking perversion. The final destiny of the country is still in suspense, and it is unable to foretell what tomorrow will be its very soul.

PART II

THE ECONOMIC SITUATION

CHAPTER XI

THE *rôle* of labour is not the same in America as on other continents. By perfecting the organization of labour and by the use of machinery, industry has ceased to rely upon brawn to an extent of which we in Europe have no conception. As a result the workman is changing in character as he gets further and further away from the old type of artisan. This is easy to understand in theory, but to adapt oneself to the transformation, one must be acclimatized to the American atmosphere. Another equally important difference between our homogeneous countries and the United States is that the cosmopolitan immigration of the last century has created in America an astonishing racial structure of trades and occupations suggestive in some ways of the Middle Ages or the Orient. Paradoxical as it may seem, the most advanced form of industrial civilization exists side by side with a social geology which Western Europe had entirely forgotten, at any rate up to the War.

The history of American labour is a perpetual process of parcelling out immigrants to the various trades according to their origins, their capabilities, and their tastes. The last to arrive does the most inferior, the most fatiguing, and the worst-paid work. In time he moves to a higher grade, and another race replaces him in the unskilled jobs and the slums. This economic structure was first begun after the Napoleonic wars, when the Irish came over to work as navvies. In time they became bosses, contractors, politicians, policemen and lawyers. The Germans and Italians replaced them, and in their turn also moved up and left the rough work to the Orientals and Latin-Slavs. Finally, after 1914, this source also dried up, and the southern negroes and the Mexicans arrived. Now, however, the list is closed.

In the industrial towns of New England every race lives in its own quarters as in an oriental bazaar, where the different types of foreigner each have their own alley. Here we have the Polish quarter, the home of Kosciuskos, and the Irish quarter, where every other person is called Murphy, Sullivan, or Donelly. In the Italian streets, overflowing with fruit, raisins, and tempting *salami,* is housed a horde of Cannelli, Fratelli, and Sbarboro. With the French Canadians we find brick churches, not unlike the spinning-mills, and a solid block of Beaudins, Dandurands, and Picards grouped about priests dressed like Protestant clergy who talk the good old French *patois* of the soil. The Americans—there are a few!—occupy the business quarters and live in expensive houses of eccentric design. Similarly, society is divided into horizontal layers that correspond to this mosaic. On the top we have the descendants of the original settlers and the early immigrants, along with the wealthy Jews. In the middle are the Irish politicians, the Italian merchants, the Greek restaurant-keepers, and the Jewish retailers, and at the bottom all the southeastern Europeans and still more Jews. In surrounding country districts, which were once American and Puritan, the Poles are farming fruit in the Connecticut valley, the Fins growing vegetables in Massachusetts, and the Portuguese cultivating cranberries on Cape Cod.

If we turn to the Pacific Coast, we find that in California the formation of the labouring class is very similar. When the country was first opened up about 1850, and afterward, Chinese and Indian labour was employed in the mines, ranches, and the construction of the first railways; but the Indians soon disappeared, and the Chinese were forbidden to enter the country. The western pioneers were unable to fall back on the Irish, Germans, and Italians; for these races rapidly became prosperous and so were not available for long. The country was forced to employ the Japanese, but this immigration also was soon stopped; so they turned to the Mediterraneans and the Slavs and even to immigrants from western Asia. Finally the Mexicans brought up the rear in their tens and hundreds of thousands.

Each group found its own level in an occupation suitable to its abilities and fitted itself into the great American checkerboard of trades and races. For example, peach-growing is in the hands of the Portuguese, Greeks, Fins, Japanese, and Sicilians. Cotton is chiefly cultivated by negroes and Mexicans, artichokes by Portuguese, grapes by Italians or Armenians, apples by Slavs from the Danube, strawberries and cantaloup melons by Japanese, rice and sugar-beets by Japanese and Hindus. Dairying is done by the Swiss, the Germans, and the Italians, while the restaurants are run by the French, the Greeks, the Italians, and the Dalmatians. The pick-and-shovel work on the railways is done by Mexicans. The real Americans direct the large agricultural and industrial developments, or are employed as skilled workmen. They are the guiding factor of the whole economic structure.

The 1920 census confirms this division by occupations. Out of the total population employed in productive work, 49.3 per cent. are of American origin, both parents being American-born. The foreign-born, including those born in the United States of foreign parents, represent 38.7 per cent., and the coloured races 12 per cent. Now though the Americans are in the majority in the professions and the skilled and industrial trades,[1] they are in the minority in

	American-born
[1] Professions	62.5%
Farm hands	58.4%
Clerks	55.7%
Civil servants	52.5%
Merchants	51.7%
Transportation	51.0%
Mechanics	59.4%
Electricians	58.3%
Carpenters	53.8%
Compositors	50.9%

all the rest. In mining, for example, foreign and coloured labour accounts for 55.3 per cent., of whom 34.6 per cent. are foreign-born. In the great manufacturing and mechanical industries they are 58 per cent., 28.3 per cent. being foreign-born, and in domestic service they are 70 per cent., of whom half are coloured. Certain trades are almost monopolized by immigrants: almost three-quarters of the bakers and two-thirds of the garment-makers. In the iron and steel industry the labouring class is made up as follows: 14.6 per cent. negroes, 45.1 per cent. immigrants, 13.3 per cent American-born of foreign parents, and only 27 per cent. real Americans.

Among the following, over half are alien or coloured: masons, foundry workers, grocers, metal polishers, chauffeurs, textile workers, boot and shoe workers, builders, metallurgists, butchers, plumbers, and painters. Many of the chief industries could not have existed at all without definite help from the foreigner. The construction of the railroads would have been extremely difficult, and even today, owing to the lack of foreign recruits, the mining and metal industries are distinctly handicapped. Cotton would have been in the same plight without the negro, and though this did not apply to the mechanical farming on a vast scale in the western corn and wheat belt, it is typical of market-gardening and horticulture, which require a special type of genius and a devotion to the soil that America does not possess.

This brings us to the fundamental difference between the American and European conception of work, and from this perspective we can see that Europe and Asia have certain things in common. Organization appeals to the American, for he loves team-work and co-operating with machinery. He is perfectly at home wherever it is possible to use machinery, and if he is aware that this excessive division of labour limits his personal interest in the final achievement, he does not seem to regret it. On the other hand, he is

quite out of his sphere with solitary work requiring physical
energy, patience, attention to detail, or artistic ability—in
short, the work of artisans and gardeners such as the French
or Chinese. The American youth, and even the assimilated
foreigner, will not do hard manual work. He considers it
beneath him, for instance, to milk cows or plant beetroots.
He wants quick returns and overlooks results that can be
obtained only slowly.

He has the greatest contempt, and he does not conceal it,
for the humble artisan who concentrates for days and even
weeks on one object, which, in the end, is entirely his own
creation. The Americans also despise the peasant who is
forever bent over a patch of soil which he cultivates with
religious zeal. When working in their factories, their banks,
and even as elevator boys, they consider themselves immeas-
urably superior. They certainly do not realize that the
French and Chinese civilizations are two of the oldest and
finest in the world. The peasants in both countries collaborate with the soil and the seasons, study every phase of the
climate, and often have an individual grasp of the philosophy
of life that reveals the meaning of what they are doing in
the broadest possible aspect. I have often tried to explain
this point of view to Americans, but they have usually
laughed; for to them a peasant is a backward type, a relic
of the Middle Ages. They do not worry about the disappearance of the artisan, and the regrets of a French individualist on this score seem quite incomprehensible.[2]

It is easy to see the kind of labour that will become scarce
by the restriction of immigration. Northern Europe sent
skilled factory workers in the past and will continue to send
them to a certain extent in the future, but southeastern
Europe is no longer allowed to contribute its navvies, farm
hands, gardeners, and small craftsmen. In the reduced im-

[2] This opinion, especially in so far as it applies to the French peasant,
may be partly because in English "peasant" originally meant a serf attached to the soil.

migration of 1925, out of a net total of 202,000, there were
42,000 skilled workmen, all from Great Britain, Ireland, and
Germany, but only 15,000 farm hands. Actually 15,000
more factory workers left than came in. In the immigration
of 1926 there were only 10,000 real labourers. When the
effect of the resort to negroes and Mexicans—necessarily
only a temporary expedient—is exhausted, there will have
to be a general reorganization of labour. In fact, this reorganization is already taking place.

As was perfectly logical, the first result of the new immigration policy was a rise in wages, especially for manual
work. The employer is forced to economize his personnel
at all costs, and, although he has done so for fifty years,
the problem is becoming critical, as the time is fast approaching when the use of machinery will have reached its limit.
This limit really does exist. The scarcity of labour will
then affect the cost of production, and competition in world
markets will be much more difficult. The authors of the
immigration laws foresaw this danger, but they considered
it less important than the rapid assimilation of the foreigner
and the formation of a homogeneous people. As long as
high wages are justified by increased output on the part of
a limited number of workers, the new régime will add to
the material comfort of the masses without creating unhealthy economic conditions.

A workman is far better paid in America than anywhere
else in the world, and his standard of living is enormously
higher. This difference, which was noticeable before the
War, has been greatly accentuated since, and is now the chief
contrast between the old and the new continents. In 1925–26
an unskilled labourer earned an average of $3 to $5 a day,
or about 40 cents an hour. Skilled workers earned from $5
to $10, and in certain special trades even more, thanks to
exceptional circumstances or particularly efficient trade
unions. For example, during the building boom of 1925–26

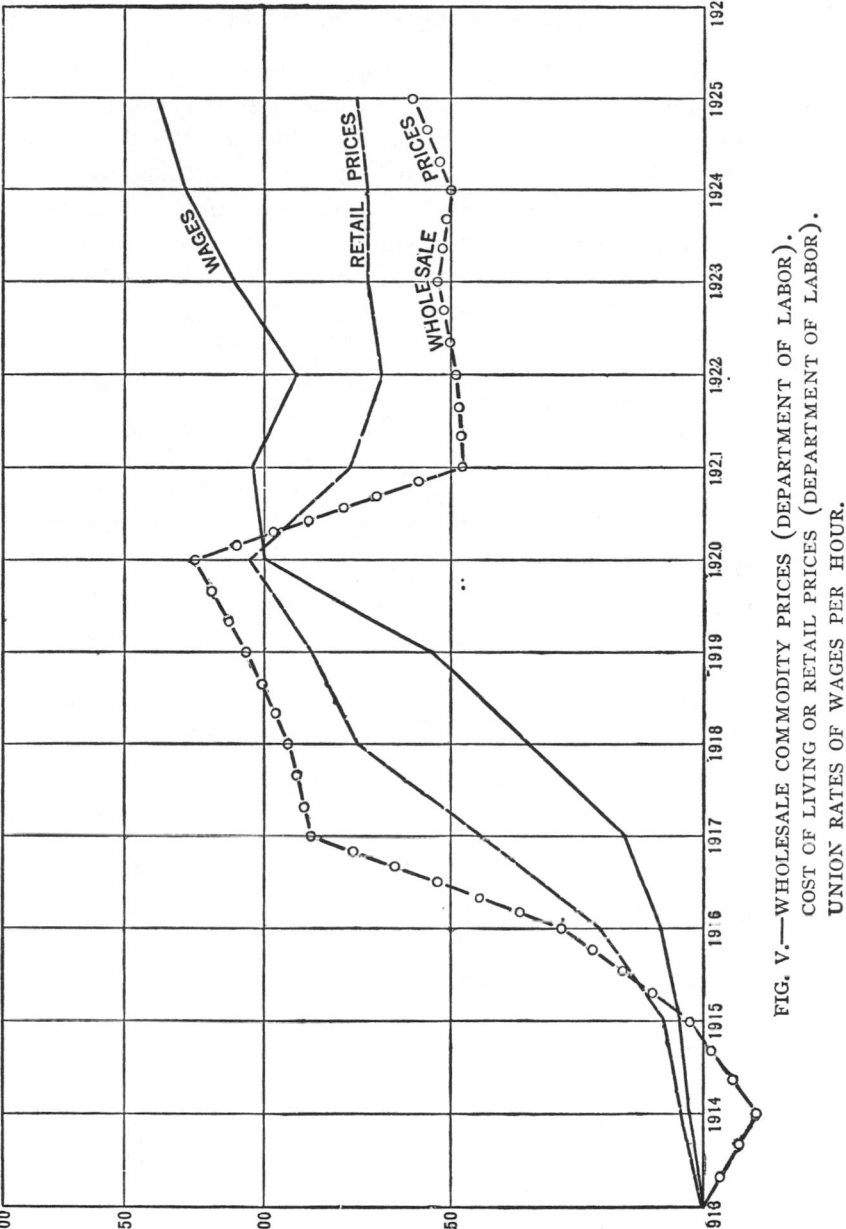

FIG. V.—WHOLESALE COMMODITY PRICES (DEPARTMENT OF LABOR).
COST OF LIVING OR RETAIL PRICES (DEPARTMENT OF LABOR).
UNION RATES OF WAGES PER HOUR.

bricklayers earned as much as $15 and $17 a day in New York and other large cities. Let us note in passing, however, that a cotton spinner in the South receives $2 a day and his lodging, compared with about $4 without lodging in the New England mills. A farm hand made about $46 a month, apart from his keep, and $3 a day during the harvest, whereas a talented ten-year-old child can make $150 a week in a Los Angeles cinema studio. In short, work is well paid. The saying, "The strength of your arm is your capital," is no mere figure of speech in America!

These observations also apply if we take the cost of living into account and obtain the purchasing price of wages as in the chart on page 155. As can be seen from a cursory inspection, the wholesale and retail price curves show the same general post-war conditions in the United States as in any other country with a sound monetary system. Wholesale prices rose rapidly up to 1920, followed after a certain interval by retail prices; but early in 1920 the wholesale prices fell tremendously again, and the retail prices soon reacted in a lesser degree. In 1922 the stabilization of both was achieved at a level about 150 per cent. of the original wholesale price level and 170 per cent. of the retail. The corresponding curve for Great Britain is very similar.[3] It is in the graph of wages, however, that the American position is absolutely unusual. Up to 1920 nothing abnormal occurred, for, as elsewhere, wages advanced soon after prices, until in 1920–21 they caught up with the retail prices. Since then the wage curve has been astonishingly independent, for instead of dropping off slowly in sympathy with the decline in prices, it unexpectedly remained almost stationary throughout the 1921–22 crisis and then definitely started to climb again, although prices remained steady considerably lower down. By 1925 the distance between the two curves

[3] See *Post-War Britain,* by André Siegfried (Jonathan Cape).

was very marked, the index for wholesale prices being 159, retail prices 173, and wages actually 238.

The obvious conclusion, which is borne out by every-day experience in America, is that the working-man is receiving a real wage considerably above pre-war standards. During the period of rising prices his purchasing power was reduced, inasmuch as wages increased only after a certain delay. In 1918 his purchasing power was only 76 per cent. of what it had been in 1913, and in 1920 it still required 5 per cent. more to re-establish itself. Since 1921 the reverse has been the case, for the purchasing power of wages rose to 137 by 1925, or one-third higher than the so-called normal years before 1914.

These figures were drawn up according to the trade-union wage rates per hour, which are comparatively high; but in the industries in which labour is only fairly well organized we find the same tendency. In 1924, for example, the purchasing power of wages in the cotton trade was 147, and in the woollen trade 176, both being industries which pay badly and will eventually have to catch up with the others. Even in the boot and shoe industry, which is going through a long period of depression, the increase in the purchasing power of wages is about 25 per cent. above 1913. Similarly, it is 149 for blast furnaces, and 138 for railroads.[4] There is thus undoubtedly a real improvement in the condition of the working classes since the War. In the decline in prices that has made it possible, we must point out the abnormal factor of exceptionally low food prices, which are the result of a prolonged agricultural depression that cannot last forever.

The reasons for this increase in wages are clear enough, though it is difficult to determine their respective importance. The immediate cause seems to be the restriction of

[4] Ethelbert Stewart, U. S. Commissioner for Labor Statistics: "Are average rates keeping pace with the increased cost of living?" Monthly Labor Review, January and April, 1926.

immigration, which has increased the value of workers generally by limiting the number available. The rise in the value of unskilled labourers is particularly marked, for they are now at a premium, whereas, in comparison with skilled workers, their wages were kept at a relatively low figure before the War, owing to the continual influx of low-class immigrants. Also, the new conditions have coincided with a period of deflation, during which, according to all precedents, wages fall more slowly than prices. These explanations are insufficient, however, if we do not realize the underlying factor which has allowed this increase in wages—nominal or real—to be healthy. The real wage of the working class has also increased in England, but there it has been at the cost of a dangerous crisis which is threatening the country's very existence, because production has not gone up in proportion. In the United States the magnificent improvement in the conditions of the working class has been possible, has even been normal and simple, because it has coincided with an increase in production, resulting partly from abundant natural resources, and partly from greater individual output on the part of the workers. Add to the marvellous natural wealth of the country the development of machinery, more efficient organization in the factory and office, steadier workmen under prohibition, and we find that higher wages can be distributed without raising the cost of production, and even while lowering it.

These are the phenomena which we must keep in mind if we wish to understand the extraordinary prosperity of the United States. After all, Europe is only a modest peninsula without the wonderful resources of this massive continent. Also, its workmen are apt to imagine that it is possible for them to earn more and yet produce less. They are not interested in results, and it is only too often from their wages that the employer tries to obtain a reduction in costs. Such ideas are out of date in America, where the workmen

enter wholeheartedly into the task of production: "We hold
that the best interests of the wage earners, as well as the
whole social group, are served, increasing in quantity as well
as quality, by high wage standards which assure sustained
purchasing power of the workers and, therefore, higher national standards for the environment in which they live and
the means to enjoy cultured opportunities." [5]

On his side, the American employer considers that he
ought to pay his employés well, and, accordingly, public
opinion is very hard on him if he refuses to do so, on the
ground that he forces the community to shoulder charges
which it should not be called on to bear. A bad reputation
in this respect reacts on sales and is therefore a consideration that employers dare not neglect. Further, the more intelligent leaders of industry know, without having to be
told, that if a country has a large home market and a perfected economic organization, good wages help in the reduction of factory costs, and that it takes two or three un-
derpaid workmen to replace one that is highly paid. [6]

Recent experience has also taught them that a well-paid
worker is soon a valuable customer and that in this way the
money spent on wages returns to industry. Prosperity, the
logical consequence of high wages, helps to send wages still
higher; for a workman, if he is well-to-do, works less and
may even disappear from the labour market, thus increasing
the chances and possibilities of those looking for work.
The situation will be sound as long as the increase in wages
corresponds to an increase in output, and this is a lesson
from which the Old World could easily profit.

Taken all in all, the American worker is in a unique position. There is no common denominator with which to compare him with the workers of other continents, for his

---

[5] Resolution passed at the forty-fifth annual convention of the American Federation of Labor, 1925. See the report of the convention,
page 271.

[6] Henry Ford, *My Life and Work*, page 168.

wages, when reduced to a gold basis, are often ten times as much as those of even a European. Even when we make allowance for the lower purchasing power of money and the longer hours of work in America,[7] the discrepancy is still enormous. In some ways life in Europe, even among the common people, may be more refined and may offer advantages which are not available for certain classes in America, such as the newly arrived immigrants of the big cities, the northwestern farmer who has been almost ruined by the recent depression, and the "poor whites" in the South. Nevertheless, North America, including Canada, is overflowing with abundance and enjoys a standard of living quite distinct from that of Europe. Statistics may allow us to measure it approximately, but it is impossible to realize it fully unless one sees it with one's own eyes. It is this difference in the level of existence, more than anything else, that separates the American outlook from the European, and it even reacts on the moral and social attitude toward life. It is almost trite to say that the rich and the poor, even among nations, can never understand each other completely, but this has been particularly true since the War.

It is impossible to describe the American standard of living without going into every detail of life. Let it suffice that European luxuries are often necessities in America, and where Europe, and especially Asia, will stint, America consumes without reckoning. One could feed a whole country in the Old World on what America wastes. American ideas of extravagance, comfort, and frugality are entirely different from European, as we soon discover if we ask what Americans mean by economy. In America the daily life of the majority is conceived on a scale that is reserved for the privileged classes anywhere else. Except for the slums of the large cities and the negro and Mexican quarters, it is not too much to say that practically all houses

7 In 1923, 53.9 per cent. of the labouring class in America worked more than a forty-eight-hour week.

are equipped with what in France is called *confort moderne*. Bathrooms and central heating are considered so indispensable that no one would rent a house without them, and to ask any one to climb four flights of stairs would be outrageous. They would think that they were back in the Dark Ages!

As for the means of communication, we find them carried to a degree of perfection that is nothing short of marvellous; in fact, they are part of the minimum amount of comfort required by every one. The use of the telephone, for instance, is very widespread. In 1925 there were 15 subscribers for every 100 inhabitants as compared with 2 in Europe, and some 49,000,000 conversations per day. The United States owns 61 per cent. of all the telephones in the world, and Europe only 28 per cent.[8]

Wireless is rapidly winning a similar position for itself, for even in 1924 the farmers alone possessed over 550,000 radios. These were not merely for amusement, for they were widely used to follow market prices and official weather forecasts. It is, however, in the automobile industry that we find the most striking signs of wealth.[9] Statistics for 1925 show that in America there were 19,954,000 cars, including 2,442,000 trucks, out of a world total of 24,565,000. Europe had only 2,676,000, of which 903,000 were in Great Britain and 735,000 in France. In other words, the United States owned 81 per cent. of all the automobiles in existence, or one for every 5.6 people, as compared with one for every 49 and 54 in Great Britain and France. Even this figure of one car to every six persons does not fully express the situation, as it does not take into account the South, where the negroes hardly ever have cars, nor yet the large cities, where a car is often useless on account of the traffic.

The truth is that in the West, and especially on the Pacific

[8] Annual report of the American Telephone and Telegraph Company. New York, 1926.
[9] Facts and Figures of the Automobile Industry, National Automobile Chamber of Commerce. 1926 edition.

Coast, every third or fourth person has a car. In California there is one to every 3.3 persons, and in Iowa one to every 4.08, or one to every family. It is quite common to find a working-class family in which the father has his own car, and the grown-up sons have one apiece as well. In the middle class both the husband and wife will have their own cars, not luxurious cars with hired chauffeurs, but modest vehicles driven by the owners. In 1925 the average cost of a car was only $825; of a Ford, only $450. Second-hand cars were to be had for $150 or less, for the American is very changeable and quickly tires of a thing after he has bought it. In practice, cars are generally sold on the part-payment plan; so almost every one, except in periods of depression, can afford them. Three or four years ago Europe marvelled at the idea of working-men going to the factory in their own cars, but it never attracted any attention in America. Around buildings under construction, government offices, or factories, cars are parked by the hundred.

The share that the American people are absorbing of the world's production of raw materials and foodstuffs is increasing at a rate which is none the less great because during the past few years we have become accustomed to their enormous consumption. The European purchaser is only a poverty-stricken parent in comparison. Though its population does not exceed 6 per cent. of the world total, the United States consumes almost three-quarters of the available supply of rubber and gasoline, two-thirds of all the raw silk, and one-quarter of the sugar. In 1923 the American *per capita* consumption of gasoline was twenty-six times as great as that of France.

In the general distribution of the products of the earth, the Americans are like the wealthy—or rather the sons of the wealthy—who consider it only natural that their slightest whim should be satisfied. In fact, this is the chief object of the community; and they are perfectly sincere and ingenuous in their conviction that it is not only normal but justified. Economy is nothing to be proud of, and the classic frugality of the Italian immigrant is considered un-American and an obstacle to his assimilation. The perpetual production of new articles, the unlimited publicity that makes them known, the use and abuse of instalment purchasing, which lets people have the article first and pay for it afterward, be it a radio or a house—in all these ways the community soon takes back a man's earnings. He does not worry, however; for he knows by experience that he will soon make more money, and besides, he believes that the resources of the country are unlimited. Hence his ill-concealed contempt for poverty-stricken and overpopulated Asia, and even for old-fashioned Europe, where people live in old houses and go to work on foot.

During the past few years an important evolution has taken place which may mean a change in the habits of the people. Hitherto the working-people hardly ever saved money, although the more prudent bought life insurance and a few owned their homes. Now, however, that wages have increased more quickly than expenses, a workman will first present himself with a car and then a house, not to mention life insurance. The prosperity of the past few years has been so extraordinary and so widespread that a surplus remains, and a new phase of saving and investment has begun, which is most unusual for the United States. A working-man is often a proprietor and even a capitalist. The first stage is the traditional practice of depositing money in the savings banks, where the increase has been enormous:[10]

	Total Deposits	Per Capita	Number of Depositors
1914	$ 8,729 millions	$ 89	11,386,000
1924	$20,874 "	$186	38,868,000

[10] "The Present Economic Revolution in the United States," Thomas Nixon Carver (Little Brown & Co., Boston, 1925).

In ten years the total deposits and the *per capita* amounts have doubled, and the number of depositors has tripled—an increase that has been mainly accomplished by the efforts of the working class. The increase in life insurance is even more astonishing. In 1912 it was estimated that the total reached the sum of $500,000,000, but in 1925 there were 83,000,000 policies, representing $60,000,000,000, of which over two-thirds were owned by the working class.[11]

But savings banks and life insurance were not sufficient to absorb the excessive wealth which kept on accumulating. The more prosperous workmen now create an investment class in the full sense of the word. Before the War only wealthy people owned capital, but since then the rich have multiplied tremendously. If any one is hard up today, it is the semi-rich, those who spend $30,000 to $40,000 a year. As social life with all its obligations becomes more and more expensive, they find it hard to make both ends meet, with the result that they have very little ready cash. But the workman, who is really well paid, is in a very different position; for·at the end of the year he often has a substantial balance to his credit at the bank. He then purchases stocks or bonds and becomes an important customer for the bond salesman.

In 1910 there were 300,000 owners of railway securities. Now there are more than 800,000, and the increase is to a great extent due to the investments of the employés of the railroads themselves. It is estimated that 630,000 people have invested in the telephone companies, and in a general way the public is turning to other public utilities as well, such as gas, electricity, tramways, etc. The companies themselves are furthering the movement by utilizing their large and constant approach to their employés and customers to place their own securities. By interesting the local community in their stocks and bonds, they create be-

[11] Estimated by David F. Houston, former Secretary to the Treasury, *World's Work*, January, 1925.

tween themselves and their public a valuable link, which almost amounts to a system of co-operation.   Many of the
more important industrial companies favour the purchasing
of their shares by their employés.   In 1923, 16 per cent.
of the staff of the U.S. Steel Trust were shareholders.   The
proportion was as high as 33 per cent. in the Goodyear Tire
and Rubber Company, 75 per cent. in the International Har-
vester Company, 95 per cent. in the Firestone Tire and
Rubber Company, and almost 100 per cent. in the Proctor
and Gamble Manufacturing Company.

Doubtless the capitalization of most of these companies
has been planned and organized to prevent employés from
obtaining control of the enterprise.   Nevertheless a democracy of capitalists is being built up among the people, a
democracy that will be conservative because it is satisfied.
The Liberty Loan campaign during the War did much to
educate the public, and prohibition, together with the marvellous prosperity of the country, also causes saving.   The
American workman, when he realizes that society assures
him a comfortable income, is ready to accept the existing
organization of industry.   He has made an excellent place
for himself in industry; so he has no wish to destroy it by
stirring up a revolution.   Lord Randolph Churchill said
forty years ago that if you wish to make democracy conservative you must give it something to conserve.   What the
Americans have to conserve is their standard of living, and
a sacred acquisition it is in which they will allow no reduction, and which they will defend to the uttermost against
both the competition and the surreptitious invasion of other
continents.

CHAPTER XII

THE question that Europeans find most intriguing is whether America will be able to withstand international competition and at the same time maintain her enormous wages and exceptional standard of living. Possibly we are not aware of the immense effort that has been made since the War to adapt American industry to the change in the labour market, by installing the very latest equipment. One is almost tempted to state that Europe with her intelligence, technical perfection, and high civilization could adopt the same policy and also profit by her lower wages and less pretentious mode of living. Such reasoning, however, overlooks the fact that America is different both geographically and politically, and therefore, with less effort and skill, has been able to accomplish things that have been beyond the Old World altogether.

The most important point in the philosophy of American production is the home market of nearly 120,000,000 people. The United States may be the most protectionist country in the world, but it is equally true that inside its implacable tariff wall is an area of 3,000,000 square miles in which there is absolute free trade and which thus constitutes by far the largest entirely free market in the world. Mass production is the logical result. American industry has been built up on broad lines from the very beginning, for it enjoys not merely the entry, but the privileged use, of this enormous market which hitherto has shown an unlimited capacity of absorption. As goods go from the Atlantic to the Pacific without a barrier, a factory can be located at whatever point is mathematically the most favourable, be it Boston, Los Angeles, or St. Louis. Within this closed area the sound laws of free trade, which are distorted everywhere else, hold good. America solves her economic problems by economic methods, and nothing interferes with her common-sense ideas of production. Having no international rivalries such as poison Europe, she can take a large view of things. This is her chief advantage and in fact is the only way in which modern industry can realize its maximum achievement.

This, however, is only one aspect of the question. Organization of industry is one thing; standardization of the product is another. In older civilizations, where tastes vary according to local customs and refinements of culture, industry is obliged to furnish a great range of models and cannot specialize on a limited number of articles. On the other hand, the 100,000,000 individuals in the United States are astonishingly alike. They all speak the same language, with fewer different accents than are to be found in England; they all live in exactly the same way and are little influenced by the differences in their climate. The immigrants at first keep a little of their own originality; but owing to the sharp rupture with their traditions, their children fall into line without resistance. With such a stereotyped clientele, industry is not obliged to prepare an infinite number of complicated products. A limited number of models suffices, repeated indefinitely and varying only according to certain fixed principles.

As if the natural similarity of the American people were not enough, "big business" has set to work to accentuate it still further by scientific advertising. Under the direction of remarkably intelligent men, publicity has become an important factor in the United States, and possibly even the keynote of the whole economic system. With the technical help of scientists, economists, and psychologists, they have built up a science of publicity. Attracting customers for existing models is not sufficient; so they have hit on an original idea of their own; namely, to "educate the public" or to direct public taste along certain definite channels. By accustoming people to a small number of well-known brands, they facilitate the mass production of an article at a low price. A typical advertisement is designed to appeal to the whole country, including Canada; for American advertising is more than national, it is continental. The public lends itself readily. Though an American always pictures himself as being as free and unbridled as a prairie pony, in reality he is the most docile of men and is moulded as easily as clay by "national publicity." The following quotation from Sinclair Lewis's *Main Street* is no exaggeration:

"Nine-tenths of the American towns are so alike that it is the completest boredom to wander from one to another. Always, west of Pittsburgh, and often east of it, there is the same lumber-yard, the same railroad station, the same Ford garage, the same creamery, the same box-like houses and two-storey shops. The new, more conscious houses are alike in their very attempts at diversity: the same bungalows, the same square houses of stucco or tapestry brick. The shops show the same standardized, nationally advertised wares; the newspapers of sections three thousand miles apart have the same 'syndicated features'; the boy in Arkansas displays just such a flamboyant ready-made suit as is found on just such a boy in Delaware, both of them iterate the same slang phrases from the same sporting-pages, and if one of them is in college and the other is a barber, no one may surmise which is which."

Advertising is important in the reduction of costs, for like machinery it works for simplification and increased output. Being constantly in the public eye, which it cannot deceive for long, it is bound to maintain a certain incontestable level of morality in order to keep its credit; but all this so-called "education" is really inspired in the interests of the seller. It is therefore uncertain, in spite of its service to the community, whether in the last analysis it is working for the good of civilization. To standardize the individual in order to standardize the things it is intended that he should buy is to lose sight of the fact that goods were made for man and not man for goods.

There is nothing unsound in reducing the cost of production by standardization, nor in transferring to the worker in the form of increased wages part of the saving effected and later taking it back by selling him goods. This is a complete cycle and is healthy as long as the country lives independently on its own natural resources. The idea is as clear as crystal, and no doubt that is why it is accepted with such enthusiasm. If one is operating on a basis of a few articles and an unlimited number of consumers, the slightest progress pays automatically, as every one knows. In the Ford works, for example, the most minute economies give tangible results: [1] "We put more machinery per square foot of floor space than any other factory in the world, because every foot of space not used carries an overhead expense," says Henry Ford.

Every employer knows this, but is the game worth the candle? It is not only habit and routine that restrains so many Europeans, and especially the French, from imitating, but rather that they have found that in a limited market these laws cannot function fully. To adapt the Old World to the essentials of mass production, it would be necessary to suppress not only the economic frontiers which too often separate the raw material from the factory, and the factory from the consumer, but also the political frontiers which perpetuate distinct types and stages of civilization side by side. After all, the very nationalities which a man from Kansas or Nebraska will good-naturedly advise us to sup-

[1] Henry Ford, *My Life and Work,* page 90.

press as out of date and incompatible with the Fordization of Europe are our inheritance, and they bring with them their own languages, customs, and intellectual culture. Yet from the economic point of view, this development of personalities is a handicap, and it would be preferable to pass every one through the same mill. We of the Old World tell ourselves sadly that in Europe mass production and civilization do not go together.

American industry is evolving a school of thought which will throw light on the fundamental conditions of its existence, on the methods that have been worked out by experience, and on the moral factors which will determine its place and its mission in the community. It is an important moment in the development of the nation, for it signifies that it has now reached maturity. The days of the pioneers were its childhood, when the country was developed by individual methods with difficulty and delay. Later, after the Civil War, and especially after 1880, came the period of youth, when its capacity for action and efficient organization were suddenly increased tenfold. Groups were organized to exploit the virgin resources which still seemed inexhaustible, but they had no general scheme and resembled the vigorous initiative of conquering expeditions. Progress, however, though unorganized and fantastic, was rapid. It was the time of the formation of the great trusts and the instinctive reaction of society against them, and it lasted until the beginning of the twentieth century.

During this stage of American development, the civic virtue and economic morality of the leaders of industry did not advance as fast as their material success. By the lack of balance between their methods, which were already skilled, and their ambitions, which were still unfettered, they recall the *Conquistadors* in many ways. Although they realized that industrial production ought to be organized rationally, the trusts strangled their competitors by methods that were closely akin to piracy. They preferred to fleece the consumer rather than to serve him, as if they did not realize that their interests coincided with those of the community. Throughout American society, particularly in the West, the chief object in life was to make the greatest amount of money in the shortest possible time. People hurried about like restless nomads, as if they would soon have to be moving farther on.

It was an age of incredible daring which anywhere else would have spelled ruin, of uncontrollable ardour and thirst for gain, of intense speculation, legendary captains of industry, and powerful perfidious trusts, of "booms" and of "panics." Among so many astonishing victories and such feverish and rapid growth, we must not overlook the disasters. There was heart-breaking ruin for the defeated competitor, bitterness on the part of consumers, sharp encounters between employers and employés further complicated by sanguinary strikes, and unbelievable squandering of natural resources. Even with its efficient organization, no industry in the world was more anarchistic at that time than the American, or was so given to fratricidal battles, in spite of its highly developed spirit of co-operation. It was also incredibly extravagant, although the methods had already been introduced that were later to develop into mass production.

Little by little the successes of this heroic age diminished, and a reaction against exploitation set in among business men. By the end of the century the West was no longer a land of adventure beyond the frontier of civilization. People had begun to adopt the idea that industry and commerce were more or less public functions involving responsibilities and duties toward the community. In a sense this was a Puritan tradition, but the War hastened this evolution by putting industry for the first time at the service of the nation. Production was now looked upon as a unit, and as a national rather than an individual affair. The colossal efforts for the co-ordination of productive activity, carried out under the direction of the government, clearly showed the many abuses from which American industry was suffering; for previously their natural advantages had been so great that they had no conception of the opportunities they were losing.

At the close of the War, a commission appointed under Herbert Hoover, Secretary of Commerce, to study the problem of waste in industry, came to the conclusion that production could be considerably increased and costs reduced—sometimes even halved—by a sensible policy of economy. For a generation they had been organizing their factories, but this determination to economize was something new. In the enthusiasm of their youth and prosperity, they had never felt the need of keeping a check on themselves, but now that they were approaching maturity, they began to realize that the country's resources were not unlimited.

The point of view of the public also altered perceptibly. Following the leadership of the government, workmen and employers both undertook to establish their enterprises on a normal, healthy, and durable basis. They wished to safeguard industry from depressions and social troubles, and to assure a steady market for it. The general aim was stability, and "service" was the catchword of the moment. This was the first application of a doctrine which was advocated not merely by the authorities, but by the public and the producers as well. It was an excellent example of the ability to concentrate on a common goal which is so characteristic of American society and in such striking contrast to other countries, where, alas! the best efforts are all too often spent on destruction.

A study of the way in which American industry has been adapted to the new conditions would require a whole book, and moreover a technical knowledge which I do not possess. The main lines, however, are visible. Economy of personnel is the first and most pressing item on the program, as from now on the labour supply will not be inexhaustible. Increase of individual output consequently becomes vitally necessary. The results obtained in this respect during the past twenty-five years and especially since the War are clearly shown in the following table, in which the year 1899 has been taken to represent 100 : [2]

	1899	1914	1919	1923
Power	100	220	278	336
Production	100	156	198	285
Number of workmen	100	134	161	190

The significance of this tabulation is that by an improvement in methods, production has been increased more quickly than the number of workers. Thanks to the efficient use of power and labour, a given article can now be produced by fewer operatives. This fact, which applies to all industries, explains how wages have risen without jeopardizing the economic equilibrium of the country.

No less important is the methodical selection of personnel. This is an old American theory that has been put in practice for many years in the larger factories, and rightly or wrongly, has been associated with the celebrated name of Taylor. It has been systematically and often ruthlessly pushed to an extraordinary degree of perfection. Thoughtful people have occasionally protested that an excess of output must wear out the human material, but the masses, hypnotized by their high salaries, did not realize at first the exhaustion that follows extremely monotonous work, and so did not offer any serious resistance. Those who were not able to fall in line went off, but they did not slam the door. The truth is that Ford, that prince of industrial output, has created an immense impression all over the country. The

[2] Figures taken from the National Industrial Conference Board.

Americans admire efficiency so sincerely that they close their eyes to its perils.

This attempt to adapt the personnel to its duties has recently been carried still further. The intelligence tests invented by the French doctors, Binet and Simon, which we prudently subordinate to the interpretation of the examiner, have been taken up with enthusiasm in America. These tests are used in the schools, the universities, the factories, and the large stores, where it is considered that they give an automatic and decisive indication of the possibilities of the individual. They are mechanically inscribed on each personal record, and ever after they pursue the unfortunate victim like a police record that can never be effaced. This test decides whether a boy is capable of becoming an artist, a book-keeper, or only a messenger, and whether he is likely to be advanced in the future or permanently kept in an inferior position. Some professors attribute even more importance to the test than to examinations. Today many of the big industries employ their own psychologists to determine and measure the aptitude of their staffs. Many prominent people consider this one of the most fruitful attempts ever made to classify the capacities and vocations needed in the various professions and trades. What earlier generations left to the whim of the individual, society in future will decide scientifically in accordance with the technical rules. (The eugenists apply the same reasoning to reproduction.) This love of the automatic, which is also found in the diagnoses of American doctors, is irritating to a European, for we still delight in the spirit of finesse. These ideas are remarkably like the dreams of the early Socialists and are likely to be most dangerous if their execution is confided to professors who have no sense of humour.

When production is no longer regarded as a brilliant adventure, but becomes a difficult science, then we must adjust our conception of the ideal leader. Experience, intuition, and decision are still valuable; but they do not suffice. The problems are now so complex that alongside of the manager a veritable general staff is required. Whether it is a case of purchasing raw materials and machinery, of the employment of workmen and the relationships of the staff, of the domestic or foreign market, of the movement of prices and the general business situation, each question must be studied separately according to its own technique, and then adjusted to its proper place in the scheme of things. This means a great change in the relationship between employers and their employés.

In a sense specialization becomes less and less necessary for the workman, for semi-skilled men are now all that is necessary at the machines, men who after a few weeks' instruction never rise much above the level of unskilled labourers. In the Ford or the McCormick works they spend their whole lives piercing holes in tin plates, or tightening up the same screw in the same place. It would be difficult to choose leaders from among them, and as Ford himself remarks, they are often satisfied with this material existence without responsibilities, and do not want promotion.

On the other hand general culture based not only on experience but on education is becoming more indispensable at the top of the ladder. As a business grows, the problems that must be confronted become broader and require minds that are more alert, keen, and highly trained. The time is past when a youth is initiated into business by sweeping out the office. For the directors, the general secretaries, and the assistants that surround them, America sincerely believes in economic education. This does not mean simply a business-college course in book-keeping, commercial correspondence, economic geography, etc., but an education which will turn out young men of broad culture. This may seem singular when applied to the Americans, whom we usually consider deliberately practical; yet the demand for such culture is today nowhere more insistent than in the executive circles of New York, Boston, or Chicago. The remarkable School of Business Administration at Harvard University is the most interesting of the institutions designed to supply such instruction.

Remarkable progress in the economics of business is being made partly as a result of experience, and partly through the help of economists and statisticians. The English were the first to study foreign markets and to work out the laws of monetary exchange, and today they are still considerably in advance of any one else in this respect. By their traditions the Americans have been more inclined to study their own home market, and little by little, with incontestable skill, they have built up a science of their own. Nor has it been entirely left to the professors and scientists. The Wall Street banker, the director of a Chicago department store, and the Los Angeles real estate agent may be seen every day studying their charts and following the slightest changes in the curves showing wholesale and retail prices, wages, and rates of discount. In periods of calm they endeavour to forsee business storms and depressions. A convention was recently held in Chicago of morticians—the noble but far too expressive name adopted by undertakers in the United States—who met to discuss the dangers that were threatening their profession by the persistent falling-off in the death rate! All the large companies and many of the smaller ones employ their own statisticians, who, like economic meteorologists, observe the financial temperature and note the daily readings of the thermometer, barometer, and wind-gauge of business. The directors devote part of their time to studying the curves that are, put before them, and they believe implicitly in economic science. In this as in their other occupations, success is due to organization.

Not merely was a general reform in industrial methods

required, and also desired by industry and by the public it served; but it was sponsored by the government with rare intelligence and moral authority. The name of Herbert Hoover, the greatest Secretary of Commerce the country has ever had, is associated with this program of national economy. His efforts and breadth of vision are reminiscent of Colbert. It is now over twenty years since the Americans first realized the urgency of conserving their natural resources, which were being pillaged by uncontrolled exploitations. Their present policy is to eliminate waste even in the smallest details of manufacturing.

Out of this vast program let us quote as particularly significant the efforts of the Department of Commerce to reduce the number of different types produced by each industry, and to concentrate on a limited number of standard sizes and shapes for materials which previously had been subject to a chaotic variety that was both useless and uneconomic. For example, investigations showed that no less than 78 sizes of baskets were employed in grape-picking and that without inconvenience they could be reduced to 11. There were 210 different shapes of bottles which could be reduced to 20; 175 kinds of automobile wheels, reduced to four; 66 shapes of bricks, reduced to seven; 287 kinds of tires, reduced to 32. The government collaborated with the trade, and although these simplifications were only suggested and not imposed, they were immediately adopted with enthusiasm, and are now accomplished facts. Since 1921, in fifty different articles the Secretary of Commerce has reduced the useless complexity of models by at least 73 per cent.[3]

This indicates a new relationship between industry and the State. Thirty or forty years ago the first trusts were the forerunners of mass production, but they often used

[3] Annual report of the Secretary of Commerce, 1921, and following years. *Simplifications and Standardization, a Means of Reducing Waste*, a booklet published by the American Chamber of Commerce, 1923.

their powers to obtain monopolies. The government fought them on this point and therefore did not appreciate what they were accomplishing by their efforts toward concentration. The distinction is now clearly drawn between the two points of view. Monopolies are as unpopular as ever, and the laws against them still exist; but the State has learned by experience that if the community is to be well served, production ought henceforth to be organized according to a general plan, though not necessarily concentrated in a few hands. Out of this theory of collaboration has grown the doctrine of "service"—the indispensable password of those who wish to justify their profits.[4]

A good deal of twaddle is talked on this subject. With their optimistic outlook and enviable prosperity, the Americans like to tell you in their self-satisfied way that "service" is an essential condition of profits, and that the great manufacturing and distributing companies are not there only to make money, but mainly to serve the community. In fact, they maintain emphatically that this is their first consideration; and one has to smile when the stodgy business man piously declares that "service" to the community is his one and only passion, while he draws up a wonderful balance sheet. He may possibly believe it, for the American deceives himself very easily. At any rate it "listens well," so that their literature—standardized also!—sings the praises of American business and repeats *ad nauseam* its profes-

[4] The *American Mercury* (Nov., 1925) humorously points the contrast between the people who give "service" and those who do not. "In service, one finds bankers, druggists, grocers, superintendents of schools, proprietors of gents' furnishing stores, teachers, professors in third-rate universities, butchers, owners of Ford garages, proprietors of shoe stores, grain and feed dealers, vendors of stationery and school supplies, ice, coal, and wood dealers, dentists, proprietors of soft-drink emporiums, agents for hygienic corsets, boarding-house keepers, insurance agents, proprietors of lunch rooms, advertising solicitors, station agents, secretaries to associations, promoters of daylight mausoleums, realtors, and postmasters. Not in service, one finds cow-boys, actors, bootleggers, opera singers, prize-fighters, lumbermen, head waiters, pool champions, baseball players, stick-up men, writers, newspaper men, gangsters, sculptors, soldiers, prostitutes. acrobats, and doctors."

sions of faith.   The eloquence of the Chambers of Commerce—those modern temples for the worship of economic
progress—is saturated with this idea, which seems to be a
practical substitute for social morals.

"Service" is a combination of the civic virtue of the
Protestant, the materialism of Bentham, and devotion to
progress.   It is not a Catholic conception, for though we
find it in England, Switzerland, and Scandinavia, it does
not flourish in Latin Europe.   It is not attractive to the
intellectual or the artist, who are accustomed to work individually, but it is very pleasing to the merchant, with
his sense of credit.   He hopes by conscientious "service"
to keep his customers and sell them again next year.   Bae-
deker, that great philosopher, advised giving good tips,
"but only if you intend to return."   In the end, "service"
is the doctrine of an optimistic Pharisee trying to reconcile
success with justice.   Such ethics have their purpose, for
they advocate honesty, good manners, and kindliness.   They
are a marvellous expression of the practical intelligence of
the American, as well as his sincere idealism and ingenuous-
ness.

Thus by the concerted action of the government, the
manufacturers, the workmen, the consumers, and the general public since the War, the United States has been able
to put under way a doctrine of production adapted to the
economic needs of the time.   Germany is the only other
country that has tackled the problem with the same fore-
thought, method, and daring.   England, in spite of her excellent craftsmen, is hindered by her trade unions, and
France by her politicians.

CHAPTER XIII

THE SYSTEM AND ITS LIMITATIONS

MACHINERY cannot accomplish everything; therefore any system which depends on it is bound to be limited, for a time inevitably comes when the active intelligence of the worker is needed, as distinct from the mechanical repetition of the automaton. It will then be discovered that the shortage of labour prevents further expansion of the industry, which in addition will be loaded down with high wages. This peril can already be seen in the distance, although the limit is being pushed back almost indefinitely by American ingenuity, which is increasing the field of machinery to an extent almost unheard of in Europe. We undoubtedly lack courage and faith in this respect, and yet in the end America will come up against a blank wall beyond which further progress will be impossible, at any rate for the time being. No factory can be expanded indefinitely, for, as any manager will tell you, production costs increase after a certain point, and the law of diminishing returns makes itself felt. For instance, in the iron and steel trade, which has been brought to a remarkable point of perfection, a certain irreducible minimum of labour is still required. This same difficulty is apparent in agriculture, where machinery is less subtle. There are no signs yet of a machine to pick strawberries!

The Americans are so bound up with their machines that they are losing interest in making anything that cannot be turned out by mass production. Market gardening, fisheries, and the lesser trades are left to the foreigners. Even where they are past masters, we find the same indifference if the volume is too small. For instance, the special steel required for a Gillette safety-razor blade is imported from Sweden, for the total amount used is too small to be financially interesting to men who know how to make money only on a large scale. All this has created an economic situation in which the cost of anything hand-made tends to increase and in the long run contradicts the general principle that prices are lowered by standardizing the product; so it is difficult to say which of the two factors will be the more important in the end.

A more serious objection to the system is that standardization is quite unsuited to a whole group of industries in which the extreme development of machinery is not only useless, but even detrimental to the creative genius on which they depend. We now enter an entirely different field, where French workmanship is the criterion. Here the value is in the originality and finish of the article, and competition requires not the standardization of a few types, but a higher level of perfection and a greater variety of models. The spirit of this kind of industry is in direct opposition to the American system, for mass production destroys the value of an article where distinction is the main attraction. Contrast the American textile mill with only 14 designs on 800 looms with a similar mill in Lyons, which turns out 81 on only 200 looms. French strength and invulnerability lie in creative instinct and the quality and individuality of the product. The French are in fact stronger when labour is less mechanical and more personal and artistic.

The same applies to agriculture, for here again French exports are by no means the staple raw produce of the farm, but are generally highly cultivated articles on which knowledge, taste, and even affection have been lavished. How different are the standardized food-stuffs exported from countries where cows are milked by machinery, and peaches peeled by dipping them into a chemical solution! The superiority of the French article depends on the patient labour and traditions of the peasant, as well as on his inborn taste. There is no use attempting to Americanize an individualist like the French gardener. Four acres of French soil tilled with unremitting devotion yields more than forty acres exploited by the industrialized farmer whose labourers are in no way attached to the soil and only think of finishing their eight hours' work. In short, whether we consider silks or agriculture, the French system is that of an age-old civilization. As a result of years of experience, they have worked out their own particular culture, which depends less on social ideas like credit and "service" than on professional pride in work well done.

The conclusion is that wherever the machine, the series, or the organization can triumph, American genius will triumph with it. But it is not adaptable and will not give the maximum output when, instead of disciplined co-operation, constant individual initiative is needed, and an intelligent appreciation of the finished product, as well as artistic ability and unremitting care. Now it is these very qualities that the American civilization, with its passion for social discipline, is tending to atrophy. In certain special lines of textiles, for example, the Americans admit that they can compete with Europe only when they invent a machine to diminish the amount of attention demanded from the worker. On the other hand, they are not sure of themselves when they try to make to order expensive articles that cannot be standardized. By turning the worker into a cog in a vast machine, they have robbed him of the intense mental activity of the artisan or even the peasant who can think in terms of the finished product, be it a clock, a fruit, or a flower. Thus, wherever standardization is not essential, America does not lead, and is in fact exceedingly vulnerable. The enormous tariff wall and the position of her industries in relation to foreign competitors show where she is unchallenged, but they also show where protection is urgently necessary.

We know already that wherever mass production by perfected machinery and scientific organization are required, the American cost of production is so low in spite of high wages that they can easily compete in the world markets. In fact, these industries no longer need a tariff; for their real protection lies in special conditions which do not exist to the same extent in Europe, such as abundant natural resources, plenty of capital, and a home market that is so large and so uniform that it is admirably suited to standardized or, in this case, economical production.

This first series of industries can be divided into different categories. At the top we have those in which the inventive genius of the American has made its mark: typewriters, book-keeping machines, calculators, cash registers, and other labour-saving devices, agricultural machinery, cinema films, etc. Their incontested superiority is based not only on quality and price, but on inventions which have been stimulated by the increasing needs of the community for labour substitutes.

Next comes an extensive and varied group of articles which, though not specifically American, can be produced cheaply enough by mass production to assure an advantage over, if not complete immunity from, foreign competition. In this category are automobiles (except *de luxe* cars), boots and shoes (except the high-grade), machinery in general, hardware, electrical fittings, canned foods, drugs and toilet accessories, musical instruments (except organs), etc. Of these the higher grades are manufactured as well if not better in Europe, but market conditions in America make production more economical there.

Finally, we have a special category of articles which are not only susceptible to mass production but are specially made to fill the peculiar needs of the American market, and are therefore hardly exposed to foreign competition. For example, we have agricultural implements specially designed for the chief American crops, such as wheat, cotton, fruit, and vegetables; automobiles designed for farm use with changeable spare parts; sanitary porcelain developed to a degree unknown in Europe, and an infinite variety of electrical labour-saving devices for the home which are absolutely essential in a country where domestic servants are fast disappearing. All these industries could stand free trade, though possibly not without certain adjustments in the quality of their products.

In the middle of the nineteenth century, conditions in England were unrivalled anywhere for manufacturing, and Cobden and Peel reaped the full benefit of the fact by abolishing a tariff which had become useless. In the industries which we have just enumerated, the world centre of cheap production has now deserted Europe in favor of the Great Lakes region of North America. Many New World employers who are aware of this have admitted to me privately that they no longer need the protection of their Chinese wall. Nevertheless, the industries that have definitely renounced protection and do not benefit by the 1922 tariff are very few in number: agricultural implements, typewriters and other office machines, boots and shoes, boot and shoe machinery, and a few others. This movement is principally confined to enterprises which export extensively and are therefore afraid of reprisals, but all the rest remain protectionist and protected. This is partly due to habit, partly to fear of the unknown, and partly to dread of demoralizing competition with countries with a depreciated exchange. In other cases, although protection may not be required for the poorer qualities, it is still needed in the high-class end of the trade. For instance, expensive cars need the tariff; but Ford is absolutely independent.

The chief reason, however, is that the Americans feel

that provided it does no harm, it is just as well to be protected, even if it does no good. The great majority of
manufacturers work almost exclusively for the home market,
and even when they do export they bother very little about
the needs of the foreigner, as only an unimportant part of
their production goes abroad. Nothing short of becoming a
great exporting country for manufactured goods will change
American opinion in this respect.

When we leave the articles in which their genius is most
successful, however, we find that they have no marked
superiority over Europe. Protection there is not a luxury
but a stern necessity. To start with, there are the many
specialized articles that do not lend themselves easily to mass
production. In the New World everything that is made to
measure, whether it is a dress or a machine, is labouring
under a handicap. Although American engineering is undeniably first class, when it comes to intricate pieces of
machinery, the order often goes to England, France, Germany, or Belgium—hence the protective tariff!

In all the better grades of textiles and knit-goods, America
defends herself by means of exceedingly high duties, varying from 40 per cent. to 60 per cent. *ad valorem*. Protection is equally necessary wherever Europe is also equipped
for mass production, and has in addition the advantage
of a lower wage level and better technique. This applies
to the textile industry and especially to woollens. Although
European political conditions hinder development on a vast
scale, yet the number of factories which are being equipped
with modern machinery is increasing every day. Occasionally capital from overseas is contributed, for Ford, Mc-
Cormick, and others have opened up American factories
in several European countries in order to install themselves
behind the tariff walls and to profit by cheap labour. Over
and above their immense home market, the chief advantages
which enable the Americans to meet European competition

are their optimism and confidence, their absence of hampering routine, and the way in which they are perpetually im-
proving their methods. Whenever these are not sufficient
they have their tariff to fall back on.

This defensive attitude is even more pronounced in the
case of the third category of industries, many of which
sprang up during the War and hence are sadly lacking in
technical background. Scientific instruments, optical glass,
chemical dyes, toys, and other delicately made articles in
which Germany has specialized for fifty years, hardly survive without state assistance, for they are still infant industries in America; and the arguments advanced by Alexander
Hamilton, Henry Clay, and President McKinley still hold
good. This policy was to assure the economic independence
of the New World in a whole group of industries. At
present America is afraid of Europe in this connection,
and therefore the latter should not consider itself definitely
relegated to second rank by its young and vigorous rival,
who is labouring under such serious handicaps as an excessively high standard of living and a lower level of individual culture.

Agriculture is a form of production that cannot be in-
vigorated to the same extent as industry by standardization
and the use of machinery. Between 1899 and 1924, the
total population of the country increased 50 per cent., while
those employed in industry increased by 162 per cent., as
against only 40 per cent. in agriculture. Agricultural production depends directly on the area tilled and the amount
of labour involved; so in contrast to manufacturing, its
possibilities are distinctly limited. Though industry is still
far from reaching the point of diminishing returns, this
law is beginning to be felt in agriculture. In spite of technical improvements—and there is no telling what American
genius may do—farming costs seem to be too heavy, unless
either the yield or the selling price rises in proportion. In

1924 the average level of industrial prices was 162 per cent. as compared with 1914, whereas the price of farm produce only rose to 134 per cent. although the farmer was paying salaries at a level of 184 per cent., agricultural implements at 182 per cent., and taxes and interest at 245 per cent. Obviously he was farming at a loss. In 1925, which was a most prosperous year throughout the whole country, the farming situation scarcely improved. The index of farm produce was 144, whereas the average index for farming costs was 168. The low selling price was not due to favourable output, but rather to the effect of world prices on a partially export industry. As a result the farmers no longer believe in free trade, but wish to serve a protected home market and to dispose of their surplus by dumping. This is not the attitude of an infant industry, but of one that is mature and is beginning to adopt the point of view of an old country.

The possibility or impossibility of exporting at remunerative prices is implied in the above analysis. The industries where American genius shines can stand free trade, for they are able to hold their own in any market. Take for example the incomparable position in the world today of American typewriters and agricultural implements. The same applies to certain articles which, though not necessarily of American invention, have been standardized and produced on a large scale. They can export large quantities of the poorer grades of automobiles but cannot compete abroad with the better makes, which in fact are actually invading their market from Europe. Those industries that are specially fitted for the needs of the American market also enjoy a privileged position in other countries that are similar in climate, customs and industrial conditions. Canada is the most favourable outlet, and to a lesser degree the other British Dominions. On the other hand articles which cannot be standardized or which require special technique, as well as certain branches of agriculture, are all in a difficult position. The first two types will not be likely to build up an export trade for some time to come, but in agriculture the tendency is more and more to concentrate on the home market.

We can thus classify American achievements according to their adaptability to mass production, which in the United States is a *sine qua non* of success. Unless the output per man can be increased by machinery, the industry goes to the wall. On the whole, American industry has solved this problem. From 1899 to 1919 production rose from 100 to 198, although the number of workers only increased to 161, but this improvement was by no means general.[1] In the following industries, however, production exceeded increase in personnel.

Metal trades in general	Gloves	Canned fruits
Automobiles	Knit goods	Explosives
Hooks and eyes	Silks	Artificial fertilizers
Blast furnaces		

In the canning industry, which happens to be exceptionally well organized, the output actually rose from 100 to 354, while labour only increased to 164. The increase of production over labour in the following has been limited:

Rice milling	Jute	Gasoline	Hats
Condensed milk	Tin	Bricks	Bicycles
Fish canning	Ice	Chemicals	Cottons
Butter	Coke	Paper pulp	Wagons
Salt	Glass	Paint	Woolens
Cheese			

In several other industries, however, such as packing-houses, tanning, perfumes, and dyes, production has not

[1] "The Graphic Analysis of the Census of Manufactures, 1849 to 1919," published by the National Industrial Conference Board.

kept up with the increase in labour.   To this last category must be added agriculture as a whole.

Thus American exports depend on comparatively simple conditions, and because the country is self-supporting they are not taken seriously.   The day will come when they will be forced to export, and then they will be obliged to adjust their prices to the world's level and to admit that their standard of living depends to a certain extent on that of other countries.   Can their present superb economic independence last forever?

CHAPTER XIV

AMERICA'S ECONOMIC INDEPENDENCE

AMERICA can maintain her exceptional standard of living as long as she buys or sells abroad only a small part of what she consumes or produces. She can remain isolated while her abundant natural resources enable her to do without imported raw materials which she would have to pay for by exporting manufactures. In the last analysis her standard of living depends on the wealth of her soil.

In 1923 the United States only imported 7.9 per cent. of her total consumption, which is extraordinarily little compared with England, which before the War imported 35 per cent. of her food-stuffs and 64 per cent. of her raw materials. The future of England is linked up with the rest of the world, and as a result she is instinctively and chronically worried, whereas a superb complacency reigns on the other side of the Atlantic. Without making a detailed study of American resources, let us point out a few salient facts to explain the situation. In 1924 the United States produced:

38%	of the world's coal
70% " " "	petroleum
38% " " "	electric power
54% " " "	copper
40% " " "	lead
33% " " "	iron ore
75% " " "	corn (maize)
25% " " "	wheat
30% " " "	cereals (other than wheat)
55% " " "	cotton
53% " " "	timber
33% " " "	tobacco

Now, though these quantities vary from one to three-quarters of the world's supply, yet the area of the country only represents 5.7 per cent. of the land surface of the globe. America thus has an exceptionally large share of the world's wealth, which is the first and most obvious reason for her astounding prosperity.

A scarcely less important reason, however, is that owing to her geological formation and varied climate, she is equipped with almost every natural resource she requires. The Americans normally have more than enough copper, lead, silver, petroleum (a most precarious possession), cotton, wheat, tobacco, and meat. They have sufficient coal, iron, corn, oats, and horses, in all of which their domestic trade is enormous, although the export figures are ridiculously small. These are family matters which have nothing to do with any one else, for if America were to be cut off from the rest of the world, she could continue to live and prosper as far as these products are concerned. Gaps do occur, of course, whenever she produces too little of some things and consumes too much of others, as in the case of wool, linen, wood, sugar, and petroleum. The waste of such natural resources as timber and petroleum, which have been senselessly exploited for generations, has now shown the bottom of the cup for the first time. Up to the present the American people have been still in the bloom of their youth and so have believed themselves to be immortal. Now they are beginning to realize to their sorrow that even the reserves of the New World are limited. Also, there are certain products which cannot be grown in the American climate, and others which can be obtained only with difficulty, owing to labour conditions. In this category come tea, coffee, cocoa, rubber, all tropical plants, and silk, which can be cultivated only by a painstaking people. By dividing up their imports into groups, we can clearly outline their requirements:

Imports in 1925

Raw and semi-manufactured materials 58.6%
Food-stuffs 22.0%
Manufactured goods 18.8%
Sundries 0.6%

Thus both manufactured goods and food-stuffs yield first place to raw materials, in which are included, in the following order of importance, rubber ($430,000,000), silk ($396,000,000), coffee, sugar, wool, furs and skins, tin, wood pulp, etc. These are enormous figures admittedly, but even the $4,000,000,000 total imports is an insignificant amount—actually less than 10 per cent. of the total consumption of the country. This explains and justifies their extraordinary feeling of independence when they consider England, mistress but also slave of the seas, and Europe, where the soil cannot completely feed either the population or the factories. Can one marvel at their condescension or their sigh of relief when they compare themselves with others?

Nevertheless, the tendency of their imports, if not their actual composition, should give them food for thought.

	Imports	
	1875–79	*1921–24*
Raw materials	26.6%	53.1%
Food-stuffs	41.3%	24.8%
Manufactured goods	32.1%	22.1%

As the country becomes more industrialized the proportion of raw materials in the imports increases. Since 1890 the appetite of the factories has increased even more rapidly than that of the people, until the two together seem to have exceeded the capacity of the natural resources. The result is a growing dependence on foreign products, either raw or partly worked. American consumption is so voracious and is increasing so quickly that thinking men and especially the government are becoming anxious. The volume of imports in 1925 was double the 1910–14 figure in the case of timber and sugar, and had almost tripled in silk and wood pulp. Rubber imports were 8 times as great, crude oil 9 times, newsprint 12 times, mineral oils 41 times. In 1899 the domestic forests furnished 78 per cent. of the wood pulp, but only 43 per cent. in 1923. Everywhere the trend is the same. The exporting trades are tending to diminish, but imports have swelled to an absolute flood.

The American public is proud of these fantastic figures, for to them they express wealth and widespread prosperity. The government, which sees further into the future, has adopted an alarmist attitude and preaches moderation and economy. But it might as well try to make water run uphill as to alter the optimism of this people who have always been accustomed to superabundance. Unfortunately, just at the moment that they first discovered that their resources did have limits, they were busy celebrating with a blast of trumpets the infinite possibilities of machinery and organization. Like Massillon's characters who know that they are mortal but refuse to believe it, the Americans may know that their petroleum and timber cannot last forever, but they too refuse to believe it.

The export figures also reveal these same tendencies, but curious to relate, they encourage that optimism, according to which the fears of the past over what was going to happen have always been overcome in the present. The exported percentage of America's total production amounted to 8.5 in 1823. This is not higher than the percentage of the total consumption that was imported. This is important, for it means that the country absorbs practically all it produces. The War had the effect of temporarily increasing exports to 15.3 per cent. in 1919, but since then it has returned to about where it was in 1914 (9.6 per cent.). Nevertheless, the exports have actually increased, for between 1914 and 1923 they expanded to 49 per cent., but at the same time production also rose still faster, to 55 per cent.; so the home market must have absorbed the excess. At the time of the Peace Conference, people said that the United States could not be prosperous in the midst of a ruined world, but since then it has been proved, at any rate for the time being, that the North American continent can live comfortably on itself.

This, then, is the meaning of the small percentage exported; namely, 8.5 per cent. Its significance is even more striking when we analyze the elements of which this trade is composed, for in that average of 8.5 per cent. there are many products of which the United States are large exporters in proportion to their total production. For example, in 1925 the percentage exported by weight was:

82% of their resin
64% " " copper
57% " " raw cotton
47% " " turpentine
35% " " illuminating oils
31% " " lubricants
34% " " tobacco
30% " " wheat

On the other hand, in a whole series of important raw materials only a very low percentage or none at all were exported, as shown by the following list:

13.0% of their bacon
0.5% " " beef
0.3% " " mutton [1]
12.0% " " gasoline

[1] 1924 figures, as 1925 had not been published when the book went to press.

9.0% of their fuel oil
2.0% " " raw petroleum
5.0% " " anthracite
3.0% " " bituminous coal
1.0% " " iron ore
0.4% " " maize

The important point to note is that the percentage of manufactured articles exported, when expressed in values, remained at the very low level of 4.3 per cent. in 1923, which was even below the pre-war figure.[2]

Exports amounted to a large proportion in only a few standardized industries, such, as, for example:[3]

53% of their motorcycles
34% " " typewriters
24% " " sewing machines

The next on the list shows a big drop:

10.0% of their cotton knit goods
5.0% " " pianos
3.8% " " automobiles (7% in 1925)
2.0% " " boots and shoes
2.0% " " cotton yarns

In 1925, the composition of the export trade by categories was as follows:

Raw materials and semi-manufactured goods 43.1%
Food-stuffs 18.5%
Manufactures and sundries 38.4%

[2] The Department of Commerce in giving this figure considers that it is a little low, on account of the inevitable repetition in the calculation of the total industrial production.

[3] Estimated by the Department of Commerce (Foreign Trade of the United States in the calendar year of 1925, page 18).

The country exports a considerable amount of raw materials and manufactures, but relatively little food-stuffs. Out of a total export trade of $4,818,000,000, certain items are quite formidable:

Raw cotton	$1,060	millions
Mineral oils	421	"
Automobiles	309	"
Machinery	234	"
Wheat	234	"

As in the lists of imports, we must not forget that here also these colossal quantities are nothing in comparison with the total economic activity of the country. The export of automobiles may amount to $309,000,000, but the home market already absorbs 93 per cent. of the national production; for America alone represents some four-fifths of the automobile clientele of the world. The motorcycle industry is the only exception, as over half its production goes abroad; for the Americans, all having their own cars, are content to leave the motorcycle to the modest foreigner!

American industry, therefore, is not developing an export mentality very rapidly, as it is concentrating on its home market and not looking to the sea as an outlet. This is shown by the way that the country is being divided up into zones with the centre of gravity steadily moving farther west from the region south of the Great Lakes, where it has been for the last twenty-five years. No one in that immense territory between the Alleghanies and the Rockies is at all concerned without outlets abroad. They are self-supporting and prosper without a thought for the rest of the world. It is here that we find the greatest contrast between America and Great Britain, where the leading industries export over half of their total output (75 per cent. of their cotton, 66 per cent. of their iron, 50 per cent. of their wool). The English are always preoccupied with foreign affairs and anxiously follow the international level of prices, the saturation points of the market, and any wars or revolutions likely to ruin their customers in other countries.   Now the Americans, on the other hand, are content to study their own home market, where they know by experience they have a purchasing power that is almost limitless.   This explains the nervousness of the British in contrast to the confidence of the Americans, who need not manœuvre for position, because they know that in their own domain they are sailing in deep waters.

This is the normal result of the perfectly sound situation which we have just described, but what are the chances of its enduring?   In this connection a detailed study of the export trade of the past fifty years is very significant:

Exports

	1875–79	1910–14	1915–20	1921–25
Raw materials	34.1%	33.1%	17.6%	27.4%
Raw materials, partly worked	5.4	16.5	16.0	12.7
Raw food-stuffs	20.3	5.9	9.6	9.7
Manufactured food-stuffs	24.3	13.8	17.6	13.9
Manufactured articles	15.9	30.7	39.2	36.3

This table shows that raw materials are becoming less important at the same time that manufactured goods are rapidly increasing.   The War stimulated the export of food-stuffs and manufactures, but this was temporary and artificial.   Otherwise the general trend is absolutely clear.   The character of the American export trade is changing as the manufactured or semi-manufactured article supplants raw materials.   In 1891, for example, cotton, petroleum, meat, and wheat accounted for 75 per cent. of the foreign trade; but in 1925 they were only 39 per cent. of the total.

We must beware of jumping at hasty conclusions. We might reasonably expect that this obvious and undeniable revolution in the foreign trade would have altered the psychology of the people, but this is not so. Up to now the Americans have sold their raw materials only to foreign countries that could not do without them, and therefore they have had little experience in the rude school of international competition. The outlook of an exporter does not come by simply shipping out cotton, copper, petroleum, and wheat, but can be acquired only by the more difficult marketing of manufactured goods. They probably do not even realize the immense advantage they enjoy from their exportable surplus of national wealth, which they use to pay for the importation of things they lack, such as coffee, tea, silk, and rubber. Thus their exports of manufactured goods are more or less optional, whereas cotton is as useful to them as coal is to the British.

Meanwhile a far-reaching and unmistakable change is taking place which is gradually reducing the importance of the sale of raw products and food. Before 1900 over 25 per cent. of the wheat was exported, but this figure fell to 15 per cent. by 1910–14, though the War and its after-effects have since brought it up to about 30 per cent. As soon as Europe has regained her normal independence in regard to food, the growing population of the United States will absorb a very large part of their own wheat crops, which are not likely to increase. Nor should we be astonished if the next generation of Americans should cease to export food-stuffs altogether and actually import them, even wheat. This tendency is already visible in the case of several important raw materials, such as petroleum, wood, and wool. Raw cotton is rather different, for notwithstanding the fears of our European pessimists, America will probably have a large export surplus for some time to come, provided they do not deliberately restrict their production. In spite of the boll weevil, their production can be increased beyond the requirements of the home market.

The movement toward industrialism is irresistible; in fact, it has been developing ever since the Civil War, as the following figures show. The rural population dropped from 71 per cent. of the total in 1880 to 54 per cent. in 1910 and 48 per cent. in 1920. In 1850, 63 per cent. of the working population were actually engaged in agriculture, but only 33 per cent. in 1910 and 26 per cent. in 1920; but the industrial population rose during the same period from 15 per cent. to 27 per cent. and 30 per cent. This is perfectly normal and in accordance with the evolution of the country, for as American products become industrialized, it is only natural that each purely agricultural operation should have an industrial counterpart in the city. Though it may be demoralizing from the social point of view, yet it is a perfectly normal development for this new community. The final effects of this change are bound to be important. America is organized for standardized mechanical production and is handicapped whenever these methods cannot be applied. Raw materials and food-stuffs, therefore, tend to become dearer and less easy to export, especially to countries with dense populations, lower wages, and less ambitious scales of living.

These symptoms herald the approach of a certain maturity in which the present plethora of wealth will give place to ordinary comfortable circumstances. Instead of paying for their needs by exporting what is superfluous, the Americans will soon be obliged to export manufactured goods in order to obtain in exchange certain raw materials and foods which may have become indispensable. When that time comes, they will be in the same position as the great industrial countries of Western Europe, in which imports and exports are absolutely necessary for their existence. Happily, however, that day is still far off, nor is it likely to be very

stringent.   Still, when the Americans do have to depend on
international markets, like England and Germany, their
present splendid isolation will be over.   They have a bitter
lesson to learn from the law that liquids rise to the same
level in communicating vessels, an axiom which they still
only dimly comprehend.

On various occasions already it has looked as if the glut
of over-production in the home market would have to be
relieved by the export of manufactured goods.   In the Mc-
Kinley tariff of 1890, Blaine forsaw this trend and suggested his famous reciprocity plan to obtain foreign outlets.   It was with the same idea in view that after McKinley
had become president of the Republic in 1896, Senator
Kasson was instructed to negotiate a series of commercial
treaties, to which, however, the Senate objected.   Twenty
years later, after the depression of 1920–21, the experts
again considered that industrial America was over-equipped
and could regain her prosperity only by enlarging her foreign market.   The capable civil servants who direct the
Department of Commerce, the U.S. Chamber of Commerce,
and several other institutions of the same order still believe
that this is necessary, possibly not for the present, but most
certainly for the future; and in the exporting industries
and those on the point of exporting, this view is shared.
In no other country is the export policy of the future being
so systematically prepared as by the responsible people in
the United States.

We must, however, admit that events once again seem
determined to falsify these warnings.   The home market
has repeatedly approached saturation, but each time it has
taken on a new lease of life and an appetite and elasticity
which even the most optimistic dare not prophesy.   On several occasions a wave of immigration poured millions of
new consumers into the country; at other times new regions
were opened up necessitating vast new equipment; or again,

unexpected mechanical improvements stimulated production and so increased wages until the purchasing power of whole classes of society was increased.   Finally, the somewhat un-orthodox system of partial payments has lately wrested new customers from the future by discounting their earnings. Each of these factors taken separately appears exceptional, but for several generations they have succeeded one another or have been renewed, except during a few short periods of depression.   It recalls the quotation from Pascal: *L'imagination se lassera plutôt de concevoir que la nature de fournir.*[4]

We can hardly wonder that the American public is not worrying over the absorbing power of their home market, for the spectacle that is renewed daily is more eloquent than any argument.   Two tendencies can be observed in the way American policy is evolving: first, we have the men who, having reasoned out the situation, are preparing their country for an international economic future; and secondly, the public and most of the employers, who are only interested in their apparently insatiable home market, and whose optimism seems justified by events.   At the end of the War, Europe thought that the United States would link up closely with the rest of the world; but this the Americans always instinctively dread.

[4] "The mind tires more quickly of originating than nature does of supplying."

CHAPTER XV

AMERICA AND WORLD TRADE

THE Americans have made a place for themselves in the economic structure of the world corresponding to their needs and their power. The nature of their commercial intercourse with other continents is determined by strictly logical considerations which give the clue to their policy.

In their foreign trade we can trace three principal export currents, according to their destination. First and most important are the manufactured goods that go to countries of lower economic development. These are either articles in which America specializes, or else the cheaper grades of manufactures which they turn out by mass production, but which are also made in Europe. Their machines, cheap cottons, and standardized hosiery and knit goods penetrate the markets of South and Central America and Canada, Asia, Oceania, and even Africa, so that in relation to continents that are either younger than they are, or much older, but being rejuvenated, they fill the *rôle* of an industrially superior country, just as Europe did in the past toward America herself. The statistics of the Department of Commerce [1] show the proportion of manufactured goods in the imports from the United States of the different continents, as follows:

South America 72%
Asia and Oceania 53%
Africa 68%
North America 46%

[1] All statistics in this chapter are quoted from the *Commerce Year Book, 1924* and *Foreign Trade of the United States in the Calendar Year 1925,* both published by the American Department of Commerce.

The second current is of a different type and consists of exports to countries that are more developed economically, as, for example, to the Old World—the term "old" is only too true in this respect! Manufactured goods hold a relatively small place in this trade, amounting to only 20 per cent., for Europe both makes and exports them herself. All she asks here are American inventions, such as typewriters, in which they excel, and certain articles of mass production like the Ford car. In other industrial products, and especially the better grades, there is no reason for the Old World to apply to its prodigious young rival. On the other hand, as America is still young and fairly overflowing with raw materials, exhausted and over-industrialized Europe is only too glad to have recourse to such a bountiful source of supply. Therefore raw materials and semi-manufactured goods amount to some 53 per cent. of European purchases in America, and food-stuffs to 26 per cent. The greater part of the American exports of cotton are sent to Europe, and also copper, meat, and wheat. In this the United States fulfils the *rôle* of a young country ministering to an older one.

Finally there is a third current of trade directed to countries where the climate, customs, and in certain cases the economic age are similar to that of the United States. This is particularly true of Canada, and sooner or later Australia, South Africa, and the Argentine will also be inevitably drawn into her commercial orbit, though to a lesser degree. The American article is as suitable to the needs of these markets as if it had been specially designed for them; so no wonder that Canada, her Siamese twin, should purchase from the United States everything from coal to magazines, almost as if there were no frontier between them. In 1925 Australia and the Argentine were the two chief importers of American automobiles, and one need only visit California and Australia to realize that they could not long be indifferent to each other. They have the same climate and outdoor sports, the same industrial conditions and scarcity of labour, the same boundless possibilities, and the same menace from over-populated Asia. Although they are under different rule, the economic atmosphere in all these countries is similar, and it is bound to develop into a familiarity which will be expressed first in trade and later in the interplay of politics.

These three currents can be broadly summed up statistically: In 1923 America exported only 28 per cent. of her manufactures to Europe and the remaining 72 per cent. to other continents, while in raw materials and food the situation is exactly reversed, Europe taking 70 per cent. and the rest of the world 30 per cent.

The simplest of reasoning suggests that a complimentary classification exists in imports, for since America has now become the leading industrial nation of the world, she does not require foreign manufactured goods. Indeed it is high time she was independent of them, but as we have shown, her intensive industrial life does not always correspond to progress. In respect to everything above medium quality her taste is far behind the European, just as Europe is far behind the skill of the Chinese in some respects. The United States, therefore, purchases, and will continue for some time to purchase, the finer qualities of textiles, certain specialized machines, prepared foods, and all manner of novelties; for the New World is the great market of the luxury trades. Manufactured articles thus make up 40 per cent. of American imports from Europe. The Old World still has rich natural resources in certain regions which America taps whenever she lacks them, and thus she fills the rôle of a developed country purchasing raw materials from economically young provinces that happen to lie in a worn-out continent. Examples of this are American imports of paper pulp from Scandinavia (and eventually from Russia), tobacco from Greece and Holland, silks from Italy, and raw wool from Great Britain. This explains how no less than 24 per cent. of Europe's sales to America are made up of raw materials.

As far as the rest of the world is concerned, except for a few artistic specialties from the Far East, America is merely an insatiable purchaser of raw materials. She empties Asia of her raw silks, the British and Dutch East Indies of their rubber, Cuba of her sugar, and Canada of her wood pulp. She takes a large share of the Australian wool crop, of Chinese furs and nuts, of Brazilian coffee, Chilean nitrate and copper, and Mexican petroleum and minerals. In a word, she relies on the Pacific countries for raw materials, and on the rest of North and South America for both raw materials and food. But in her imports from these regions, manufactures are almost non-existent; for with the exception of Japan and Canada, they have no exporting industries. The exports of other North American countries show only 11 per cent. of manufactured articles, Asia and Oceania 17 per cent., both South America and Africa only 1 per cent. In relation to the latter, though some are younger and others older, the United States occupies the position of an elder country that buys raw materials and pays for them in manufactured goods.

This relationship is really perfectly logical, but its complexity is due to the fact that the age of the United States is not always the same in her different economic activities. Industrially America is mature; as an exporter of cotton she is young, and as a consumer of wood she is old. From this arises an interplay of reciprocal dependencies not unlike the evolution of Europe during the nineteenth century when she colonized the whole planet. In the future, whether we call them colonies or not, America will be dependent on her external sources of supply.

All this indicates the future trend of the relationship be-

tween the Old World and the New. If Europe is to continue to sell her high-class goods to the United States and
to buy in return articles of mass production, a certain balance of exchange will be created in the industrial world.
Can there be a genuine interchange of raw products between
the two continents that will be either normal or lasting, if
the requirements of both exceed their own resources? In
this respect both will eventually turn more and more to the
rest of the world, where they will compete with each other
as purchasers. As statistics already show, America is fast
becoming the economic centre of the world by sheer weight
of wealth, but when her industry tries to conquer the international markets, the low wages and finished technique of
Europe will prove formidable obstacles. The rivalry will
be less a direct struggle than competition to obtain a third
market in which to purchase raw materials or sell manufactured goods. Judging by the place that American commerce has won for itself in the past fifty years, Europe
will probably not long continue to occupy a dominating
position, either as a market for, or as an exporter to,
America.

The division of American exports by continents is as
follows:

	1875–79	1910–14	1915–20	1921–25
Europe	81.6%	62.3%	63.9%	52.6%
North America	11.3	23.1	19.4	24.4
South America	3.3	5.6	5.4	6.8
Asia and Oceania ..	3.8	7.8	10.1	14.6
Africa	0.0	1.2	1.2	1.6

As this table shows, the relative importance of European purchases apart from the War years has been steadily
dwindling, although when expressed in dollars they increased by 72 per cent. between 1910–14 and 1921–25. In
the same period exports to the rest of North America,

Oceania, and Asia increased respectively 145 per cent., 196 per cent., and 312 per cent., although the total increased only 103 per cent. Taking the lower purchasing power of gold into account, we see that the European clientele has scarcely increased at all, and it is the other countries that show such great progress. Therefore, if we disregard the swollen orders of the War, the reconstruction of Europe does not appear to the American public as essential to their prosperity. All predictions for the future must be based on other markets than the European, for it is to them that the methodical and weighty efforts of American policy are turned. They are endeavouring to capture the markets of the world, not by the charm and originality of their goods, but by superior organization and reciprocal trade.

The declining importance of Europe is clearly shown in the following division of American imports by continents:

	1875–79	1910–14	1915–20	1921–25
Europe	49.4%	49.6%	20.8%	30.4%
North America ...	25.1	20.6	30.2	26.4
South America ...	13.7	12.2	17.6	12.2
Asia and Oceania..	9.9	16.3	28.7	28.9
Africa	1.9	1.3	2.7	2.1

According to these figures the War dealt a fatal blow to American imports from Europe, although as in the case of exports, when expressed in dollars, they increased 25 per cent. between 1910–14 and 1921–25; but with the decrease in the value of gold, this is really a decline. The products which the United States will need in the future—rubber, silk, sugar, and coffee—do not come from Europe. Between 1910–14 and 1921–25 purchases in Canada increased 235 per cent., in Asia 265 per cent., and in Oceania 212 per cent.—in fact, America can do without Europe more easily than without South America or Asia.

The trade returns show the exact relationship of the United States vis-à-vis the various other continents. With South America, Asia, and Africa, the balance is unfavourable to the United States; for during the period 1921-25, imports exceeded exports by 42 per cent., 89 per cent., and 2 per cent. respectively. The reason is that these undeveloped regions cannot absorb large quantities of manufactured goods, but America is forced to look to them for raw materials. With Europe, North America, and Oceania, on the contrary, the balance is favourable, as imports amount to only 45 per cent. of the exports in the case of Europe, 85 per cent. in the case of North America, and 38 per cent. in the case of Oceania. In other words, the Americans sell to Europe twice as much as they buy, and three times as much to Australasia. The people of these latter countries, and also of Canada, are similar in customs to the Americans, and therefore they consume their products. Europe, however, is a worn-out continent, and obliged to obtain at any price the raw materials and foodstuffs that she vitally needs. This unbalanced trade is bound to be abnormal and unhealthy to some extent, and this very lack of reciprocity is the outstanding characteristic of the relationship between Europe and America at the present time.

The War was partly responsible for the creation of this new series of economic bonds between regions that previously had not been in direct contact. This is a far-reaching change in the relationship between the continents. By its wealth, its size, and its material attraction, the North American continent is claiming first place in the economic world, a place that had been accorded without question to Western Europe during the past three centuries. True, the Americans leave to Europe the control of certain regions— colonial empires of European countries in Africa, Australasia, tropical Asia, and southern, western, and Russian Asia

—and also certain international economic activities which do not attract them, and for which they are neither particularly gifted nor equipped.

For over a century the United States has been building up an international system independent of Europe, and since the War this tendency has been conspicuous. A whole group of countries, including Canada and in particular Central and South America, which formerly gravitated more or less about the Old World, are now turning for good or ill to the United States. This attraction is also being felt in the Far East and Australasia, and we may even expect that one day South Africa will be influenced by this distant force. The Pacific and the whole American continent is destined to be the future field of economic activity of the United States, with the Panama Canal as the main artery, just as the Suez Canal is the route to the empires over which Europe is still sovereign. The two zones, be it noted, do not interfere with each other. The two canals scarcely compete, and from this we may infer that the old-time unity of the world is splitting up into two parts.

The United States does not appear to be striving to dominate the world, as Europe in her limitless ambition long dreamed of doing. Nor does she wish to emulate England and become the universal merchant of the four quarters of the globe. In spite of their intense self-satisfaction, their frank and almost brutal self-interest, and, even more dangerous, their self-appointed duty toward humanity—in short, with everything that goes to make up imperialism—the Americans are the most continental people in the world, and far more domesticated than adventurous.

During the nineteenth century they lavished their genius on the development of their immense territory and on the building up of an industry unrivalled in its power. They demonstrated their superiority whenever it was a question of organizing for cultivation, production, or scientific salesmanship in their home market, and more recently in the skilful development of a perfected banking and monetary system, a domain which they had hitherto neglected.   In all these activities America has undoubtedly added to the list of human achievements, but the genius of the international merchant, that marvellous gift of the Venetians, the Dutch, and the English, seems to be lacking.   Is it simply that they are not interested, that they find more profitable activities at home, or is it because it requires so much technique and tradition?   Or is it because they are more attracted by simple operations and are always in a hurry?   Or possibly it may be owing to the geographical situation of the country—massive, inarticulate, and isolated between two oceans which cut it off from the more densely populated parts of the globe—which does not lend itself to the subtle and flexible combinations which mean so much in the international market.   As a result of all these conditions, the United States has not followed England and become an international clearing-house.

The real international clearing-houses are those which receive merchandise from every part of the world and redistribute it not merely within their own country but in others as well.   London and Liverpool both do this, but none of the American ports has as yet assumed the *rôle* to any extent.   New York does receive enormous quantities of goods, but only to reship them to her insatiable home market, which absorbs everything and gives back nothing. Of such international re-exports as there are, three-quarters are destined for Canada; but that can hardly be called a foreign country.   In this respect the contrast between Britain, the island, and America, the continent, is very striking.   Re-exports amounted to 17 per cent. of British exports in 1913 and 16 per cent. in 1925, but American re-exports only amounted to 1.5 per cent. in 1913, 2 per cent. in 1924, and 1.9 per cent. in 1925, and consisted almost entirely of raw sugar.

Instead of trying to develop their own activities in this field, the Americans until fairly recently accepted Great Britain as the middleman for a considerable proportion of their foreign trade. For example, they have always purchased their rubber, tea, furs, and raw silk in London, although none of these are British products. Although this brokerage is still continued on a very large scale, there are signs of an important change. When the British middleman was temporarily paralyzed during the War, the American demand for several of these raw materials grew at such a rate that they naturally went direct to the primary market for them. Though they still buy heavy quantities of furs, tea, and wool in England, they are now buying by far the greater part of their silk and rubber direct from the countries of origin. The British middleman was immediately affected, and the drop in their re-exports since the War is largely due to the decline in their shipments to the United States from 27 per cent. of the total re-exports in 1913 to 17 per cent. in 1924. The position in the rubber market is particularly interesting. In 1910–14 America bought 32 per cent. of her raw rubber in England, 35 per cent. in Brazil, and 8 per cent. in the British and Dutch East Indies. In 1925 her English purchases fell to 11 per cent. and her Brazilian to 4 per cent., whereas her direct imports from the British and Dutch East Indies rose to 81 per cent. The British did not really lose, of course, for they own most of the islands; but the change in policy is significant.

We must not exaggerate the importance of this evolution, however; for though the United States may free herself from the middleman, it does not necessarily mean that she will create her own re-export trade. The volume of her imports is so great that she can make a direct appeal to the producer, but she buys not to resell, but simply to absorb; and there are only two parties to the deal, not three as in the British trade. The American spirit is much more continental than international, which accounts for the fact that well-situated ports like San Francisco, New Orleans, and even New York are becoming re-export centres exceedingly slowly.

On several occasions London has worried seriously over the possible competition of New York, but to my mind unnecessarily, for the two cities have little resemblance. Geographically New York is not so favourably situated as London to be a distributing centre. Europe is too far away, and North America is too busy exporting her own raw materials to be interested in the products of other continents. This is especially so under the Fordney Tariff, which like the McKinley–Dingley and the Payne–Aldrich Tariffs before it, does not create a favourable atmosphere for free transactions. Thus what to London is vital and essential is almost a luxury to New York. Americans are apt to despise small profits unless driven to them by necessity, and international commerce often means great risks and narrow profits, to which must be added infinite patience, varied and meticulous technique, an inherited aptitude, and a detailed and almost personal knowledge of the chief markets of the world. Neither their personality nor their traditions fit the Americans for this *rôle,* as their gifts lie more in the line of agriculture, manufacturing, and wholesale distributing within their own country. To create a commercial centre like London takes not years but decades. London carries out the function of world intermediary to perfection, and has built up incomparable business institutions which could only be replaced by people who are both adaptable and subtle, and with years of practice in a trade which cannot be improvised.

In spite of the loss of a certain amount of ground, British commerce is still making a vigorous resistance, and her only real weakness has been in her monetary position. Up to the War, London was universally accepted as the financial clearing-house for all commercial undertakings, owing to the stability of the pound sterling, which was an essential condition of the smooth working of the system of bills drawn on London. Nine-tenths of all international transactions outside of America were done in sterling, but this supremacy has since been seriously impaired; for the dollar, in its triumphant stability, is now the chief international currency, in competition with the somewhat precarious pound sterling. The United States does not, however, seem especially eager to wrest from England this commercial financing that the latter is so keen to undertake, even for American exports of cotton and wheat. The Americans have made no attempt, at any rate up to the present, to establish a régime of international credits to deal with European purchasers direct, but have contented themselves with financing their own producers by means of bank credits, a business in which the War Finance Corporation took a very active part for some time.

In Europe we often regard the dollar as the sworn enemy of the pound and imagine that New York is trying to undermine London's position. This idea I regard as false, for although the Americans are carrying out a growing number of transactions direct, in the long run they conform with the British system, in which they have considerable experience, and also implicit confidence. The fact that these two Anglo-Saxon peoples are accustomed to extend credit to each other is really at the bottom of their close relationship. This régime naturally produces a certain amount of rivalry and friction which the European press is tempted to exaggerate. Of course the broker must not abuse his privileges, and it would be very imprudent of him, for instance, to repeat his high-handed restriction of rubber too often.

If the British Empire were to fall, America would consider it a catastrophe for herself, since her contact with the greater part of the globe is made through the intermediary of the British. Such a disaster would, of course, cause the principal British Dominions to gravitate around the United States; but she would be forced to create an equipment to deal with exchange and international transactions, in neither of which has she had much experience. Her ambition may yet bring her to this point, and certain superficial reflections may cause her to rejoice over the misfortunes of John Bull; yet we are wrong if we believe that she wishes to precipitate them. Even in her pride in the strength of her superb economic growth, America always remembers that she is of Anglo-Saxon origin, and she has great respect for the British civilization from which she emerged.

CHAPTER XVI

FOREIGN LOANS

AMERICA emerged from the War as much changed financially as commercially. Whether the transformation is permanent, or whether it is only the result of over-hasty expansion which has artificially brought about conditions not normally due for decades, of one fact we are certain, and that is that in 1914 the Americans were in debt to Europe and now Europe is in debt to them. The question is, how was this balance of trade and finance reversed?

Before 1914 the foreign trade of the United States showed a heavy annual excess of exports. Being still financed by the Old World, they paid their interest in goods; and astonishing as it seems, in spite of the complete reversal of the debt situation, this favourable balance of trade still survived several years after the War. An exceptional sequence of events explains this phenomenon, which, however, cannot endure indefinitely. There had been a remarkable expansion during the first fourteen years of the twentieth century, but the War and the boom of 1919–20 gave American exports an extraordinary impetus, though imports did not grow in the same proportion; for Europe had nothing to sell. This fabulous excess of exports resulted among other things in choking America with half the world's gold supply. After 1920 imports began little by little to regain their old importance, as the following table shows:

	Exports	Imports	Relation of Imports to Exports
1900–04	$1,429 millions	$ 919 millions	64%
1910–14	2,166	1,689	78
1915–20	6,261	3,223	51
1921–25	4,397	3,450	78
1925	4,309	4,228	98

Thus exports tripled during the War period though imports only doubled, but since then imports have gone on increasing and exports have fallen off slightly. During the 1921–25 period we may say that the balance of trade has returned to the 1910–14 level.

If we take account of the lower purchasing power of gold we find that American sales abroad increased about 30 per cent. over the so-called normal years before the War. It is quite possible that if the War had not intervened progress might have been even more rapid, and occasionally Americans, who are almost embarrassed by their orgy of wealth, are inclined to use this idea to justify themselves in the eyes of ruined Europe. At any rate there is no doubt that the crisis gave the United States a much larger share of world trade than before. Before 1913 they only claimed 12.9 per cent. of international exports, but by 1924 this proportion had increased to 17.8 per cent., although the increase in their sales had been quite normal. The reason is that the exports of other countries had declined, British exports, for example, only reaching three-quarters of their pre-war volume. It may possibly be only temporary, but American commerce has won a more important position for itself in practically every market in the world.

Until Europe regains her normal productive capacity, American exports will remain relatively high.[1]

[1] Estimates and figures taken from *Foreign Trade of the United States in the Calendar Year 1925*, page c, published by the Department of Commerce.

The American Share of the Imports of Various Countries

	1913	1924
Argentine	15%	22%
Brazil	16	24
Chili	17	23
Peru	29	39
Mexico	48	72
Cuba	56	67
Canada	65	65
Great Britain	18	19
France	11	14
Italy	14	24
Germany	16	19
China	6	18
Japan	17	27
India	3	6
Australia	14	28

The effect of the War on imports is quite different. During the War their expansion did not keep pace with exports, because Europe, engrossed in the struggle, could not continue to sell while she was sweeping up everything available in other markets. Since then, however, imports have more than made up for the ground lost. On the basis of 1923 prices—that is to say, considering volume but not value—the increase in imports between 1910–14 and 1924 was 50.2 per cent., but only 26 per cent. in exports. If the balance of trade expressed in dollars reflects this phenomenon incompletely, it is because of an exceptional anomaly in the movement of prices. In comparison with 1910–14 the average price of exports increased 69.5 per cent., but of imports only 43.1 per cent. The Americans are lucky enough to be able to buy cheap and sell dear. Now that the price of cotton is falling, however, and rubber is rising, the whole situation may be modified within a few months.

The United States is logically and irresistibly approaching the time when she will no longer have a favourable balance of trade. This occurred for the first time in 1926. Chance circumstances have retarded this reversal of the situation by several years (in this the War must be considered an exceptional circumstance). First of all, Europe until quite recently paid practically none of her War debt; but when she is able to pay it, she can only do so in the form of increased exports, which will mean increased American imports. At the present time the American tariff arbitrarily prevents this by reducing the volume of foreign purchases. In the second place, Europe has partially denuded herself of gold, not merely during the War but ever since, to buy overseas certain products that she could not do without. She must have meat, cereals, cotton, and petroleum. If she again becomes even partly self-supporting as regards food, and if she succeeds in developing an immense cotton-growing area in Africa, she will purchase less corn and cotton from America.

Finally, whenever the gold shipments or the exchange of goods was insufficient to pay for European purchases, the surplus was converted into credits. During the boom of 1920 they took the form of short-term credits, but more recently they have been converted into long-term investments. Thus the relationship between American investments in Europe and their excess of exports is very close. If the European client had to pay for American merchandise in gold or goods, he could not have bought at all. Hence, thanks to the favourable trade balance which has existed for several years, the United States has artificially prolonged a youthfulness in its export trade quite out of keeping with its maturity in other directions. The American public does

not appreciate this, for they are still under the impression
that the country is only now approaching manhood.

They are deceiving themselves, however, for the balance
of payment and the distribution of American investments
abroad show that their relationship to the non-European
world is that of an elder brother, while in regard to Europe
they are the strong man in his prime supporting a con-
valescent grandfather. The Department of Commerce has
prepared a balance sheet for 1925 to show America's relationship with the rest of the world:[2]

	Credits	*1925*
		(*Millions of Dollars*)
Excess of Exports		666
Interest on Inter-Allied Debt	160	
Private Interest and Dividends	355	
Motion Picture Royalties	75	590
		1,256
	Debits	
Services to Tourists		560
Immigrants' Remittances		310
Ocean freights, Missions, etc.		63
		933

The strictly commercial balance is found to be favourable,
but the other entries on the contrary show a deficit of
$343,000,000, which reduces the final surplus to $323,000,-
000. The Department of Commerce has estimated the
movement of capital resulting from these transactions as
follows:

[2] *The Balance of International Payments of the United States in 1925,*
by F. W. Ryan, preface by Herbert Hoover, Secretary of Commerce,
page 3.

Movement of Capital   *1925*

Outgoing

New Foreign Loans, exclusive of refunding 920
United States Paper Currency 62
                                                   ———
                                                   982

Incoming

Sale Abroad of Outstanding Securities 461
Principal of Inter-Allied Debt Repaid................ 27
                                                   ———
                                                   488

There is thus an excess of outgoing capital of $494,-
000,000, which shows that the United States invests abroad
more money than foreigners invest with her, although Europe is paying back a small proportion of the principal of
her War debt. In the end the excess of exports is paid
for not in gold but in securities, and in this way part of
the great wealth of America is sent across the ocean.

The above can hardly be compared with pre-war figures;
yet they instantly suggest certain important changes. In the
first place, contrary to the conditions in 1914, interest on
capital invested abroad considerably exceeds that on capital
invested in the United States. Freight charges for foreign
shipping used to be a considerable debit item in the balance
sheet, but this has ceased. On the other hand the expendi-
ture of American tourists and the remittances made by immigrants to their families are far more important than ever
before, and together offset to a large extent the unfavourable balance in European trade.

Another significant fact is that though Europe formerly
paid for her excess imports by the interest on her capital
invested in the United States, she can no longer do so at the
very time when she most needs this method of payment.
Since 1914 the Old World has only been able to carry on by

sending over gold or opening up fresh credits, and the stocks of gold and foreign securities that have accumulated on the other side of the Atlantic as a result are one of the most important factors in the situation.

Up to the War the United States absorbed foreign capital, but now it lets its own overflow. Over and above the $12,000,000,000 lent to the Allies, and the foreign securities which they had accumulated before 1920, new investments abroad in the six years ending 1925 actually amounted to about $6,000,000,000.[3] Therefore, if we total up the foreign investments at the end of 1925, apart from loans to the Allies, we obtain the impressive figure of $10,405,000,000. Thus American foreign investments have almost tripled since the Armistice. It was, of course, the exceptional circumstances arising from the War that brought about this extraordinary change.

This enormous overflow of American capital in search of employment is an absolute paradox, for here is an immense country, only partly inhabited and with its natural resources incompletely developed; and yet its capital is going abroad to find remuneration. It ought to be used within the country, as was the case up to 1914. Apart from money invested in Canada, Mexico, and South America, foreign loans were quite unusual in the past, except in Europe. Occasionally a millionaire would seek safety by investing part of his fortune in gilt-edged securities abroad. In those days Europe had an excess of wealth which she could not use at home, and therefore was glad to co-operate in the development of mines, railroads, and other enterprises in the New World. The American investments in Canada, Mexico,

[3] American foreign investments:

1920	....	$1,445	millions
1921	....	1,092	"
1922	....	963	"
1923	....	417	"
1924	....	909	"
1925	....	1,175	"

Brazil, and the Argentine were really only apparent exceptions to this rule, for American money really remained on the American continent. Canada especially possessed a ready banker in her rich neighbour. Since on both sides of her artificial frontier one found the same men, the same companies, and the same interests, this was not a genuine case of investment abroad. Europe was the real foreigner, and she did not attract American capital.

The situation was modified, first by the War, and again, after the Armistice, by the difficulty in making Europe pay for the excess of American exports. If the Americans had not consented to accept partial payment in securities, their export trade could not have continued on the same basis. The exports were therefore the main cause of their investments.

We must now explain why it was that American capital was willing to be expatriated contrary to all its traditions. The reason lies in two circumstances, both exceptional, but complementary to each other. Europe on the one hand needed the money to recuperate more than America needed it to continue her own development, and therefore Europe offered a higher rate of interest. On the other hand, by a mere coincidence, the capital requirements of America were temporarily below their normal level. Their industry had been equipped and over-equipped to cope with the extraordinary demands made upon it during the War and the boom of 1920, and its capacity was now beyond its normal outlets, as is shown by the following figures: [4]

Industrial capacity (1923) .. $83,764 millions
Actual production (1923) ...   60,106
Percentage of production 71.8

Under these circumstances there was naturally a surplus over and above the large issues in the home market, and

[4] National Industrial Conference Board, Wall Chart Service, No. 117.

this was available for foreign investment. This stream of capital was more or less precarious, as the causes that created and maintained it could easily disappear, more especially as foreign investment is not in accordance with the psychology of the American, who is as insular—provincial or continental, if you prefer—in his investments, as he is in his ideas.

It is true that the War altered the American attitude somewhat on this subject. In spite of their spendthrift habits, the general prosperity of the country has created a democracy of small capitalists resembling in many ways the French investors before the War. They had the same desire for security along with high interest, the same absence of any consideration apart from their revenue.

The French *rentier* was never afraid of expatriating his money, but to convert the American meant upsetting all his traditions. He knew nothing about foreigners, and moreover he did not trust them. He had always been taught that Europe was a worn-out country, demoralized and with no future, and that the wisest thing was to avoid it. In the surcharged atmosphere of the War, his repugnance was temporarily overcome by the official propaganda which busily directed his attention to Europe and endowed the Allies with every virtue on the list, to their intense astonishment! When peace came, the bankers profited by this new attitude for a time; also, the immigrants who were still unassimilated naturally showed a keen interest in their particular countries of origin. For example, there is always a Czecho-Slovak market in the States for a Czecho-Slovak government loan, and the Italian loans are supported by the Italian colony. Over and above any question of sympathy, the rate of interest offered was always very attractive, and even a slight increase in the rate brings the capital of a host of small investors across the Atlantic in search of employment.

In these unprecedented conditions the companies con-

nected with the issue of foreign loans have developed enormously. Their attitude of mind curiously recalls the great
French banks of deposit prior to 1914. Now the chief desire of the English is to help on their export trade and to
buoy up their international commerce on the strength of
their finance. Such motives scarcely exist among the French,
who simply say, "We have capital available, and it must
be invested to the best advantage." We look in vain for
a far-sighted policy such as is so apparent among the London bankers.

The composition of the foreign dollar investments emphasizes their financial character in contrast to the commercial
character of similar British investments. At the end of
1925, American foreign investments consisted of 43 per
cent. government and municipal bonds and securities guaranteed by the states, and 57 per cent. industrial stocks and
bonds. If we except Latin America the proportions were
just the reverse, 57 per cent. going into state securities and
43 per cent. into industrials. It is especially since the War
that state loans, or securities guaranteed by the state, have
predominated in American foreign investments. In 1925
they actually accounted for 69 per cent. of the total. In
British foreign and colonial investments on the contrary,
state loans only accounted for 33 per cent. in 1913 and 40
per cent. in 1925. The English lent their money as merchants, but the Americans purely from investment considerations, and in this they resembled the pre-war French. In any
case this exportation of capital, in spite of its volume, made
up only a small fraction of the total issues of the country.
In 1925, it amounted to about one-fifth of the total of
$6,000,000,000 that was invested. In 1913, when British
credit was functioning normally, no less than 82 per cent.
of their investments went abroad; and in 1924 they still
amounted to 60 per cent. Although England seems inclined
to reserve a larger proportion of her capital for her own

devolpment, America is gradually drawing into her banking orbit a host of countries which were previously served by British finance. Yet in contrast to the London market, New York is still continental and not international.

The subdivision of American foreign investments by continents is most enlightening. The following estimate was made by the Department of Commerce in 1925:[5]

Latin America	$4,210,000,000	40% of total
Government securities	22%	
Industrial securities	78%	
Canada	2,825,000,000	27% of total
Government securities	41%	
Industrial securities	59%	
Europe	2,500,000,000	24% of total
Government securities	73%	
Industrial securities	27%	
Asia, Oceania, etc.	870,000,000	9% of total
Government securities	60%	
Industrial securities	40%	

The first conclusion to be drawn from this table is that the United States is concentrating two-thirds of its attention on its own continent, and Europe occupies only a secondary position. The next conclusion is that loans to American countries are largely commercial, whereas loans to Europe are chiefly to governments, municipalities, or state institutions. The paradox in the present relationship of the United States and the Old World is that normally the latter should be the silent partner, but her ruin has reversed the *rôles*.

What American money is doing today for the victims of the War is not so much investment in new productive enterprises as saving governments and picking up bargains

[5] *The Balance of International Payments of the United States in 1925* page 15.

at low prices. She has done it with a certain amount of conviction, because her foreign investments have proved a profitable outlet for her surplus capital. In spite of individual profits, the transactions taken broadly seem to run contrary to the logical evolution of economics. A young country, even though gorged with wealth, should not be giving financial aid to a competitor who is quite as developed and from whom there is no chance of obtaining later either raw materials or customers for manufactured goods.

The situation is entirely different when we examine the relations between the United States and the rest of the American continent. Whether it be Canada or Latin America, the intercourse is both healthy and normal; for here the highly developed country is building up the younger ones where her industries will logically find a market.

Without seeking it, the United States has become the universal treasury. New York bankers now have interests and credit all over the world. They control enterprises everywhere and hold at their mercy governments which they can reduce to bankruptcy with a stroke of the pen. This power, without precedent in history, has come upon them suddenly and without preparation. Only a dozen years ago the great American financiers were preoccupied with their own affairs, their own railroads, mines, and industrial consolidations. Foreign transactions were quite secondary. The English bankers with their years of experience in international matters were equipped to treat not merely with the great companies of the world, but also with governments. Only yesterday the leaders of Wall Street had none of this experience, but although they are acquiring it rapidly, the financial and political traditions of such markets as London, Amsterdam, Frankfort, and Vienna embrace a knowledge of which America in her sudden coming of age is still unaware.

There are grave dangers, both financial and political, in

this situation, which could never occur to the same degree
in British finance. British methods of lending abroad follow a definite system, for they usually grant credit accounts
in order to obtain new markets. This means an exchange
of services and a moral equality between the borrower and
the lender, for the borrower is able to offer in exchange an
outlet for goods. But in the case of the American loans
to Europe, what have we to offer? Europe buys in the
United States only what she must—wheat, cotton, and petroleum. The American knows this so well that instead
of feeling thankful for their European clientele, they regard it a favour to serve them. Under these conditions the
position of the New York money-lender is frankly that of
a creditor watching his money, or a rich man charitably
helping a poor man in the hope of getting his loan back
in the future.

In this lies the danger that America may feel she can
do as she likes without consideration for any one else. She
can act as arbitrarily as she pleases. She can strangle whole
peoples and governments, or she can assist them on her
own terms. She can control them and indulge in the pleasant sensation of judging them from her superior moral
height, and then impose her verdict. This is bad not only
for Europeans, who are humiliated, but also for Americans;
for their sovereign independence makes them less and less
willing to accept international obligations. Always being
sought after as the rich are by the poor, and always giving without receiving, tends to destroy any consideration for
the borrower, such as arises from free exchange on an equal
footing. They are gradually and surreptitiously assuming
the *rôle* of a missionary bailiff or of an ambitious man in
search of power, and from this may arise a new and subtle
imperialism unlike anything we have known before.

CHAPTER XVII

THE MONETARY POLICY

AMERICA would probably have been industrialized much less rapidly if the War had not taken place, and therefore we may assume that as a result the country reached maturity earlier than otherwise. In normal times her exports of food-stuffs and raw materials (wheat, cotton, etc.) would likely have fallen off, instead of increasing as was the case during and since the War, so that from this aspect the War prolonged her economic youth. At the same time the upheaval in the world's money-markets drained the gold out of Europe into America; and so, although no real inflation occurred, the development and industrialization of the country was redoubled in intensity. Also a part of the wealth that was being created overflowed the confines of the country in the form of foreign investments. America is still young in that her abundant natural resources require a constant increase of capital to develop them, but on the other hand she has been forced into maturity—possibly only temporarily—and is now lending her money abroad through lack of sufficiently lucrative employment at home.

Thanks to the balance of these two simultaneous although contradictory phases of youth and maturity, the country has been able to remain an exporter and a creditor at the same time, and to absorb the gold of the Old World while she has been lending capital back to it. This precarious adjustment, which is obviously due to the War, explains her high degree of prosperity in spite of the ruin in Europe. The question now is whether she can consolidate her enormous lead in front of the other continents and especially

Europe. We must make allowance for the abnormal causes of this prosperity, although the Americans themselves are convinced that it is permanent and they will not hear of any readjustment of economic levels throughout the world that requires the slightest sacrifice on their part.

The visible sign of Europe's poverty and her wealth is this enormous increase in the American gold reserve. Except for a surplus of gold exports in 1919–20 and in 1925, it has never since 1914 ceased to flow in a perpetual stream into the United States. In August, 1914, their stock amounted to $1,887,000,000, by December, 1924, it had risen to $4,570,000,000, and it has remained ever since about $4,500,000,000. Almost half of the world's supply is now concentrated in North America.

At first it was difficult to measure the exact effect of this congestion—the term is not too strong. American pride, of course, was flattered; but the experts were anxious. Nor was it without a certain jealousy that Europe insisted that America would suffocate herself with her inordinate gold supply. Some people believe this yet, but they overlook the fact that America is young and growing vigorously. If production had remained stationary while the stock of gold visibly expanded, or if an imprudent policy of credit had discounted its full value, there would have been real inflation and a sharp rise in prices. This was avoided, however, partly by her wealth, partly by the wisdom of her government, and partly by fortunate circumstances.

M. Rist, who is an authority on this subject, has clearly shown how an enormous increase in the gold reserve, coinciding with a great increase in paper money and bank deposits for the financing of the War, resulted in a decided decrease in the purchasing power of the dollar. By July, 1920, the dollar had shrunk to 48.9 per cent. of its 1914 value. This fall represented a decrease in the purchasing power of gold itself, for the paper dollar did not depreciate in relation to the gold dollar. Like other countries the United States had been compelled to emit paper money, but the fortuitous arrival of fresh gold had enabled her to keep it convertible. Though the government and the Federal Reserve Board have not followed a policy of extreme deflation, their methods have been very sound. The absorption of the war loans by the public relieved the banks and was a form of financial deflation. The restriction of commercial credits after the slump of 1920, the increase in the discount rate, the throwing back on to the banks of the instruments of credit used to prop up issues during the War and the boom period, were all methods of credit deflation. There was no corresponding reduction in currency, and therefore we cannot say there was any genuine monetary deflation.

The decline in the purchasing power of the dollar in 1920 was, however, both monetary and economic; monetary in that it was caused by the congestion of gold and war-time inflation, and economic in that it was the result of the situation in the commodity markets after the Armistice. Also the fall in prices—or the rise in the value of the dollar—after the slump of 1921 was partly the result of a world-wide economic liquidation and partly of a policy of financial retrenchment. Between May, 1920, and May, 1921, the index figure for wholesale prices fell from 247 to 145. The percentage of the gold reserve, which in March, 1920, had fallen to 40 per cent. of the notes and deposits, had climbed back by the autumn of 1921 to over 70 per cent. The purchasing power of the dollar if calculated on a basis of retail prices increased from 48.9 per cent. of its 1914 value in July, 1920, to 61.3 per cent. in July, 1921, and since then has oscillated around this level, being 59.3 per cent. in July, 1925, and 59.2 in July, 1926.[1]

This rapid and brilliant monetary reconstruction was less

[1] Calculated according to wholesale prices. the purchasing power of the dollar in comparison with 1914, was 42.2 per cent. in 1920, 68 per cent in 1921, and 62.8 per cent. in 1925.

the result of accentuated deflation than because the gold stocks were perpetually being fed from abroad and therefore tended to rise to the level of the former inflation, which, though restricted by a prudent policy, had not been entirely absorbed. All this took place during a world-wide economic depression in which prices were being lowered through the adjustments of supply and demand. M. Rist shows that immediately after the War an irreducible minimum of inflation existed in the United States as elsewhere. It was corrected partly by an increase in the gold stocks every year after 1915 and partly by the constant economic development of the country, so that it was finally overtaken and justified by the creation of new wealth, and the situation was balanced on a new basis.

In other words, the policy of the government since 1921 has taken this into consideration. The 1920 boom was liquidated by a fall in prices that was almost vertical, and the credit inflation was overcome by the severe resistance of the Federal Reserve Board; but no attempt was made to restore the purchasing power of the dollar, for they accepted the reduction in the value of gold as an unavoidable legacy of the War. Wholesale prices fell from their peak of 247 in May, 1920, to below 150 in 1921, but they neither tried to force them back to the pre-war level of 100, nor wished to raise them again even to satisfy certain interests. They aimed at stability at a practical level, and this aim has been magnificently achieved; for the dollar has hovered around a purchasing power of 60 per cent. of its 1914 value according to retail prices, and wholesale prices have held firm, having been 150, 153, 145, 157, and 152 in the month of June each year from 1922 to 1926. The balance was thus maintained between the various interests at stake, for the farmer demanded a rise, and the consumer wanted a decline. Wall Street was still recuperating from the effects of a too sudden change in level and was intent on a stable market. The prudent policy of the government was thus largely dictated by influential circles in the East.

International considerations also carried weight in determining this policy, for on reflection the authorities decided to avoid further sharp deflation, if such had ever been their intention. They decided that to restore gold to its former value would make it all the more difficult for Europe to restore her currencies to a parity with the dollar, for the goal would be just that much further away. To retard the monetary re-establishment of Europe would only put off the payment of the war debts and interfere with the purchase of American goods. When the pound sterling finally rejoined the dollar at par, it was partly because the dollar (gold) had lost two-fifths of its previous value. The return of the dollar to its former level would only have widened the gulf between the two continents.

The real temptation, however, lay not in exaggerated deflation, but in the other direction. The Federal Reserve Board was most anxious to prevent their compact mass of gold, which started accumulating again after the slump, from becoming the cause of a new period of inflation with rising prices. Responsible men in American finance often hazard the idea that this gold supply is the result of exceptional circumstances and therefore should not be considered as a definite acquisition. Occasionally it is suggested that in the long run it would be better for it to depart. It is hard to believe them, however; for, as Rochefoucauld says, *on ne souhaite jamais ardemment ce qu'on ne souhaite que par raison.*[2]

However, the Federal Reserve Board outlined a policy of prudence based on this hypothesis that the gold was only acquired temporarily and also on the fear of a further increase in prices. They decided not to utilize the gold at their disposal to its fullest extent in building up their new

[2] "One never desires very ardently the dictates of pure reason."

credit structure. It is interesting to note how far these ideas have been put into practice. In accordance with the wishes of the powers that be, the stock of gold was partially sterilized. Some of it was used for credits, but the rest was simply put into circulation in the form of gold certificates, which replaced the Federal Reserve notes as they were retired. This injection of gold cured the previous inflation and consolidated the position without causing fresh inflation. The policy of the experts was thus carried out.

The presence of this $4,500,000,000 in gold has, however, made itself felt in spite of official caution, and it is a question whether in any country the intoxication of such a mass of precious metal could be avoided. The stock of gold is there, every one knows it, and they never stop talking about it. Even though it is not fully utilized, it is undeniably a potent force in the rise in the economic temperature of the country. But after all, in spite of what has been said, the gold is needed; for the possibilities of America are immense, and she requires a stock of gold as a reserve which she can fall back on for future development. Europe with her savings is no longer a sleeping partner in America. Instead, in order to pay for her fantastic war purchases, she has had to send her gold back across the Atlantic. The effect was the same, for the Americans first used it to consolidate their inflation; and now that their development is so rapid, they need it to keep pace with their enormous expansion. The gold stock, therefore, has been virtually incorporated into their system, and they would see it go with the greatest uneasiness.

This intoxication has been less apparent in the economic world than in financial speculation. The abundance of funds in the money market after 1924 did not entirely correspond to the sudden growth in savings, although the latter was both real and imposing. It also reflected an expansion in bank credit which was really caused by the presence of the

gold, which seemed to be determined to make itself felt.
The Federal Reserve banks relaxed their severity a little
and adopted a policy of cheap money. After 1924, their
discount rate, which had been kept between 6 per cent. and
4½ per cent. since 1920, was reduced to 4 per cent. and less
during the whole of 1925—the rate of the Federal Reserve
Bank of New York actually hovered around 3 per cent. and
3½ per cent. At the same time they increased their purchases of bills, and so put into circulation sums which commerce did not require. This indirectly increased the hold-
ings of the private banks until they did not know what to
do with their money. The result was increased purchases
of stocks and bonds, and more collateral loans from the
banks. We must note, however, that this inflation only took
place to a very limited extent in commercial loans from the
banks or in foreign loans. It was especially directed toward
real estate speculation such as the fantastic boom in Florida, to building in general, which was extraordinarily prosperous from 1924 to 1926, and more particularly to speculation in securities, which was the most characteristic phase
of this boom up to the semi-panic in March, 1926. These
excesses were limited to certain spheres of action. Taken as
a whole, commerce was prudent, and economically the country is healthy; for only the financial speculators got out of
control. Thus the gold fever, which the country was determined to ward off and in which they all but succeeded,
caught them in the end, but only in a restricted crisis.

When we regard the latent menace of inflation from the
European point of view, we are apt to forget that coincident
with the increase in the stock of gold, the national production expanded as much if not more and provided a strong
influence in the opposite direction. Every year a growing
quantity of products were thrown on the market, and this
acted as an antidote to any dangerous germs of inflation that
may have existed. It must be noted on the other hand that

the manufacturers and merchants—not the farmers as yet
—need the banks less than before, for prosperity has given
them working capital. Also with the improvement in the
technical organization and means of transportation and distribution, they no longer find it necessary to keep as large
stocks on hand as in the past. For some years now, in spite
of the increase in business, genuine commercial loans have
been moderate.

This explains the fact that in spite of the plethora of
gold, the basic tendency of wholesale prices has not been
on the up grade since 1921. The characteristic feature of
the curve is its stability between the indices of 145 and 160,
every attempt to rise being checked by an increase in production.

	Wholesale Price Index	Farm Produce	Wood	Iron and Steel	Hardware and Manufacturing
1913	100	100	100	100	100
1920	226	218	307	219	192
1921	147	124	163	148	129
1922	149	133	183	135	122
1923	154	141	207	162	144
1924	150	143	184	149	134
1925	159	158	186	138	130

This table shows that the tendency is working toward an
increase in the cost of raw and semi-manufactured products. In these spheres machinery cannot be used to its full
extent, and therefore wages weigh heavily on costs. This
is the case in agricultural products and wood, but the reverse
occurs when machinery and organization are more important than wages, as for example in iron and steel and in
manufactured articles. It is noticeable that the prices of
agricultural products, which decreased more than industrial
products during the 1921 slump, are now rising steadily,

although industrial prices still tend to drop. The general result is a remarkable balance in wholesale prices, for their
variations taken as a whole have not amounted to 10 per
cent. since 1921.

This stability was desired by the government and the leaders of the business world and is the reward of the policy
of the Federal Reserve Banks. One cannot admire it too
much, for quite apart from its fine technique, it is the realization of a magnificent conception.

PART III

THE POLITICAL SITUATION

CHAPTER XVIII

As the best energies of the Americans are absorbed by production, politics can never be more than a secondary interest. The real creative efforts of the people, therefore, are to be found neither in the state nor in the political parties, but in the community, which expresses itself in its own particular way. It is most important to bear in mind that these three forces are not in the same relationship to each other that they would be in Europe, and we are liable to be led sadly astray if we are not clear as to what they stand for.

In an earlier chapter I emphasized to what extent the Calvinist spirit has penetrated American conceptions, and I have shown that to the Protestant American, the state is less a self-contained organism than a simple method of expressing the will of the people. We might even go so far as to say that in the eyes of a conscientious Protestant it is merely the guardian of the morals of the community, for he would never dream of considering it superior to the body of citizens taken as a whole. In this respect the American conception of the state is the antithesis of the German. The American view is so distinctly national that its opponents are usually foreigners, like the Lutherans, who are unaccustomed to seeing the government subordinate to religion, or the Catholics, who claim for the family—in reality for the Church—an independence which the civil community is always trying to usurp. Out of this arise two schools of thought: the American or Puritan, in which the individual is subordinate to the group, and secondly the foreign, in

239

which the excessive ambitions of the community are re-
sisted.

A European in America is rather puzzled when he comes
to look for the state. The Federal government represents
only certain strictly limited aspects of sovereignty, for civil
legislation is almost entirely vested in the State legislatures
which make the laws governing the daily life of the people.
In domestic politics, the equivalent of what Europeans call
the state is to be found less at Washington than in the capitals of the forty-eight States, which form a polyarchy in
which each unit jealously defends its independence.

In spite of the enormous area they cover, it is easy to
govern these sparsely populated republics, some of which
have been in existence less than fifty years. In a sense each
resembles Rousseau's conception of the community, for their
citizens are all fully alive to their duty to society. In some
parts there are still people who remember the days when the
pioneers opened up the country before the States were
formed. Under such circumstances it is difficult to distinguish the state from the majority of its citizens, of whom
it is really the reflection. No one has ever considered it as
a distinct entity that could impose its will on the community.
On the contrary the majority of citizens wish to live in a
certain way and are ready to use the law to force their
standards on unwilling members. Even in this, however,
the state is only a passive agent; for it is the community
that really functions. This explains the extraordinary way
in which the State legislatures supervise the customs of the
people even to the smallest details. These moralizing laws
could never be applied—and as a matter of fact they are
applied seldom enough—if they did not express to some
extent the will of the people. Whenever they are imposed
from without, like prohibition in the East, they fall flat.

Lack of permanency in the administration is another result of this direct type of democracy that exists in America

and particularly in the West. This deprives the state of much of the prestige that it enjoys in Europe. Once you make most of the chief administrative posts elective, you have no stability among the men who embody the power of the state. In certain western capitals, not a single person of the preceding administration survives after a few years. The governor, the heads of departments, and even minor officials are replaced by new faces whenever there is a change of party. In France the *huissier de ministre,* and in England the permanent under-secretary, are symbols of the continuity of the state; for they survive cabinets and even régimes. They have no counterpart in the United States where, apart from a few centralized administrations, there is no traditional civil service, especially in local politics. Even at Washington, secret government policies—in so far as they exist at all—are perpetuated less by the departments than by the continuous influence of certain groups of individuals, who, be it noted, are nearly always of British origin. This is a striking illustration of the jealous way in which the Anglo-Saxon keeps the real power in his own hands.

As the government is only the reflection of the community, it would be quite possible for the latter to express itself otherwise. This is a subtle distinction which leaves a loophole for the intrusion of Fascism. In the beginning, when the state and the community were one, the pioneers carried out their own decisions without troubling about the legality of their acts; for they used force whenever any one refused to comply with the commonly accepted rules. This tradition of direct action, which at first was confused with the functions of government, has never entirely disappeared. It still continues, one day in harmony with the law and the next opposed to it. In the so-called interests of society, a group of citizens usually comes forward spontaneously, but with no mandate whatever, to execute the law—often an unwritten law which they declare to have been broken. This applies to the first Ku Klux Klan in the South after the Civil War, and also to the second, which has carried out the same tradition in the last ten years.

The cases of officious policing which occur at intervals can be linked up with the same inspiration. A good example is the famous deportation from Bisbee, Arizona, in 1918, when a group of anti-revolutionaries plotted together to drive out certain anarchists whom they considered undesirable. One night all the anarchists were rounded up in their homes, and without trial were forcibly conducted to the border of the State. In August, 1925, at Fargo, North Dakota, we find the same treatment meted out to some harvesters who belonged to the I.W.W. In both cases an organized minority took action independently of the law, on the plea that they were serving the interests of the community. Similarly the defence of the South against the negroes openly defies the Federal Constitution, but it receives the tacit approval of the whole white population. Is this the same as Italian Fascism? Or is it not rather the survival of the rough and ready methods used by a primitive government, the recollection of which has not entirely faded away? At any rate there is a certain amount of confusion between the legal organs of government and the spontaneous champions of popular opinion. Whenever it approves, the public shuts its eyes to this distinction, and the judges, who are only elected, think twice before opposing. It is only during times of crisis or when race hatreds are kindled that these cases of direct action are numerous, although a certain number of incidents are always occurring in the South and West. The interesting point is that they always say that they are acting on behalf of the public, which they regard as sovereign. It is important, therefore, to ascertain how public opinion is formed and how it expresses itself, for nothing is more vital in a country where there is no appeal against it.

It is of course a recognized fact that public opinion is not spontaneous. In the United States even more than in other countries organized minorities can direct it, restrict it, and exploit it. In the past, geographic decentralization made it flexible. The local newspaper, which was generally directed by the oldest inhabitant and edited by citizens of equally good vintage, represented and also influenced the attitude of the district.[1] These newspapers formerly had considerable personality, but they are changing rapidly with the growth of the standardized press with its syndicated features, its telegraph news, its extensive editorials, and national advertising. Diversity in public sentiment is tending to disappear, and as in no other country it is being remorselessly brought into line with accepted standards. In the same way the stage, the movies, and the billboard all have to submit to a standardization which is fast wiping out local and class distinctions.

The great newspapers, as every one knows, live entirely by their advertising. Logically, therefore, they are bound to fall sooner or later under the influence of high finance and big business, which pays for publicity. Whenever an editorial contradicts their views, the captains of industry can easily exercise a little pressure. "Your editorials are not up to our standards," they write; and the editor, realizing what he is up against, gives in. Otherwise the paper goes to the wall. The national interests thus possess an effective means of moulding the public to their own ends by withholding what they think it should not know and presenting each subject from the desired angle. A rigid code is soon built up from which there is no escape, though people are soon unaware of its existence.

[1] *In Our Town,* by William Allen White, gives an excellent portrayal of the power of the press in a small Kansas town twenty years ago.

Distinct from the business interests are the associations. Their influence is immense and is often parallel to and allied with "big business." In this country where the chief lever is group initiative, every movement sooner or later crystallizes in a committee, an association, or a league. Whether it is an association of ex-soldiers, an anti-saloon, anti-cigarette, or anti-opium league, a missionary society, or a committee created to put a bill through Congress, the method is always the same, i.e., to act upon public opinion and the authorities by the concerted action of a group of citizens.

Nowhere else in the world are associations so powerful as in the United States, and especially if they have some social or religious propaganda in view. The good will, the funds, and the devotion at their command are enormous. With their excellent equipment and ceaseless and varied activity, they are the real expression of the community, and they enable it to carry out definite programs of reform. The reverse of the medal, however, is almost alarming, for their unrestricted influence on public opinion is positively dangerous. An Anglo-Saxon community is a veritable hotbed of fanatics who know no scruples in imposing their favourite nostrums. Publicity, which is reduced to an exact science, provides an automatic means of reaching the masses. The temptations are too great, and the weapons too efficient.

The power of propaganda is all the more irresistible when the capitalists and the reformers combine forces, especially as it is unnecessary to have public opinion behind a bill to get it through either the Federal or the State legislatures. All that is needed is a vigorous association with access to the local or national moneyed interests through which the support of the press is obtained. Once this is arranged they set out to capture one of the parties or some individual Congressman. If the party has not already been won over to the opposition by some equally efficient association it nearly always comes round, provided the attackers have enough ammunition. In the end, the public is more or less phlegmatic and easily led; so the struggle is left to the minorities, and the best organized wins. Prohibition could never have been passed otherwise.

The ambitions of the associations know no limit, especially when they are intent on uplift. Their authority is all the greater because they demand support in the name of the welfare of the community. The individual must therefore be protected less against an all-powerful state, as conceived by Herbert Spencer, than against the community itself. In no other country can the public be so successfully manipulated by experts, or is it so liable to be carried away in times of excitement. In older nations where the civilization is more subtle, the currents of public opinion break down or wear themselves out against established institutions that have grown up like fortifications throughout the centuries. The family and the clan are both impregnable to outside influences, and so are certain universities where independence of thought is encouraged. The same applies to such bodies as the army, the church, the law, and also to certain groups of intellectuals who are indifferent to public opinion.

In the United States, such barriers exist only where assimilation has not taken place. The Roman Catholic Church, for example, keeps aloof and depends on the attitude toward family life that is still held by those races which have not yet been Americanized. It acts as a brake to some extent, but all the other institutions—the universities, the Protestant churches, the business world, and society—seem to be ready to swell the tide of popular opinion and work for the common goal. This may be splendid national discipline, but it is also a latent power which can be terrifying if it breaks loose and annihilates all opposition. We must not forget that, west of the Alleghanies at any rate, there is no intellectual aristocracy capable of thinking for itself and courageously opposing the masses. If there were, it would be crushed.

In this land of exaggerations, where ideals are pushed to extremes, public opinion is a formidable weapon. The methods of organizing it, crystallizing it, and inflaming it to the point of hysteria are so well understood and the technique is so perfect that, given the malleability of the people, there appears to be no limit beyond which they cannot be led. Look at the way they were manipulated during the War, when, without exaggeration, they were bamboozled every day and everywhere as a matter of course!

The real strength of these propagandist associations lies in their energy and the fact that they are continuously being renewed. The political parties in contrast are mere machines without life or initiative, intent solely on getting into office. They are essentially passive and lack both the aptitude and the desire to create. They are little more than a mechanism for registering votes and except in name have nothing in common with the political parties of Europe.

The enormous size of the United States easily accounts for this. In spite of the fact that the Americans are more uniform in their habits than any other modern people, their country is so large and so varied in climate and development that the same point of view could not possibly exist on the coasts of the Atlantic and the Pacific, the Great Lakes, and the Gulf of Mexico. It is therefore almost impossible to draw up a program which will enable a single political party to satisfy the interests of the different regions. Each district sees things in its own light, and the result is that political parties are little more than coalitions of various geographic units. The Democrats of New York and New Orleans or the Republicans of Pennsylvania and Wisconsin may have the same label, but they have little else in common. Above all they are Easterners, Westerners, or South-

erners, as the case may be, just as in the Labour International the French and German Socialists are French and
German first and Socialists afterward. A congressman in
American Federal politics is not merely a legislator, but also
a plenipotentiary to a sort of League of Nations. The basis
of the parties is always local, for in them can be discerned
the viewpoint of the South, the East, the West, and the
Pacific. Beyond this there is no unity. The country is too
big.

Under these circumstances party platforms are inevitably
reduced to their lowest common denominator. Any interests or aspirations which cannot be fitted into this narrow
framework or harmonized with the rigid views of the politicians must develop outside the party machine, which is
expected only to furnish a practical means of achieving success. It is an indispensable tool and nothing more. One
therefore applies to the party or to its specialized personnel
as one would in business to a bank or a transport company.
A leader of a movement will enter into a contract with the
party in order to achieve his ends, but he will not sell himself to it body and soul. It is useless, therefore, to look
in the parties for political ideals or underlying tendencies,
or even for a common outlook among their leaders. In the
Republican party we find a conservative like Coolidge and a
demagogue like Borah, not to mention a radical like La
Follette. The Democrats in their turn are represented by
an Irish Catholic like Al Smith, or a Protestant and friend
of the Ku Klux Klan like McAdoo.

The situation will be clearer if we consider each group as
a coalition of incongruous and varied elements whose only
chance of getting into power lies in banding together. At
each election there is a new and different combination, the
important question being to decide where the emphasis is
to be placed; that is to say, which section of the group will
be authorized to speak officially in the name of the party

and to use the powerful ammunition at its disposal. As may be imagined, this is the subject of bitter dispute. According to this conception, the party is like a shell into which any political creature may crawl, or better still, like an omnibus in which one travels with all one's bags and baggage. The wily ones reserve seats in the omnibuses of both rival companies, in order to make sure of getting there.

The politician, however, will not take assistance from every Tom, Dick, or Harry, nor will he back a movement without due consideration. With unrivalled psychological skill, he watches the electoral sky and bluntly shoves aside anything that may injure his career. He takes his cue from influential quarters, now a bank, a railway, or a propagandist association; or again from a powerful church whose membership probably includes bankers and railroad directors; or it may even be a colony of Italians or Poles who are still half-European. In this way, our parasite undeniably sifts the sands of public opinion and fills a useful *rôle* in the life of the nation.

We will not find the equivalent of French parties in the official American political parties, but in the groups formed by the various interests, or better still among the numerous propagandist associations. It is the latter that best represent what the French call "political currents." Very often the point at issue is not included in the platform of either the Republicans or the Democrats, for more often than not, the cautious politicians of both parties have side-stepped all burning questions and are busy working on the same reforms. In short, they invent makeshift platforms in order to avoid discussing their real ones. Meanwhile, the real clash of opinions and interests is being vividly expressed in the Ku Klux Klan, the Anti-Saloon League, the American Chamber of Commerce, the American Federation of Labor, and various Catholic societies, for these are really the counterpart of the European parties. Their organization and inspiration are more flexible and varied than the French, since each group, with complete freedom of outlook, works for a single aim for which it leaves no stone unturned. They shamelessly employ the most cynical tricks of the politicians; in fact, their agents at Washington are equal to the best when it comes to electoral and parliamentary dodges. At a meeting of these lobbyists, many of whom obtain enormous salaries, we find some of the most influential men in the country.

It is estimated that the Federal capital contains over 150 central agencies of various associations and groups, and 60 of these represent political and financial powers that have to be reckoned with. A list of them is in a sense a review of the real parties underlying the official parties. And such an inventory it is of interests, propaganda, ideas, and fads! Let us give a few names.

First, in aid of "big business" and leading all the other commercial organizations in power, we have:[2]

American Chamber of Commerce
National Association of Manufacturers
American Manufacturers' Export Association
Institute of American Meat Packers
American Automobile Association
National Canners' Association
Council of American Cotton Manufacturers
Founders' Association
Lumber Manufacturers' Association
Manufacturing Chemists' Association of America
Highway Industries Association
Interstate Cottonseed Crushers' Association
Merchants and Manufacturers' Association
Southern Industrial Education Society
United States Sugar Manufacturers' Association
Western Petroleum Refiners' Association

[2] These lists were obtained from the *Introduction to American Government*, F. A. Ogg and P. O. Ray, second edition, New York, 1925.

Alongside this first group come the following:

American Railway Association
American Association of Engineers
American Bankers' Association
American Beet Sugar Association
American Bureau of Trade Extension
American Chemical Society
American Mining Congress
American Realty Exchange
American Association of Real Estate Boards
American Automobile Chamber of Commerce
National Bureau of Wholesale Lumber Distributors
National Industries Conference Board
National Merchant Marine Association
League of Commission Merchants of the United States
National Oil Bureau
National Petroleum Association
American Patent Law Association

The passage of the recent laws relating to the use of electric power, and the growing interest taken by the investor in public utilities, have attracted to Washington many representatives of the interests allied to electricity, gas, etc.:

American Electric Railway Board
National Association of Railway and Public Utilities
    Commissions
National Committee on Gas and Electric Service
National Committee on Public Utilities Conditions
Dixie Freight Traffic Association

The farmers are also strongly represented, for including the Farm Bureau, the leading agricultural organizations are:

Farm Bureau
American Agricultural Association
Eastern Agricultural Bureau

Farmers' National Council
The Grange
Cane Growers' Association
National Board of Farm Organizations
Texas Cotton Association

Then we have the labour organizations:

American Federation of Labor
National Federation of Federal Employees
National Federation of Post Office Clerks
National Association of Letter Carriers
Brotherhood of Railway Clerks
Brotherhood of Railway Signalmen
Maintenance of Way Employees
Plumb Plan League
National Women's Trade Union League
American Train Dispatchers' Association

The American Federation of Labor is, of course, the most important of these, as all the unions are affiliated with it.

Then the women's associations:

League of Women Voters
Gentlewomen's League
Congress of Mothers
National Woman's Christian Temperance Union
Woman's Section of the Navy League
Child Welfare Society

The representatives of racial groups are particularly interesting, for they shed a curious light on the local politics of the United States and the foreign influences that penetrate them:

Irish National Bureau
Poland Information Bureau
Lithuanian National Council

Lithuanian Information Bureau
Bureau of Jewish Statistics
National Association of Colored Races
Jewish Press Service of America
National Committee for Armenian and Syrian Relief
British-Canadian Society
Friends of the Ukraine
Korean Relief Society League

The all-powerful anti-alcoholic societies, headed by the famous organizations:

Anti-Saloon League
Board of Temperance of the Methodist Episcopal Church
National Temperance Bureau

In 1925–26, the organizations of liquor dealers were no longer listed as such among the Washington lobbyists, but the propaganda in favour of a repeal of the Volstead Act proves that they are carrying on their activities and are only in hiding, ready to come out if chance permits.

Next come the peace associations:

Peace League of the World
American Peace Society
American Union vs. Militarism

And opposed to them the patriotic associations:

Navy League
American Legion
Private Soldiers' and Sailors' Legion

Finally we have an interminable list of associations for propaganda and reform:

National Association for Protection of American Rights
    in Mexico.
National Association for Constitutional Government

National Civil Service Reform League
National Committee on Prisons and Prison Labor
National Committee to Secure Rank for Army Nurses
National Educational Association
National Industrial Council
National Committee for Soldiers' and Sailors' Relief
National Negro Business League
National Popular Government League
National Committee for District of Columbia Suffrage
National Patriotic Press
Rivers and Harbors Congress
National Voters' League
National Forestry Association
American Medical Society
Christian Science Association
Consumers' League
Co-operative League of America
Free Press Defense League
League for Preservation of American Independence
Osteopathic Association
Physicians' Protective Association
Prisoners' Relief Society
Smokeless Coal Operators' Association
Tuberculosis Association

We are now at the very heart of political influence, for it is generally admitted that the associations are today even more powerful than the press itself. They influence the newspapers, the parties, the government, and individual Congressmen and Senators. The system extends from the smallest county, through the State capitals, right up to the Federal government. We find them at every turn, formulating new laws, overseeing the wording of the text, and controlling votes in Congress. They bring constant pressure to bear, both indirect and direct; so the politician has no possible means of escape. Not merely do they get the laws passed, but they see to it that they are applied, and so carry

out the maxim of Thiers: *Un ordre donné dont on ne sur-
veille pas l'exécution est un ordre vain.*[3]   It is, for example,
thanks to the Anti-Saloon League that many Congressmen
ostensibly approve of prohibition, though they secretly condemn it.

The result of this system is that all really important discussions take place in the party caucus and not in the debates
between the parties.   Whenever an idea for a reform takes
shape, the promoters call on the two political organizations
to see what they can get out of them, and come to an agreement with one or the other, and often with both.   It is a
straightforward bargain without a trace of sentiment in it.
As soon as agreements have been made with both sides, the
question ceases to be a party matter, and the battle is regarded as won.   All the rest is mere procedure.

It is interesting to note that the most important legislative
measures during the past few years have not been carried
by either of the parties in opposition to the other, but have
been voted by both.   The Eighteenth Amendment, for instance, was passed in the House of Representatives by 282
votes, of which 141 were Democrats and 137 Republicans;
against it were 128 votes, of which 64 were Democrat and
62 Republican.   In the same way the 1924 immigration law
received 308 votes against 58 in an assembly in which the
Democrats had 207 votes and the Republicans 225.   Was it
that there was no opposition to these measures?   Obviously
not, but the opposition was over and done with already, and
all decisions had been made.

Thus a history of the parties is far from being a complete survey of American national life.   If a question looks
thorny they avoid discussing it, or if they feel that the public is behind it, they accept it without discussion.   It is
almost impossible to create a new party to embody an oppo-

[3] "An order given without supervision of its execution is given in
vain."

sition, for it would need the support of the whole country to succeed. This explains why the Democrats cherish in their bosom both Protestants and Catholics who loathe one another, and the Republican flag waves over conservatives and radicals who haven't a principle in common. Underlying currents of public opinion undoubtedly exist, but the electoral platforms do not attempt to give a genuine expression of them; so we must look for them elsewhere.

The country accepts the existence of a politician class who are pursuing the interests of their own parties and it pays them a heavy commission in order to be able to use their intervention and their equipment; but it does not let them handle anything vital, for in the end they are the slaves of public opinion. The real strength of the country therefore does not lie in the political machine, but in the great interests, the convictions, and the passions that make use of the machine. Were it not that the public allows itself to be led away by highly organized propaganda, it would indeed be a perfect type of democracy.

CHAPTER XIX

THE DEMOCRATIC PARTY

THOUGH the Democrats have not quite the same value as the Republicans on the electoral chessboard, yet to analyze their position is not only more instructive, but is the best introduction to a study of the psychology of the various political groups in the United States.

In its essentials the traditional program of the Democrats has been the defence of the unorganized and of the minorities; hence its lack of constructive unity. Its real function is to be in opposition, and it exists as an ever-changing coalition of discontent. To protect the immigrant against his assimilator and the individual against the state, to combat the legal and social oppression exerted by the majority, to stand up for local communities when they attempt to solve their own problems without interference from the central authority—in short, to champion the State against the Federal government—such is the spirit of the Jeffersonian tradition. We must admit, however, that it owes its vitality to the reaction of threatened minorities rather than to any theoretical attachment to eighteenth century political and philosophic thought.

Viewed from this angle, it is perfectly clear that the Democratic party will always be supported by oppressed local communities—or those who believe themselves oppressed; by the South against the North, by the western farmer against the eastern capitalist, and by the great cosmopolitan cities of the Atlantic coast against Protestantism. Their many victories are numerous but always local in character rather than national, such as the election of State governors or

State legislatures. When they obtain a majority in Congress or the rare prize of the presidential chair, it is usually because some special circumstance has given the malcontents a temporary majority. Thus the Democratic party prospers in hard times in contrast to the Republicans, whose great unanswerable argument is prosperity. It has never been a really nationalist party, for it has always upheld those who refuse to conform to established traditions.

Herein lies its innate and pernicious virus. Certain regions insist on their own viewpoint in opposition to the rest of the country, as in the case of the negro question in the South, where, although in the minority nationally, the Democrats have a local majority. Like any other majority, they are tempted to use the same practices of force, intolerance, and oppression that they condemn in their adversaries. The southern Democrats are quite exceptional, for apart from the race question they resemble the Republicans more than they do the Irish Catholic Democrats of New York. That is why this medley of opposites can never find its centre of gravity. In the crisis through which it is now passing, the most serious since the Civil War, it has been reduced quite logically to a mere coalition of regional groups all in the opposition on local issues. Of its ultimate destiny there is no doubt whatever, but the difficulty is to find a single mind to represent the many ambitions it embraces. We cannot regard it as a unit, for it includes three distinct parties, one in the South, one in the northeastern cities, and the third in the West.

To be strictly accurate, the Democrats of the South and the North have nothing but the name in common. It is tragic, but it is a fact, that wherever the negroes exist in numbers, their presence has killed or falsified the normal interplay of political life. An instinctive sense of self-preservation has forced the whites to make common cause against the blacks, for if even a few of them were to join up with the negroes, their racial balance would be compromised and their supremacy imperilled. The whites may be divided during the primary elections, but never after that. By a tacit agreement that is always respected, the successful candidate in the primaries becomes the candidate of the district and is always returned. Since apart from the negroes, who are excluded from the suffrage, there are no Republicans in the South, they have arrived at a single-party system. If the atmosphere were normal, wholesome differences of opinion would arise; but to people living in a state of war, with the defence of their race always in mind, a *union sacrée* is imperative. Their political party is like a mobilized army in the presence of the enemy, when the least dissension assumes the seriousness of a mutiny.

In this unhealthy atmosphere, where the principles of liberty are often combined with the practices of violence, it is hardly surprising that the traditional liberalism of the Democratic party should have disappeared, though it still receives ample lip-service, and stereotyped eulogies of Jefferson are the rule for after-dinner speeches. The South has naturally turned toward the nationalist ideals of the native-born American; for in no other part of the country is the origin of the race so pure. With the exception of certain Spanish and French elements, the population is of English and Scotch descent, and therefore Protestant and Fundamentalist. It is further terrified of foreign influence and of the menace of the coloured race. It was here that the Ku Klux Klan was born twice over; it is here, among the Methodists and Baptists, that the campaign against evolution has triumphed, and here also is the supreme stronghold of prohibition. Neither the rights of the individual nor his independence of thought count for much in this community, which does not think for itself and is simply determined to maintain the status quo.

Practically nothing is left of the Democratic spirit of Jefferson, except perhaps the still potent principle of state rights. In everything else these stubborn Democrats are really Republicans. This is largely because the growing industrialism of the South is converting them to protectionism, although as long as they grew only cotton they were free-traders to a man. Nowadays the sugar refiners of Louisiana and the cotton spinners and weavers of Georgia and North and South Carolina are protectionists. Editors may write blindfold or by force of habit their free-trade editorials for the front page of their papers, but on the second they demand a tariff on cotton thread, cloth, and sugar. If their Congressman does not vote for protection, he will not be nominated again.

With their suspicion of everything foreign, their good conservative fear of Bolshevism, and their Protestant anxiety over Roman Catholics, the sympathy of the South is bound to be Republican. Having at last tasted prosperity after a generation of misery, they find the prudence of Coolidge much more to their liking than their allies, the people of New York State; or, as ex-President Taft once said with penetrating irony, "They vote one way and pray the other."

Their loyalty to the Democratic party is purely local, but it is unimpeachable, as even the slightest defection would threaten the supremacy of the white race. This could never be tolerated, as is shown by the fact that their election successes are practically automatic. They would really prefer their representatives to vote for the Republicans at Washington if occasion demanded it. Also, in the cotton towns at the foot of the Alleghanies there are many New Englanders who are Southerners only by adoption; and though they vote Democrat in the State elections as if it were a sacred rite, they go Republican in the Federal elections. They are as unyielding as the best on the colour question, but otherwise their sympathy is with the big interests. What really is new is to find in the South Republicans who are respected for their money, their influence, and their social position. Hitherto the carpet-baggers and black-and-tans, and indeed any one who voted for the Republican party, were looked down on with undisguised contempt. Truly prosperity has wrought great changes in the South.

The South has altered in another respect that may not perhaps be noticeable on the surface but is quite apparent behind the scenes. On Election Day the discipline of the Democratic electors is still enforced without a single default, but when it comes to choosing the candidates, the rivalry between the various factions within the party is very keen. In the Southwest (Louisiana, Texas, etc.), it is largely a question of personalities, for the political groups are as changeable as clouds; and like the popular pickles, there are fifty-seven varieties. East of the Mississippi one can discern signs of profound social changes that have come during the past generation, but here again realities are masked by vain and misleading personal struggles.

The "poor whites" had always been disciplined and led by the aristocrats, but for a while they were taken in hand by the agitators who tried to organize and make use of them politically. At the end of the last century Senator Tilman of South Carolina took up the cudgels on their behalf against the financial interests and in so doing helped to bring about a change in southern politics. Due mainly to his intervention but also to others in Alabama and Georgia, class distinctions were accentuated and the "poor whites" brought to the fore politically. At the present time, in several of the southern States we can easily discern two separate political trends. On the one hand we have the popular composition of the electorate, and on the other the persistent conservatism of the capitalists. Were it not for the obsession of the color problem, this class antagonism might in time become important; for poverty and squalor still exist in the South in contrast to the rest of the country, and therefore there is always the possibility of a political struggle between the rich and the poor. Instead of this, we have political sterility owing to the existence side by side of two races which can never amalgamate; and in the long run this makes for conservatism. The "poor whites" are the most stubborn defenders of the rights and privileges of the race; for if they admitted the slightest infringement, they would be the first victims socially. The very logic of the situation binds them to the wealthy and dominant class, and even when they win at the polls they cannot profit by their victory. Simply say that the white race is in danger and they rally to a man, with the poorest in the lead. Any tendency, therefore, to drift toward radicalism is nipped in the bud, until one wonders whether a really democratic régime is even possible in a country where there is neither racial equality nor homogeneity.

If the Democrats of the South are mainly rural, in the East they are essentially urban. Here their strength lies in the votes of the immigrants, who are anxious to find a party which will protect them morally and materially against the distant reserve and veiled contempt of the old inhabitants. They feel the need of some touchstone that will admit them into the community before they are completely assimilated and at once make Americans of them and their children. For the moment all they ask is to be admitted as they are, with their queer bags and baggage, their misfits, shortcomings, and all. In the great Atlantic ports the traditional function of the Democratic party has been to befriend and champion these uprooted homeless and bewildered arrivals in the strange country which they hope to make their own. In this respect the party is a valuable factor in Americanization, for it stands for the hospitality of the United States.

The extraordinary and lasting prestige of Tammany Hall is derived to a great extent from its wonderful sympathy for the immigrants. The lonely, feeble exile finds in it an advisor, a protector, and a friend, and such practical assistance as he may need. The Democrats do not exclude him on account either of his race or his religion, nor do they patronize him when they help him. Instead, he meets with a human kindliness that is rare and precious. Let the pure in heart rant against the corruption of Tammany, but these leaderless, inarticulate masses of aliens will never share their indignation. They will only remember that Tammany received them as equals on their face value alone.

In this polyglot party where every race has its place, one nation above all has undertaken to guide the rest in politics. It is impossible to understand the Democrats, in the East at any rate, unless we penetrate the psychology of the Irish. Brilliantly gifted, nimble of wit, seductive, eloquent, and imaginative, they are born leaders of men. Toward the middle of the last century, the boss or gang leader in the great engineering enterprises was invariably an Irishman; for like the Corsicans, they excel in making others work for them, and they adore being in command. It was but a step from this to politics. What they had done in the factory they now repeated in the elections, but this time they worked for their own benefit. They aroused the discontented, organized them, led them out to vote, and by them and through them they obtained control of municipal affairs, which they made their own.

Political intrigues and agitations, stirring public meetings, electoral campaigns, seething masses of party agents, canvassers, and intermediaries, hours spent hanging around the City Hall or lost in a cloud of stale tobacco smoke in the lobby of a political hotel or leaning against the rail of a corner saloon drinking his glass of beer or whisky—such was the atmosphere in which our "artist" throve, a bit of a scamp maybe, and not greatly respected, and yet so irresistibly lovable! It is impossible to describe the extent of his influence in the cities of the East. I did not visit Dublin until after I had been to the States, but when I did I felt as if I had seen it all before.

We now come to the faithful ally of the Irish Democrat, the Roman Catholic Church, which also welcomes the stranger. Its thousand years of experience have given it an insight into these pitiful crowds of immigrants swarming over from the older communities of Europe. In the persons of its clergy of Irish, German, or Polish origin, it has made the same journey across the Atlantic; so when the immigrants reach the quay, it is there to welcome them like an old friend and protector. It strives to help them settle down and does not hustle or Americanize them, but in its tender solicitude forms them into groups that remain intact for years. The broad internationalism of the Church is superimposed on all these different nationalities, and every one finds in it something of his own native land. The Irish priests and politicians are two parallel forces, neither one controlled by the other, but both working together for common ideals and interests. Their respective programs are the result of similar preoccupations which logically make them allies. Both desire to protect certain customs which the Protestant assimilators wish to stamp out, but which the immigrants naturally wish to preserve. With their taste for beer, Chianti, and whisky, the Germans, Italians, and Irish are bound to oppose prohibition, because it interferes with their daily habits. The Catholic Church tacitly backs them up, for it is determined to maintain the family group intact rather than allow every one to drift into the general uniformity. In the same spirit the Democratic party defends the individual against the powerful organized economic interests; that is to say, it defends the consumer against the producer, and the common people against the trusts. It stands for low cost of living, a reduction in the tariff, and free competition, which will benefit the masses. Here again the Catholic Church is in agreement, for though it is far from poor itself, its congregation includes the poorest classes. The vested interests can and do come to an understanding with the Democrats, but it is only logical that they should apply for help first at the house across the way, for in the East, at any rate, the Democrats are essentially the party of the people, of the masses as opposed to the classes.

Having said this, we have practically exhausted all that works effectively for reform—one can hardly call it revolutionary—in Irish-American politics. The genius they have brought across the Atlantic is for opposition. "I'm ag'in' the government!" exclaims the transplanted citizen of Cork or Dublin the moment he lands in America, and all his organizing energy is henceforth devoted to the malcontents. He stirs up the unabsorbed races against the 100 per cent. Americans, the poor against the rich, the homeless against the landlords. He is a complete demagogue, who arouses the lowest passions of the mob. But we must be particularly clear on this point, for it is the root of the whole question. He may be a demagogue, but he is not in any sense a revolutionary, but really a conservative. He is most destructive when in opposition, but when in power he does not wish to build up a state of society based on new principles. The reason lies in the fact that the priest is always on hand and is listened to respectfully. The Church stands for conservative influences in every country in the world, for the family against moral anarchy, for order against license, and for property against revolution.

When the Irish Catholic captures a municipal government or a State legislature, which is all he ever succeeds in doing, he is satisfied as soon as he has rewarded his friends and supporters. He runs public affairs with a certain amount of skill and merit, but he stops there. In the end he does not overturn anything. "Big business" easily manages to have the last word in any matter which it considers essential; so in practice this demagogue acts as a vaccine against revolution.

Once outside the big cities, the cosmopolitan industrial centres, and a few large western towns, the Irish politician is out of his depth. Although only a few miles away, the farming communities and the small English and Scottish settlements escape his influence entirely. In the same way he has no hold over high finance and "big business," where the old-time Protestant aristocracy preserves its power intact. He controls the great city populations, however, except for a few foreign elements that are attracted away by other affinities, and even the successful Irish themselves who often desert the "old gang." The French Canadians generally keep to themselves, owing to their jealousy of the Irish, and this is also true in part of the Germans and Italians. The Scandinavians are Republican by temperament, and the Jews will adhere to any party that is likely to win. The negroes are traditionally hostile to the Democrats, and with reason. Still, the Civil War is now fading into the past, and they are learning to vote like opportunists for the side that offers them tangible advantages. With these exceptions, the masses of New York and Boston go Democrat, and so long as there are no internal quarrels, success is assured.

Quarrels unhappily are common, for the Irish are born scrappers. As a rule there are as many factions as there are leaders differing in temperament and social level. The "machine" relies on the lowest grade, for the better classes like to have their own special candidates. It is only through these quarrels that the Republicans ever succeed, as they did, for instance, in the Boston municipal elections in November, 1925. The Hearst-Hylan faction, with its futile propaganda, is a perfect example of the "machine." Alongside it is Tammany, another "machine," which ever since the War has followed the lead given by Alfred ("Al") Smith, governor of New York State. As a result of his unrivalled personal popularity and considerable political authority, Tammany has incontestably dominated the situation since the municipal elections of 1925. The Republicans have hardly counted at all.

Al Smith is not only an excellent governor, but has attained national prestige, partly by his honesty and his ability as an administrator, but mainly owing to his origin. This child of the pavement was born in the slum quarters of East Side New York, of common Irish parents, through whom he is directly descended from the old Irish peasantry. The enormous mass of immigrants rightly look upon him as their mouthpiece, for he is Catholic, though not the tool of the Church, a man of the people in every fibre and yet not an extremist; and above all, he proclaims a new Americanism in which the old Nordic Protestant tradition counts for nothing. In spite of his crudeness, this Irish-American stands for the best in the non-Anglo-Saxon community, and the foreign population feels for the first time that he gives them access to power and honours.

According to our analysis of the Democrats of the South and of the East, there is little possibility of their agreeing together on a common program at present. The most that can be expected is that the coalition should justify itself as a combination of minorities to protect their regional interests against the central authorities. This may be true of the New York Wets, but the Klansmen and Prohibitionists of the South are ready to ally themselves with any national majority to bring the rebels into line. The fact is, these two wings of the party have nothing in common. To the foreign Catholics of the eastern cities, the Ku Klux Klan is a daily insult, and prohibition an intolerable interference in their private lives. To the southern Protestant, New York is a Babel to be shunned like the plague by the healthy American Puritan.

The cosmopolitan cities of the Atlantic States have become the last resort of liberalism, and by a singular paradox the tradition of Jefferson is kept alive by the Catholics, the Irish, and other foreigners, who are not necessarily liberals, but merely minorities defending themselves. Though the Solid South—so called because it is always faithful—is still the electoral stronghold of the Democrats, it is in New York and Boston that their real spirit is most vigorous.[1]

Is there any hope of the West's mediating between these hostile brothers? Several times, as under Bryan in 1896 and Wilson in 1916, the party achieved magnificent victories in the West; and yet it has no normal or permanent status there. The reason is simply a matter of races. The Scandinavians and Protestant Germans who make up the bulk of the Northwest's population, are traditionally Republican, which leaves as material for the Democratic party only the Catholic Germans and the Irish, and of course the old type of American whose ancestors migrated from the slave States and brought their politics with them. Thus we have two distinct types of Democrats side by side. In spite of their local importance they are only scattered groups at best, and so the Democrats succeed only when fortuitous circumstances drive public opinion away from the Republicans. If the crops are poor and have to be marketed at a loss, or if the manufacturers in the East profit too much by their tariff, up goes the stock of the Democratic party.

A similar reaction occurs in local politics if the Republicans have been too long in power or are too intimately allied with the mines and railroads of the district. An explosion of popular fury then gives victory to the other side, but it is generally only a political somersault with no lasting results. If this continues in the future, the Democrats should have a chance of success regularly every so many

[1] The Solid South comprises the ten States stretching from Virginia to Texas, viz., Virginia, North and South Carolina, Florida, Georgia, Alabama, Mississippi, Louisiana. Texas. and Arkansas.

years. Unfortunately the revolt, instead of being directed
against the Republicans, often occurs within the Republican
party itself and benefits its own factions only. Though
Bryan roused the entire West in 1896, and a similar movement under Roosevelt in 1912 and later under La Follette
only helped the rebellious Republicans, the Democrats gained
nothing. Sometimes, as after the elimination of Wilson,
their status in national politics in the West was reduced to
a few isolated groups, although they maintained their hold
over local affairs in a few States. It is thus impossible to
determine the field of the Democratic party with any degree
of exactness, for although its influence is definite in the
South, it is uncertain in the East and altogether elusive in
the West.

In the South, a Democratic majority is assured in advance
under any circumstances. Except in North Carolina and
Virginia, where the Republicans have penetrated from the
North, the majorities are enormous, and in several counties
the opposition is scarcely represented. In the presidential
elections òf 1924, for example, the Democrats obtained 66
per cent. of the votes in these ten States. In Mississippi
they obtained 90 per cent., and even 96 per cent. in South
Carolina. Four other States on the border of the South—
Oklahoma, Missouri, Tennessee, and Kentucky—also have
the Democratic spirit, and in the same way it persists in
Delaware and Maryland, and also in the southwestern districts of West Virginia and the southern half of Ohio, Indiana, and Illinois, which were all three colonized from the
South, and where politics still show this influence.

The one exception in the Solid South is the Alleghany
Mountain region to which the coloured race has never
spread, and consequently its political atmosphere is quite different. Northeastern Alabama, northern Georgia, and the
west of North Carolina and Virginia contain strong Republican minorities, and we can almost consider the eastern

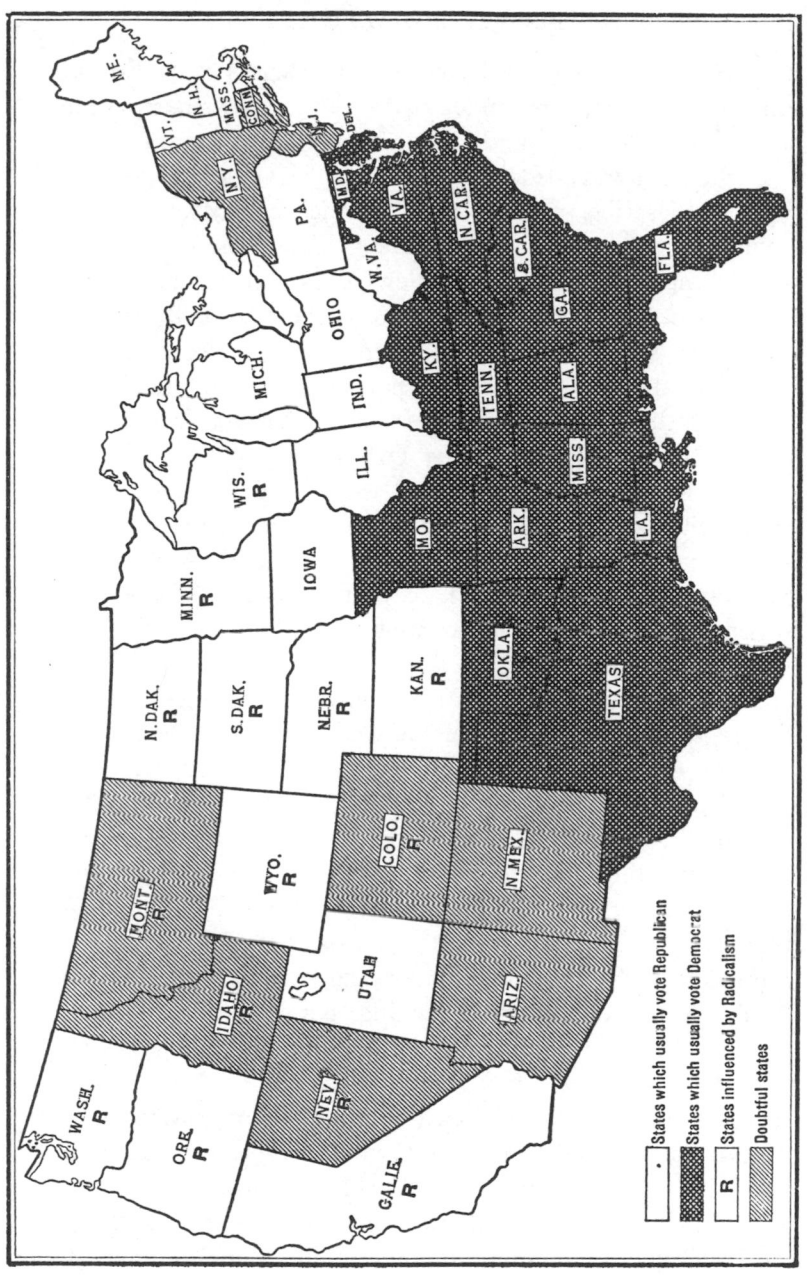

FIG. VI.

counties of Tennessee and Kentucky as Republican. Southern Louisiana also is tinged with Republicanism, for the
sugar interests are frankly protectionist.

In the East and Middle West the topography is more difficult to describe, for apart from the municipalities, the
Democrats are never sure of success. The most we can say
is that important States like New York, New Jersey, and
Connecticut are doubtful, and Ohio, Indiana, and Illinois are
even more so, though the situation becomes clearer if we
study the strength of the two parties State by State. In
the South the Democrats stand for all that is rural, national,
and deeply ingrained. In the East their following is just
the reverse, for here they attract the immigrant population
of the cities. They do not flourish in either the country
districts or the small towns of the East, and apart from
the metropolis the States of New York, New Jersey, and
Massachusetts elude them, as well as the less industrialized
parts of Maine, Vermont, and New Hampshire in New
England, where the Puritan influence still survives. The
dividing-line between the northern and southern Democrats
is quite curious. In Illinois, for example, the Chicago
Democrat is generally a city man—foreign, Catholic, anti-
Prohibitionist, or Irish—but in the southern counties of the
same State, the Democrat is a hard-headed farmer of the
old American type—Protestant, Prohibitionist, and Klans-
man.

Finally, in the West it is impossible to map out the party
at all. Not that support is lacking, but it is so spasmodic
and unstable, and because the New York and the southern
types are so mixed up and confused. In Arizona, New
Mexico, and Colorado it is easy to trace the migrations that
came from the South after the Civil War and brought with
them the old Democratic atmosphere of the Gulf States.
One feels this influence in the upper Mississippi and Missouri valleys and in various parts of the Rockies, even to

far-off Montana. At the same time we find the Irish in the mining centres and the big cities like St. Paul and San Francisco, for the Tammany spirit has penetrated even there. Here as elsewhere the peculiarly western revolt of the rural communities against the capitalist city is sometimes radical Republican and sometimes Democrat.

If we take a bird's-eye view of the Democratic party throughout the country, we are struck by its unassailable predominance in the South, its vitality in the East, and its latent power in the West. In local politics it can almost always achieve success; but to capture the presidential chair, a combination of conditions which rarely takes place is indispensable. Success in one section is not enough, for it requires a larger field. Like an ocean liner that rides steady on three waves but rolls and pitches on one, the Democratic ship can keep an even keel only if it has the support of more than one section of the country.

The southern vote, which is practically guaranteed in advance, is essential but insufficient. A combination of the South and West might just mean victory, but this has only happened once, in 1916 at the time of Wilson's re-election, when he carried Ohio and New Hampshire as well. Leaving aside the elections of 1916, and also that of 1912 when the Democratic candidate succeeded with less than an absolute majority, thanks to the division of his adversaries, we may say that presidential victory is possible only when they can add to the Solid South three or four States of the East and the Great Lakes as well as a certain amount of support in the West—in short, the Democrats of the cities.

In 1876 Tilden, a Democrat, almost became President, for besides the South he carried the States of New York, New Jersey, Connecticut, Indiana, Illinois. In 1884, Cleveland, also a Democrat, was successful, and in addition to the South he had New York, New Jersey, Connecticut, Indiana, Illinois. But in 1888 this same Cleveland was beaten, for though he had the South he failed to rally New York, Ohio, Indiana, Illinois. In 1896 Bryan, a Democrat, was defeated although he captured the South and almost the entire West; for he was unable to win over New York, New Jersey, Connecticut, Ohio, Indiana, and Illinois. Finally in 1924, Davis, the Democratic candidate, was defeated. As usual, he had the South, but the West was entirely gone, and so were the East and the Middle West, where none of the important States supported him. He did not capture New York, New Jersey, Connecticut, Ohio, Indiana, or Illinois.

The experts correctly describe New York, New Jersey, Ohio, and Illinois, as pivotal States, for any change in their status can overturn the fortunes of the party. The Democrats can succeed only when they unite, on a common platform—or a common lack of platform—the Baptists of Texas and the Catholics of Tammany Hall. Since the advent of the Ku Klux Klan and the Eighteenth Amendment, this is a ticklish problem, and yet if they fail to adopt a common national platform, they will be reduced to the impotence of scattered groups.

In 1924 when the party met to choose its presidential candidate, the impasse was nakedly revealed. It assembled in New York on June 24, 1924, with 1,446 delegates having 1,098 votes. A hopeless antagonism was immediately apparent between the East and the South, the Catholics and the Protestants, the Wets and the Drys. Should the party condemn the Ku Klux Klan by name in its platform? In all, 542 votes were cast in favour of this resolution,[2] but against it were 546 votes, representing the entire South and West. When it came to nominating a candidate there was the same impasse: 431 nationalist (we might almost say

[2] New York, New Jersey, Pennsylvania, Vermont, Maine, Massachusetts, Connecticut, Vermont, Delaware, Maryland, Ohio, Illinois, Wisconsin, Iowa, Minnesota, North and South Dakota, and Alabama—the latter owing to the great personal influence of Senator Underwood.

Klanist) votes were given for McAdoo, while the New Yorker, Al Smith, claimed the allegiance of a fervent group of 241 Catholics and anti-Prohibitionists. This left 372 votes to be divided among 13 other candidates. Ninety-eight ballots were taken, and still no one would give in. At the one hundred and third, they compromised out of sheer weariness, and in the interminable platform that they afterward drew up, they did not once mention either the Ku Klux Klan or prohibition!

This pitifully ridiculous convention is historically important, as it laid bare, beyond possibility of misunderstanding, the problem of the rights of Catholics and aliens in the American community. For the first time in the history of the country, an Irish Catholic was proposed as candidate for the highest post in the government. To nominate Al Smith was nothing short of astounding cheek in the opinion of the Baptists and Methodists of the South, but did he not have as good a right as any other citizen? It is no exaggeration to say that since his candidature two civilizations have been contending for the conquest of the government: the new civilization, industrial and cosmopolitan, of the great cities of the East, and the older, more strictly American one of the country-side and small towns.

For three-quarters of a century the immigrant population has not produced a single personality that could be dreamed of for the presidency. Al Smith, to part of the country at any rate, seems worthy of the honour, and yet an unwritten law endeavours to exclude him because he is a Catholic and does not belong to the Protestant Anglo-Scottish lineage which up to now has furnished every president, Democrat and Republican, with the sole exceptions of Roosevelt and Van Buren, who bore old Dutch names.

This brings out into the limelight the same problem of Americanization that we have met in every aspect of the national life since the War. During the last forty years a conception of life has been growing up in the large eastern cities which means an absolute break with the old Puritan traditions. The champions of the past who have taken refuge in the country districts see in this new Americanism a menace to the spiritual integrity of the nation. To send Al Smith to the White House would be equivalent in their eyes to giving the freedom of the city to the alien masses, and yet to millions of excellent citizens this frowned-on civilization represents not merely all that they know, but all that they love in their new fatherland.[3]

The very destiny of the country is at stake in this controversy, and the Democrats cannot get away from it, for it is their shirt of Nessus. If it had not been for the negroes, they might possibly not have survived in the South; for contrary to appearances, the real vitality of the party is no longer there, but in New York and Boston, where it is defending a conception of the country founded on liberty and hospitality. Nothing short of a genuine reconciliation between the East and the South, and more than a mere exchange of courtesies, will allow the Democrats to sweep the country again, for if they cannot agree on this burning question, can they ever agree on any other? This the future alone can tell.

[3] On the subject of this controversy, a very good article by Walter Lippmann was published in *Vanity Fair* (December, 1925), entitled "Al Smith, the Man of Destiny."

CHAPTER XX

THE REPUBLICAN PARTY

HAVING traced the moral and geographic boundaries of the Democratic party, it is now fairly easy to contrast them with the Republican. The latter relies instinctively on the wealthy classes and "big business," with which it has always worked. On occasion the interests have also applied to the Democrats—for re-insurance as it were—but they really only use them as a sort of spare tire, for in business the national chariot rolls more smoothly on Republican rubber.

The Republicans are the party of wealth and social conservatism, and the results of their policy can be gauged by the index of material success. Their great unanswerable argument is that they bring tangible prosperity to the pockets of all, and though there are some doubters, this is enough for most of their followers. As one might expect, the Republican party has been continuously in office apart from a few rare intermissions during the last half-century of unbroken prosperity. With wealth goes conservative thought, for as long as business is good, no one wants a change. In a new country where the individual can achieve great material results, social problems are very different from what they are in worn-out countries where additional effort gives only slight returns. In America the greatest possibility of becoming rich does not lie in the subdivision of existing wealth, for it is easier to create new wealth altogether.

Those who are already on the way to making their fortune, or who have already made it, wish only to consolidate or increase it, and their one idea is that the government should leave them alone and not hinder them, unless of course it is willing to aid them by putting the power of the state at their disposal. Though at times this system may injure the individual, as when the interests demand and obtain excessive protection or privileges, yet the Republican party instinctively feels that its function is not to oppose. It leaves to others the defence of the consumer, and does not pretend to protest against monopolies. Its *raison d'être* is to aid organized production and protect it against the foreigner by means of a high tariff wall. It has made the tariff its specialty and frankly considers that by helping business it is also serving the country. This policy holds good as long as there is prosperity for all, and so the masses put up with it. Nowhere but in the United States, with its abundance of natural resources and high standard of well-being and wages, could we find the paradox of a conservative capitalistic democracy that believes in equality. The Republican outlook exactly expresses this.

Doubts appear only in hard times. Sometimes it is the Democrats who profit, but sometimes a group within the Republican party rebels, complaining that they have not received their share of good things, or else grumbling that they have been the victims of favours granted to certain privileged classes. In this respect the Northwest, though Republican by temperament, nurses a perpetual grievance which culminates in a noisy outburst which is sometimes Democratic and sometimes Progressive, but always inspired by the same spirit of opposition. These exceptions only prove the rule that prosperity works for the Republican party, and hard times against it. "How could a man like myself be anything else but Republican?" This remark was made to me in San Francisco by an important business man as we discussed politics in his luxuriously appointed office. The Republican ticket is almost obligatory for a man who has an established position in the community, or a comfortable share of the national prosperity. For such, McKinley and Coolidge fill the bill.

The strength of the Republican party dates from the Civil War, which wiped out the South as a political influence. The real reason of its success is that its policy suits "big business," which has been in existence only for half a century at most, although the traditions of the party date much further back. Just as Jefferson was the inspiration of Democratic philosophy, so Alexander Hamilton originated the Republican doctrines. In fact, the broad outlines of the two policies were already sketched out by the end of the eighteenth century, as we can see by the controversies between Washington's two chief ministers. Hamilton was a great admirer of the British constitution, and he did not conceal his predilection for a strong central government which could impose obedience both on individuals and on local parties. His policies were in favour of order, organization, and material prosperity designed and carried out by the government. Although the whole of America was strongly influenced by Jefferson at the beginning of the nineteenth century, as even the Republican party still shows by its respect for the will of the people, yet the spirit of Hamilton proved more enduring among the Republicans; for it has a great effect on them even today, especially if they have acquired a vigorous personality by their contact with modern industry.

The great development of mass production coincided during the second half of the nineteenth century with an unprecedented immigration of all races, but this did not bring the present Republicans any nearer to the early liberal ideals. Do the economic leaders of the United States believe today in equality even of the white races? It is hardly probable. They employ every class of labour, and look upon it with the same superior detachment as a planter regards his natives. Do they even believe in popular sovereignty and the wisdom of the majority? They may accept it as a fact, but experience has convinced them that business success is based on authority and discipline, and not on liberty. Jefferson inherited his respect for man as a man from the eighteenth century philosophers, but the great industrial leaders of today, and with them the Republican party, have other ideas, for the essentials of their program are continuity of government and the organization of society.

The rank and file of the Republican party are recruited chiefly by arguments of self-interest, though there are also racial and patriotic reasons. With the exception of the South, the Anglo-Saxon and Nordic races form the main basis of the party; and if we take into consideration the native-born and the Ku Klux Klan, it is more nationalist than its rival. It is very sound when it repudiates cosmopolitanism and even relegates to second rank the glories of a triumphant industrialism. Its moral centre of gravity is located in the small towns where the Protestant traditions are still alive and memories of the past are a household word. The legend of Lincoln, that ideal type of American, brought up on the Bible and the British classics in his vigorous pioneer childhood, is still as fresh as ever. Al Smith always conjures up East Side New York, that unbelievable Babel of races; but when Republican propaganda pictures Colonel Coolidge, the President's late father, they show him singing psalms on Sunday in the humble Congregational church in Vermont, and their sentimental picture seems more in keeping with the Lincoln tradition and penetrates much more deeply into the hearts of the old-timers. We must not let the triumphs of city life blind us to the fact that it is in the tranquil backwaters of the old American towns that the men of sterling influence are created. They may be neither the richest nor the most intelligent, but they inspire confidence. The antiquity of their race and their allegiance to the God of their fathers gives them a sort of privilege.

The Republican party plays this card with greater success than the Democrats.

The more the foreigners are assimilated, the more they turn to the party that shelters the successful. The Scandinavians adopt this attitude immediately. Economic success produces the same result. Though the isolated workman and the newcomer with neither friend nor trade may turn to Tammany, the well-to-do skilled worker feels that the Republican party will protect his wage level as well as the profits of his employer. Where a position has to be defended, be it moral, traditional, or simply a question of material success, this rule works automatically. Behind the Democratic screen of New York and Boston is an ingrained Republican community, prospering in all the eastern states.

The East and the middle western States around the Great Lakes are essential to Republican victory, but they are inclined to be fickle. New England—except for Boston, which is Democrat, and Connecticut, which is doubtful—forms a zone that is almost solid. Although the country districts of New York and New Jersey are entirely Republican, these States run the danger of going over to the other camp by the weight of numbers in New York and New Jersey cities. Pennsylvania is always Republican, even including the Irish of Philadelphia. The four States, Michigan, Ohio, Indiana, and Illinois that border the Great Lakes, have a Republican basis except for the big cities and the southern country districts in the last three. Their imported southern atmosphere, coupled with the Democrats of the cities, is occasionally sufficient to swing the balance away from the Republican party. To this list of faithful States we may safely add Iowa and Utah, which were strongly influenced by earlier migrations from New England.

We must now examine the Northwest and the Pacific Coast by themselves. The States lying between the Great Lakes and the Rocky Mountains were largely colonized by

Scandinavians and Germans, and belong almost body and soul to the Republicans. So, to a lesser extent, do Kansas, Nebraska, and Wyoming. Only in the most exceptional circumstances do they go over to the other side, for their Republican allegiance is a matter of tradition and spirit. This also applies to the three States of the Pacific Coast, which, like the West, are always trying to organize a revolt within the party, though they only rarely desert the Republican cause. The deserters to the Progressives, who, at any rate in 1912, were responsible for the defeat of the Republican presidential candidate, were chiefly in the Northwest farming area, which shows that Republican thought is not always conservative and sometimes has almost a radical tinge.

In the rest of the country—that is to say, in the South and the Rocky Mountains—the Republican party is not at home. We know that they are almost non-existent in the South, apart from the few negroes who have been permitted to vote, and a few rare "poor white" politicians. In spite of protectionist leanings among the wealthy, the existence of the southern Republicans has been purely theoretical up to the present, and the only excuse for them at all is to be delegates to the party convention when the presidential candidate is chosen. If the President feels like it, he occasionally rewards them with Federal posts, as when, to the horror of public opinion generally, a negro was nominated customs officer in New Orleans. For the same reason, the negroes are heard with consideration at Washington when their protectors are in power. Election statistics cannot err in this matter, however, and they show that there are practically no Republican votes in counties with a heavy negro majority. Under these conditions the whites get together and absolutely forbid the slightest suspicion of Republicanism. It is only when the percentage of negroes is very low that the Republican party can hope for even a feeble showing.

From this geographic inventory the obvious requirements of the Republicans are comparatively simple. All they need is the solid vote of the East and Middle West. The South and West can be hostile without affecting the result, but if two or three of the larger States in the East or the Middle West were to go Democrat, victory would be precarious. Similarly, without going over to the enemy, if the northwestern States were to band together and vote for candidates of their own, their revolt might easily be sufficient to defeat the party. This occurred in 1912 in the Roosevelt campaign, and was again threatened in 1924 by La Follette. For the conservative Republicans—the real Republicans— to succeed, it is essential that no movement of discontent be allowed to snatch away the eastern cities for the benefit of the Democrats, or the northwestern prairies for the radicals. Conditions necessary to the triumph of conservative ideals are found in certain prosperous combinations from which neither the city consumer nor the agricultural producer is excluded. This happens comparatively often, for after all, a fair degree of prosperity is normal in the United States. True, prosperity rarely smiles on all the interests at once; for the eastern consumer wants to buy cheaply and the farmer to sell dear. Nor must we forget that the Democrats and the Progressives can never agree, for in spite of their name, the Democrats are quite as conservative as the Republicans.

In Al Smith we have the genuine representative of the New York Democrats. Let us now study President Coolidge, in whom the average post-war Republican recognizes his own type. Since Lincoln, America has had three great presidents, two Democrats, Cleveland and Wilson, and one Republican (but later a Progressive), Roosevelt. Republican politics, which often consist in simply letting them-

selves be swept into power on the tide of prosperity, require less exceptional ability than these men possessed. The
remarkable qualities of Taft did not appeal to the masses,
who preferred McKinley or Coolidge. The popularity of
Coolidge after the 1924 elections (the date is important,
for no one should be called popular until after his death!)
is a most enlightening paradox.

Here is a man who is popular with the public, though
possibly mostly with the lower strata. He may be less admired than Roosevelt or Wilson, but he inspires much more
confidence than either of his great predecessors. He is a
small, uninspiring man, and his restless eyes look at you
without warmth or brilliance. He is not a hail-fellow-well-
met like President Harding, nor "one of the boys" like so
many politicians in both America and France. He takes
no recreation, does not play games, but prefers long, prosaic
walks. If he rides at all, it is on a dummy horse in a riding-
school. And yet his popularity suddenly sprang up when
the premature death of President Harding automatically
made him chief executive. Both the House and the Senate
were against him then and heaped the most humiliating
abuse on him. But public opinion judged him differently,
and quickly wove about him a legend of defects and qualities
which are not usually valued by the people—first his obstinate
silence, in such contrast to the loquacity of the ordinary politician.

"I have made a bet that I would make you say more than
three words to me at dinner," a lady once said to him.

"You have lost," replied Coolidge.

After a delegation of women had held forth for half an
hour on their rights, he merely said to his astonished visitors, "Why not?"

The legend has used certain traits which are only more
or less correct. They do not interpret his silence as lack
of thought, but as a sign of depth. In America, as in Eng-

land, many people prefer an average type to real brilliance, as they feel that a man who thinks slower is safer. In point of fact, President Coolidge is a skilful, prudent politician, thoroughly honest; and as a good Protestant he is eager to do what is right. His much-vaunted personal economy inspires confidence in a country where every one is extravagant. He listens with consideration to business men and does not worry them. His personality has now become the guiding factor of the doctrine or policy of his party.

It may be that exceptional circumstances were necessary for this popularity, for normally America prefers to elect men of good presence, easy cordiality, eloquence, and magnetism. After going through the War, however, and other unforeseen eventualities, America felt that his inertia would lead to safety. By 1924 and 1925 they were weary of the lofty idealism of Wilson and the vain amiability and shallowness of Harding. After the peace treaties, they regarded European diplomats as Machiavellis, or even as a sort of Mephistopheles, but in Coolidge they had a man who would do nothing sensational. What a relief! Also, he was an American of the old type from Vermont, who had never even visited Europe. His name was illustrious, for the Coolidges trace their lineage right back to Adam, and like the Cabots, "speak only to God." The President, however, does not belong to the aristocratic branch of the family, and this pleases the people, who prefer him to be average, typical, and unpretentious. At a time when so many good Anglo-Saxons shudder to think of their country slipping down the fatal slope—girls and boys drinking bootleg liquor, crime waves, inundations of alien immigrants, and Catholic propaganda everywhere—it is a comfort to feel that the White House at least is in the hands of a Puritan descendant of Old England, who can act as a brake when cosmopolitan America tries to shake off these traditions, and who considers that he has only done his duty when he runs the affairs of state efficiently. There is a certain grandeur in his self-satisfied, conscious, aggressive mediocrity, which is an antidote to foreign and offensive forms of superiority. In this the popularity of President Coolidge is symbolic of the entire epoch.[1]

[1] In this analysis of the popularity of President Coolidge, I obtained considerable material from an illuminating article by Bruce Bliven. "The Great Coolidge Mystery," in *Harper's Magazine,* December, 1925.

CHAPTER XXI

THE PROGRESSIVE PARTY

THE rank and file of the Democratic party may follow the demagogues at times, but their policy in the long run is anything but revolutionary. Even less so are the higher-grade working-men, who in the main are conservative and almost Republican. It is quite a question whether there are any out-and-out radicals in the country, and in fact, apart from a few revolutionary aliens in the large cities and mining- and lumber-camps in the Far West, the northwestern farmers are the unique centre of radicalism.

The Northwest is peopled by landed proprietors who believe thoroughly in equality and democracy. A few of them hire men throughout the whole year, but mostly they farm their land with the help of only their families. During the harvest they are all more or less employers of labour, and although they howl at capitalism, of which they think they are the victims, yet it is from the viewpoint of employers that they consider the rights of the wage-earners. As debtors they are hostile to capital, but as employers they favour order. Their politics are intermittent, explosive, and distinctly limited in scope.

When business is good, the West goes to sleep politically, but when the margin of profit is reduced or disappears, the farmer perceives that he is really in the hands of interests more powerful than himself, and begins to protest. He is caught in the net of the capitalist much more than the European farmer, for he needs more capital, as he uses so much machinery. He is a spendthrift, and does not know enough to save or even to pay off his mortgage when he makes money. Also, as he cultivates nothing but wheat in certain areas, he runs great risks, and in fact is always in debt to the bank.

It is important to note that his outlook is due to the fact that the ever-present financial pressure comes from a distance. It is New York and not St. Paul, Minneapolis, or even Chicago that dispenses credit. The bonds which bind the farmer are even more complex, for even when he has harvested his wheat he is still dependent on the railway to transport it and on the elevator to receive and classify it. The railway and the elevator are both more powerful than he is, and he always feels that they have beaten him when the price of wheat falls, and his borrowed capital cannot stand the strain of freight rates in addition to high interest charges.

We have thus two opposing points of view: on the one hand, the local interests which do not extend beyond the boundaries of the State in which universal suffrage makes the farmer master of the situation, and on the other, the great financial powers of national importance whose decisions are entirely beyond the control of the local voters. In one of his novels, Jack London gives a vivid picture of the burden of this "golden heel." The hostility between the local and national interests is the dividing-line between the radicals and the conservatives. Wheat grows within the limits of the State or the county, and is therefore radical. The railway spreads over the frontiers of several States, and is therefore capitalist and conservative. Wheat's bitter hatred of the railroad is always causing political explosions.

This gives us the key to these periodic agrarian movements. Of course, there are mortgaged farms in the East, and the South with its cotton is also in the grip of the single-crop system; but the East has not the menace of the single crop or of drought, and in the South the negro problem and the passions it arouses stifle the radical tendencies that otherwise would appear. It is only in the Northwest that these various factors all unite to produce the mania of persecution. When they feel that they are being strangled by the banks who sternly restrict credit at a signal given two thousand miles away, the farmers rebel politically and try to protect themselves by their vote. The railway companies, the elevator companies, the mills, and, in short, all organized capital then retaliate and try in the many ways at their disposal to "control" the local legislature, the government, and the entire administration. It is a struggle between the popular will and the dominating influence of arbitrary, distant, and uncontrollable interests.

This arouses indignation and panic among the farmers, who endow the "bank" and "capital" with limitless powers of evil, and who look upon the East almost as a foreign country determined to crush them. They believe that the tariff arbitrarily raises the price of all the manufactured articles they buy, while the price of the agricultural products they sell is being systematically lowered by deflation, and all the time they are weighed down with mortgages. The political division is thus not between the rich and the poor or between employer and employé, but between the eastern creditor and the western debtor.

We need two maps to show the regions which are subject to these collective revolts. The first is the rainfall chart. Indignation is always more violent in the area where the annual rainfall is less than twenty inches, which explains why most of the agitations are started in the west of Minnesota, in the Dakotas, Nebraska, and eastern Montana. The second chart shows the races. Minnesota, the Dakotas, and northwestern Wisconsin are the country of the Norsemen, in which the basis of the population is Scandinavian and German. We no longer find the robust conservatism of the Anglo-Saxon, nor yet the erratic vivacity of the Celt, which is kept in check by the priests. The Norwegian or Swedish farmer of the Northwest is a solitary introspective individual, proud and violent, like the obstinate idealists of Ibsen. To understand him we must turn back to Nordic Europe.

Such, then, is the atmosphere in which these periodic agitations are created. They are always the same, although the title varies: Grangers, Greenbackers, Populists, Free Silverites, Non-Partisan League, Farmer-Labor party, or Progressives under Roosevelt and La Follette. These mushroom movements use the existing political organizations, but they are far broader in spirit and decline to be tamed by the discipline of a party machine. No one can obtain a permanent following from such wilful masses, for they are quite unsuitable as the basis of a third party.

The area of unrest is always changing. In the Free Silver tempest of 1896 the centre of the depression was in Nebraska, South Dakota, Montana, Wyoming, Colorado, Kansas, Idaho, Utah, and Washington; but Wisconsin, Minnesota, and North Dakota held back. In 1912, the radical Republicanism of Roosevelt succeeded in the same area, but his territory also included Minnesota, California, and Washington. Since the War, three distinct movements have arisen, none of them having exactly the same geographic origin or the same following as the others. The Non-Partisan League centred in North Dakota, the Farmer-Labor party in Minnesota, and La Follette's party in Wisconsin.

About ten years before the War, the American Society of Equity was formed in North Dakota to erect terminal elevators under the control of the farmers themselves, but their efforts failed, owing to the resistance of the menaced interests and the indifference of the politicians, who were more or less in the power of these interests. Embittered and disillusioned, the farmers decided that they could not succeed unless they controlled the public services also. As they ac-

counted for over 80 per cent. of the population of the State,
this was not very difficult so long as they voted *en bloc* for
their own program and did not divide their votes between
the two political parties. The result was the formation in
1915 of the Non-Partisan League, which was originated by
a ruined farmer named Townley. His aim was to create a
super-political organization which would make use of the
existing parties without being dominated by them. The
farmers attacked the problem with mystical fervour. "The
time will come when the State will belong to us," they said.
By 1918 the League had won all the electoral posts in North
Dakota, and, apart from a return offensive of its adversaries in 1920 and 1922, it remained in control up to 1925 and
the beginning of 1926. The election of November, 1926,
may show a change.

Material interests are the real basis of the League, for
the members are practical farmers and not theorists. Townley seems to have acquired from the Milwaukee Germans
certain second-hand ideas from Karl Marx; so a few Socialist agitators were sent to help him with his propaganda.
For a while he thought of forming an alliance with the
I.W.W.'s, but, as we have already said, the Dakota farmer
is not in sympathy with the demands of the working-classes.
During the War their leaders adopted certain pacifist ideas
and even incurred the hostility of the authorities; yet this
does not necessarily imply an international outlook, which
is in fact far removed from their ideals. The originality of
the Non-Partisan League lies in the sentimentality and mysticism of its members in addition to their quest for material
prosperity and their ready-made agitations. They are not
revolutionaries but simply anti-capitalists, and their enthusiasm and fanaticism is directed less toward making money
than toward building up a new state of society in which
they will be freed from the yoke of "Capital," spelled with
a big "C." The heroic period of the League is not over,

but its most ardent followers at Fargo and Bismarck look back on it as on a crusade, in much the same way as the Dreyfusards in France look back on the Dreyfus case.

The League started off with an ambitious program: the nationalization of the grain elevators, flour mills, railways, banks, and co-operative stores, as well as mutual assurance run by the community. In North Dakota, however, this program has only been partially carried out, and has hardly altered conditions at all. Prosperity is the worst enemy of the Non-Partisan League, for in 1924, when the price of farm products began to rise after a long period of depression, the farmers' enthusiasm waned rapidly. The League was largely a matter of atmosphere which could not be transplanted. Unless they were pure farming communities, the towns never took it up. At Fargo, "the greatest little city in the world" (sic), and at Bismarck, the capital of North Dakota, the ocean of wheat begins at the end of every street. The feeling of vast spaces is forced on one at every turn, just as in the little French ports where one breathes the fresh sea-breezes from over the Atlantic and where the principal street is the "Rue de la Mer." The East has never understood this combination of enthusiasm, bitterness, and rage, and even in the West the domain of the Non-Partisan League is restricted to North Dakota and the plateau of Montana and Wyoming. It is now only a latent force, however; but the fact that the price index of farm produce has moved up does not mean that mysticism has been wiped out altogether.

The Farmer-Labor party which works from St. Paul, Minnesota, may have more extensive ramifications than the Non-Partisan League, but it is less homogeneous. Alongside of the country radicals are real extremists and revolutionaries, in both St. Paul and Minneapolis and the western mining-towns. They are chiefly recruited from the unassimilated immigrants. They advocate a Marxian doctrine of violence and anti-religion which is out of place in America, and they try to insinuate themselves among the Progressives in order to profit by their agitations. Thus discontented farmers, embittered workmen, and idealist militant reformers, without the slightest resemblance to each other, are trying to put up a common front. Such is the history of the Farmer-Labor party. It was originated in St. Paul in 1920 with leaders of considerable ability, three-quarters of whom were Irish—Donnelly, Loftus, Manahan, and Mahoney. Its program included the liberty of the worker, a certain amount of state socialism, the nationalization of the railways, hostility to Wall Street, a vague longing for inflation, pacifism, and the usual condemnation of imperialism in all its forms. Its name indicates a desire to unite the labourers of the soil and of factory, without, however, realizing the fundamental difference between them. The city worker wants high wages and cheap foodstuffs, but the farmer, who is also an employer, wants low wages and dear farm products. The special outlook of the Northwest may unite them for a while, but though they may be able to destroy together, they can never build up. For this reason the Farmer-Labor party, like the Non-Partisan League, has never been able to grow beyond a temporary local group. In 1920 its presidential candidates received only 265,000 votes, three-quarters of which came from the Northwest, and in 1922 two Senators from Minnesota were elected under its auspices. They seem to need a particular climate, for east of Chicago or south of St. Louis they do not thrive.

Although he polled almost 5,000,000 votes in the presidential election of 1924, Senator La Follette did not succeed in creating a national third party, for his only real stronghold was west of the Great Lakes. The centre of his powerful movement was Wisconsin, a State of well-to-do farmers who go in for dairy-farming rather than wheat. The country-side is very green, and under the beautiful trees planted like a park the sleek herds graze in shady pastures. It would recall a canton in northern Switzerland, were it not for the turret-like corn silos alongside the painted wooden farmhouses that are so typically American. The basis of this rural community of land-owners is Scandinavian and German, all independent and equal, and almost all well-off or even rich. Every family has a car or cars, a telephone, and a radio. The arid zone does not begin for almost two hundred miles further West; so there is no material here for the demagogue, and if we consider La Follette a revolutionary agitator, he would be quite incomprehensible in such surroundings.

During his whole life he stood for the same program, whether it was as District Attorney in 1880 in Dane County, his first elective post, as Governor of Wisconsin in 1900, or as Senator in Washington from 1905 up to his death in 1925. He defended the elector against the machine, the common people against the domination of "big business," and democracy against control by capital—this sums up his career. Not much, perhaps, and yet in the United States enormous; for it meant nothing less than a declaration of war on the most powerful forces of his times. Ought we to call him a Socialist? Possibly his program as governor included socialistic reforms, and in so far as comparison with Europe is worth anything in the New World, he could be styled an 1848 revolutionary; for he tried to preserve in an over-industrialized community the popular ideals of the nineteenth century. The farmer, and even the factory worker, to whose world he never belonged, regarded him as the friend of the people; but the middle class were bound to oppose him, and the revolutionaries would have had to curb themselves considerably if they wished to follow him. As soon as he tried to weld these dissimilar elements into a national party, the inherent weakness of his position was immediately apparent, just as had been the case in the Farmer-Labor party.

As people's tribune, La Follette was able to gather together only a very composite electorate, even in his own State of Wisconsin. Like their leader, the Scandinavian farmers in the northwestern part of the State were Republican by tradition, and in the central and eastern districts the German farmers, though rather more Democratic, also rallied to his cause, especially after his protest against the War and the Treaty of Versailles. In the great industrial city of Milwaukee, an important group of Socialists under the leadership of Berger, a German, moved parallel with him, and often assisted him. In the same way the small commercial class supported him until they were finally won away from him by the large financial corporations. But the southeastern districts of Wisconsin, which had been settled to a great extent by New England Yankees, were always hostile. Nor was he able to carry the industrial counties north of Milwaukee along the shore of Lake Michigan, for here the employers exercise a rigid control over their non-union labour.

La Follette was a Republican born and bred who had never even dreamed of being anything but a Republican, and yet he was able to evolve out of the various elements in his State a party of his own which the bosses of the Republican machine opposed obstinately and peevishly for nearly half a century. The interesting point is that the struggle was not between the Republicans and the Democrats, but between two groups of Republicans, conservatives and radicals, both belonging to the same party.

Owing to his prestige as champion of the people, it was only natural that La Follette should have been the rallying-point of all the western radicals, and that in 1920 and again in 1924 the Farmer-Labor party should have offered to make him their presidential candidate. He refused twice.

chiefly through fear of compromising himself with the over-advanced sections, for there were communists in the Farmer-Labor party, but in his heart of hearts it was really because he hoped to receive one day the mantle from his own Republican party. But it was a vain hope, for they chose Coolidge, who is conservative in the extreme. Meanwhile the Democrats were busy quarrelling at their convention in New York and were equally indifferent to advanced thought. Finding no suitable resting-place in either of the official parties, he was compelled to seek a new and independent setting for his political career. It was with this in view that an independent movement was created by the advanced wing of the Republican party, together with a group of western Democrats, the non-communist element of the Farmer-Labor party and the Socialist party. They jointly nominated him as their Progressive candidate at their convention in Cleveland in July, 1924. It was not exactly a new party, although in most States it called itself Independent or Progressive. In California it was described as Socialist, in Colorado and Montana as Farmer-Labor and Progressive, in Connecticut and New York as Socialist and Progressive, in Missouri and Pennsylvania as Socialist and Labor, in North Dakota as Non-Partisan, in Oklahoma as Farmer-Labor, and in West Virginia as Socialist and Farmer-Labor. Thus all the opposition parties, except for such violent extremists as the Workers' Party and the I.W.W.'s, marched behind the one man and under the one flag.

The only unity in the program was the personality of La Follette. In the name of his faithful farmers, he protested against excessive industrial protection and high freight rates and timidly demanded the nationalization of the railways and water power; for the workmen he demanded the right to form unions and freedom to strike; for democracy in general he proclaimed the sovereignty of the

people as against control by the moneyed interests, and he
demanded that the Supreme Court should cease to veto any
legislation passed by Congress on the ground that it considered it unconstitutional; and finally for the pacifists (or was
it for the German-Americans?) he protested against imperialism and the Versailles Treaty. The chief defect in his
program was that it looked dangerous to his adversaries and
only lukewarm to many of his partisans. In its social legislation it fell far short of the demands of the Socialists, and
yet it exceeded the political aims of the farmers. It was
this division among his followers more than any lack of
sincerity or lofty aims on his part that proved the weakness
of his whole political adventure.

Twelve hundred delegates and nine thousand spectators
attended the Cleveland Convention with a spontaneity of
conviction which must command respect. There were no
corrupt bosses, no professional ward politicians, only simple
people, serious and rather boring. The atmosphere resembled a revival meeting, but it lacked the magnetism of a
Roosevelt or an Al Smith, for La Follette was old and
weary, and crammed with statistics. The most intense and
impassioned section of the Progressive party represented
the despairing northwestern farmers in the clutches of the
banks. The Non-Partisan League had already passed its
zenith, however, and after all, Wisconsin was very comfortably off, and unfortunately for the campaign the price of
wheat started to rise rapidly. The working-class was present to a very limited extent, for the masses were contented,
and the Socialists, though they admired the sincerity of the
man, well knew that he was not one of them. There was
none of the fanatical enthusiasm with which Bryan carried
away his followers in his Free Silver election of 1896, nor
yet the impassioned devotion which Roosevelt inspired in
1912. La Follette was a formidable parliamentary debater.

He had the soul of a people's tribune, but he sadly lacked the magnetism.

Thus, in spite of the 4,823,000 votes for La Follette in the election of November 4, 1924, the results were very restricted geographically. He led in one State only, his own faithful Wisconsin, where he secured 54 per cent. of the votes. This State was his, his kingdom, and after his death was inherited by his son. He came second with between 24 per cent. and 45 per cent. of the votes and exceeded the Democrats in the solid *bloc* of the eleven States of the Northwest;[1] he came third with 10 per cent. to 24 per cent. of the votes in five other States on the borders of the Northwest,[2] as well as in nine States of the East and Middle West.[3] In northern New England and throughout the South, he received less than 10 per cent. of the votes, for the simple reason that neither of these regions was interested in his campaign, nor did he receive more than the most indifferent support from the industrial population of the East. The only region which he was able to galvanize was the northwestern farming community, which is perpetually discontented, and which since 1920 has been in debt to the extent of mortgages on more than half of the farms. The charts of this mortgaged territory show that it coincides fairly accurately with the following of the Senator from Wisconsin. For him to carry the great industrial population in a radical movement another centre of gravity was necessary, and also much less prosperity and more widespread discontent among the working-classes.

The death of La Follette in June, 1925, made impossible the constitution of a permanent third party as many of his followers desired, and to which he himself finally agreed. His personality alone could have consolidated it into a more

[1] Iowa, Minnesota, North Dakota, South Dakota, Montana, Wyoming, Idaho, Washington, Oregon, Nevada, and California.
[2] Colorado, Nebraska, Kansas, Utah, and Arizona.
[3] New York, Massachusetts, Connecticut, New Jersey, Pennsylvania, Maryland, Ohio, Michigan, and Illinois.

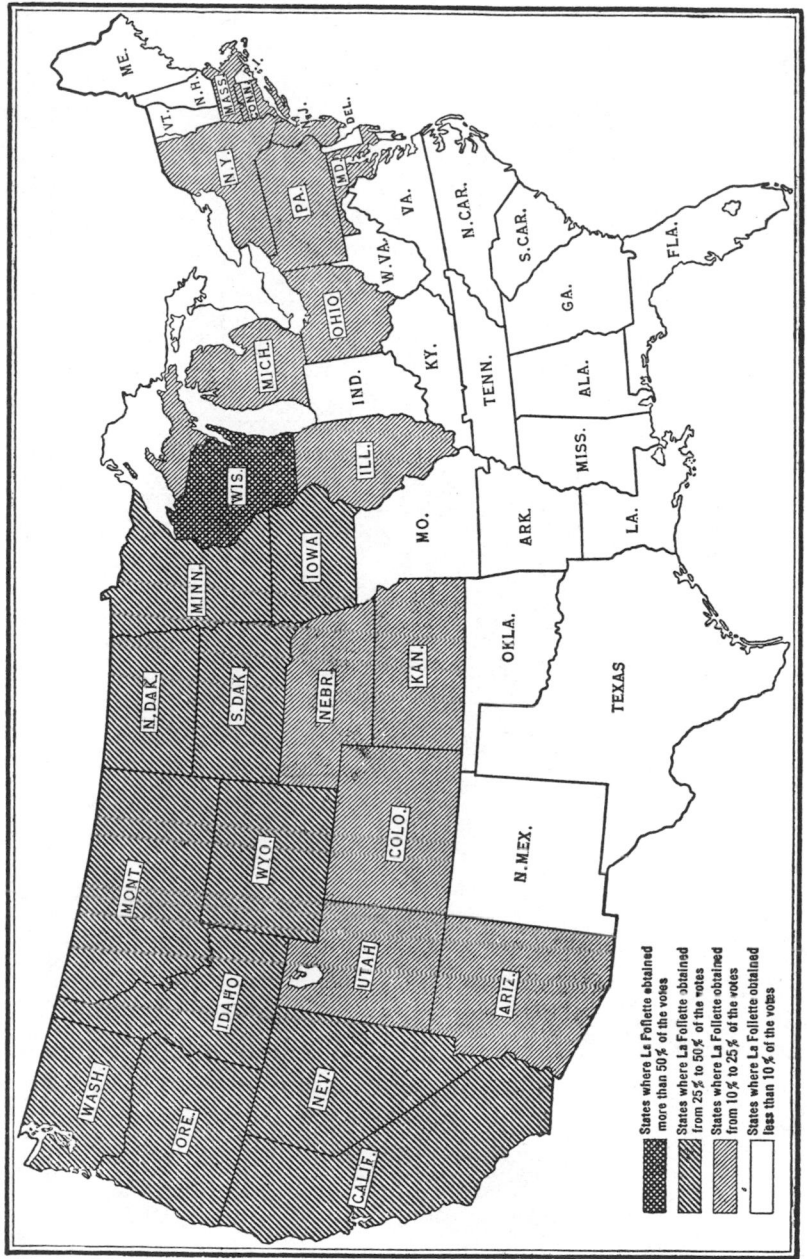

States where La Follette obtained
more than 50% of the votes

States where La Follette obtained
from 25% to 50% of the votes

States where La Follette obtained
from 10% to 25% of the votes

States where La Follette obtained
less than 10% of the votes

FIG. VII.

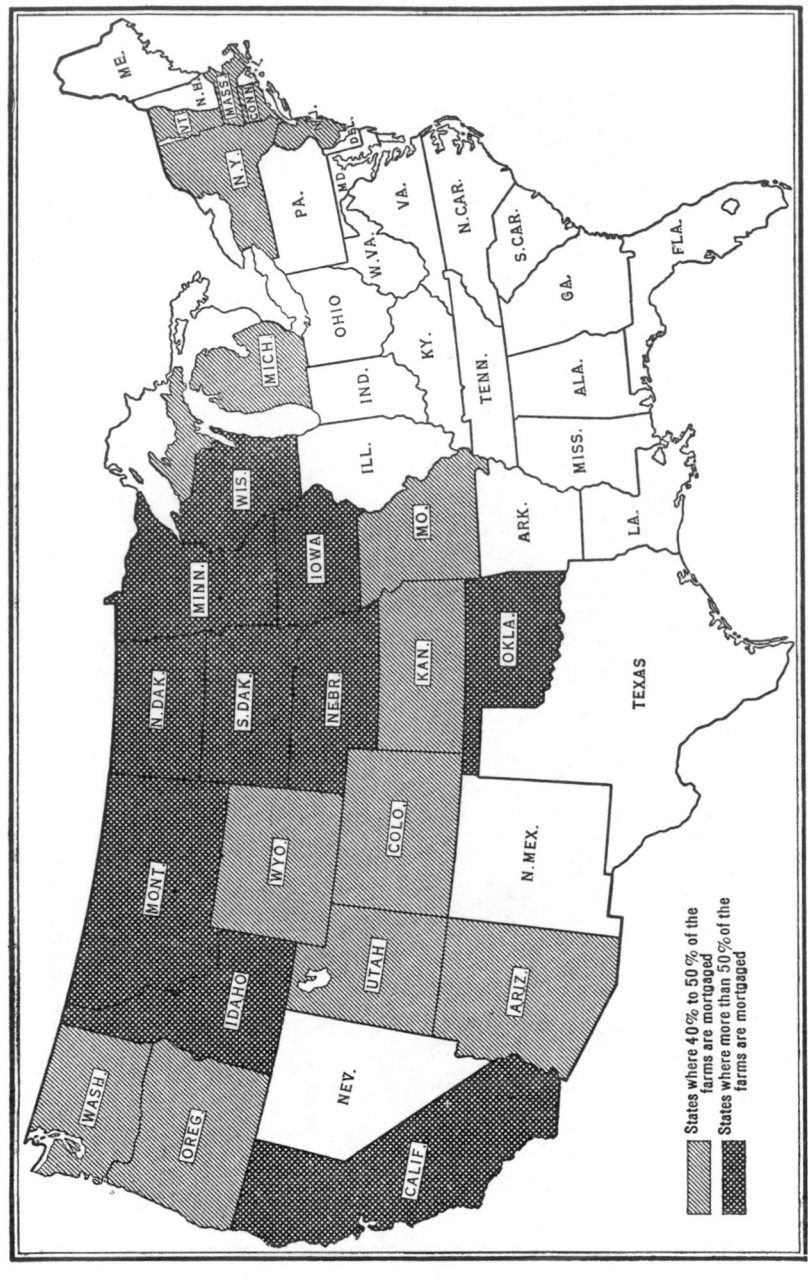

FIG. VIII.—MORTGAGE STATUS OF FARMS OWNED WHOLLY OR IN PART BY THE OPERATOR (BUREAU OF THE CENSUS, 1920).

☒ States where 40% to 50% of the farms are mortgaged

■ States where more than 50% of the farms are mortgaged

or less unnatural unity, though geographically it could never have assured him national success. Many centres of advanced thought have been in existence for years, but they are still so scattered that they are only likely to result in occasional outbursts, usually in the form of individual revolts within the confines of the two great parties.

The most difficult problem which now confronts the Republicans is to offer the Westerners a policy which will be sufficiently attractive to retain them in the Republican ranks. The West has a disconcerting disdain for orthodox political economy and is profoundly inflationist. They are always asking for subsidies to keep export prices at an artificial level, and they put forward dangerous plans based on the dumping of agricultural produce, such as the McNary-Haugen Farm Relief Bill in 1926. These methods are incompatible with sound finance, and if the eastern Republicans wish to pursue a sensible course, they run the risk of having their western colleagues desert them.

Whether the insurgents come from the left wings of the Republican and Democratic parties, from the Farmer-Labor party, the Non-Partisan League and the Socialist party, or are simply groups of farmers discontented with the price of wheat, they have succeeded in forming an unstable and rather insignificant opposition party in Congress. Their ideas are either advanced or simply fantastic, combining the most varied tendencies. When a vote is taken, one notices that certain Republicans and a few Democrats from the West link up together to oppose the majorities of their respective parties. A Progressive tendency, which stands for the outstanding characteristics of the movement we have analyzed, will continue to live in the United States; for it expresses a state of mind that is essentially American, though not advanced in the European sense of the word. Yet in this over-disciplined country, it fosters a valuable individualistic ferment.

CHAPTER XXII

PARTY POLITICS

In the preceding chapters we were chiefly concerned with the psychology and permanent characteristics of the various political parties, but to realize the situation during the postwar period and the volume of the public that each party represents, we must compare their numerical strength in the 1920 and 1924 presidential elections.

In the first place the votes cast were as follows:[1]

	1920	*1924*
Voters registered	54,166,000	56,942,000
Votes cast	26,646,000	29,139,000
Proportion of votes cast	49.1%	51.2%

The total number of votes may be further divided as follows:

	1920	*1924*
Abstentions	27,520,000—50.9%	27,803,000—48.8%
Republicans	16,152,000—29.8	15,725,000—27.6
Democrats	9,147,000—16.9	8,387,000—14.7
Socialists	920,000— 1.7	73,000— 0.1
Farmer-Labor ..	265,000— 0.5	
La Follette		4,823,000— 8.5
Sundry	162,000— 0.2	131,000— 0.3

[1] The American electoral lists are drawn up by the States, and their qualifications vary so much that it is impossible to ascertain the exact number of voters. The above figures, which are only approximate, are the result of an inquiry made by the National Association of Manufacturers during its campaign in 1920 and 1924 against abstention from voting.

Although these figures are only approximate they show that the interest taken in these elections was not very keen, for nearly half the electorate did not bother to vote, which confirms our conviction that the Americans are not greatly preoccupied with politics. The average of votes cast is considerably reduced on account of the South, for in the fourteen southern Democratic States only 31 per cent. of the votes polled in 1924—why bother when the result is known in advance! Nevertheless, even in the six New England States the proportion of voters did not exceed 58 per cent., so that the real interest of the country evidently does not lie in electoral battles.

It is equally certain that the conservative Republican party easily took first place at the close of the Wilson régime, which with all its brilliance had no future. We must not overlook the enormous mass of people who did not declare one way or the other, though it is unlikely that they would suddenly have taken an interest in politics. After the Republican defeat in 1912 due to an internecine dispute, and their further defeat in 1916 due to exceptional circumstances, the country fell back on the Republican party quite naturally as soon as the War was over, as it felt the need of stability. This was perfectly normal and in keeping with post-war conditions. The situation was scarcely the same, however; for though the Republicans were weakened by the La Follette vote, the Democrats suffered even more in comparison.

By a simple calculation based on the above percentages, we can estimate where the Progressive party obtained its 4,823,000 votes. Out of the 8.5 per cent. of the registered voters that it succeeded in capturing, the Socialists and the Farmer-Labor party provided 1.7 per cent. and 0.5 per cent. respectively, and the Republicans and the Democrats each gave it the 2.2 per cent. that they lost in comparison with 1920. The remainder was apparently furnished by those

who abstained in 1920 but decided to vote in 1924.   In this
way we can reconstruct the 8.5 per cent. who revolted,
though we must not forget that this left wing was very
mixed and unimportant numerically.   The Socialists who
voted for Debs in 1920 and for La Follette in 1924 were
astonishingly few.   At present the tendency in American
politics seems to be toward the centre rather than the extremes.

The reliable experts were quite wrong, as later events
proved, when on the eve of the 1924 election they doubted
the success of the Republican cause.   The weakness of the
Harding administration, coupled with certain political scandals, was thought to have antagonized the public; but they
underestimated the power of Coolidge as a symbol of stability.   Add to this the lamentable division of the Democrats, the disturbing memories of Wilson's lofty idealism,
the vague taint of revolution among the western Radicals;
and it is easy to see how the overwhelming support of the
organized manufacturing class gave the Republicans an absolute majority.   The two elections of 1920 and 1924 are
not unlike those of 1896 and 1900 which gave victory to
President McKinley, in that they all confirmed the fact that
the country goes Republican whenever it is a question of
stability *vs.* adventure, of a business *vs.* a political administration, or of those who merely ask to be left alone *vs.*
those who are concerned with the theoretical division of
wealth.   The country gave the same sigh of relief when the
failure of La Follette was announced that it did in the case
of Bryan thirty years before.

We must note, however, that the returns of the presidential election do not do justice to the strength of the Democrats throughout the country.   In the South they have many
more electors than is indicated by the votes cast, and also
many of them voted for a Republican who would give them
certain national guarantees.   On the other hand, elections

in which public opinion is more local and articulate have proved that the Democratic party still has remarkable vitality when in contact with the local sources of its influence. In various regions it still seems to be the persistent incarnation of a thoroughly American outlook. This is shown by the present composition of the House of Representatives and the Senate, where the difference between the two parties is much less accentuated than it was in the last presidential election, and suggests that the Democrats could quite easily capture the majority of either house at the next biennial election:

House of Representatives

	1918	1920	1922	1924	1926
Republican	240	300	225	247	236[2]
Democrat	190	132	207	183	196
Farmer-Labor			1	3	2
Socialist		1	1	2	1
Independent	3		1		

Senate

	1918	1920	1922	1924	1926
Republican	49	59	52	55	48[3]
Democrat	47	37	42	40	47
Farmer-Labor			2	1	1

We must further note that in 1924–26, out of 48 States, 24 had Democratic governors. This comprised the whole of the South, most of the Rocky Mountain region, and in the East, Ohio, New York, and New Jersey. Thus, though the Republicans may be much more powerful in national politics, the Democrats, although they are scattered, are far from negligible. They are important as an organized opposition and as expressing the local outlook of whole sec-

[2] Including a few "Insurgents."
[3] Including about eight "Insurgents."

tions of the country, but their internal disputes during the last few years have made them leave the real duty of an opposition to the rebels from the Republican party.

From this survey of the national parties we are bound to admit that political life in the United States is not to be compared with that of the great centralized countries of Western Europe. The existing institutions meet with no opposition, although the State Constitutions are constantly being revised in a very broad way. The administration also is being constantly improved, for the Americans are intent on efficiency; but the Federal Constitution is still, in spite of very slight alterations, the cornerstone on which the public relies. They will tolerate no further meddling with it, especially since the Eighteenth Amendment! As for those political problems which are genuinely debated, there is no real expression of the wishes of the people, for the issues are systematically obscured, either due to the rigidity of the party machines, or on account of the jealous attitude of the various States in defending their individual rights. Just as subterranean channels invisible from the surface may carry away part of the water of a river, so behind the problems which are officially discussed by the politicians lurk other tendencies, which though not openly admitted are probably a more direct and honest expression of the real ambitions of the public.

Two passions animated the American people at the end of the War. The first was sentimental. Whenever such subjects as the Catholic menace, evolution, or prohibition were introduced, eyes would shine and interest was immediately awakened; for these were the issues that aroused the country far more than all the rivalry of the politicians. What a beautiful map we could make showing the Bible belt coinciding with the Dry belt! If Bryan had lived, we might even have outlined a Bryan belt, feverish and turbulent. The second question is the defence of American prosperity against the menace of countries with low wages, and the resentment against foreign invasion in any form whatsoever, from immigration to revolutionary ideas. This resistance against the foreign is almost a *union sacré* with all the fervours and passions of patriotism.

CHAPTER XXIII

ANGLO-AMERICAN RELATIONS

IN the United States more than anywhere else, foreign policy is developed in accordance with the views of different sections of the country. In the thin strip of seaboard between the Alleghanies and the Atlantic which Europeans usually think is the whole of America, the people look to the east and realize that Europe exists. They are even attracted by our civilization, and occasionally go to the length of admiring it. Returning to this coast after a stay in the West or on the Pacific, one seems to breathe a European atmosphere once more. It is almost a stage between the two continents, for after all New York, London, and Paris look out on the same ocean, or one might almost say on the same street.

One discovers the typical American only further west, in that immense and nameless country between the Alleghanies and the Rockies, which lives on itself, and ignoring Europe entirely, thinks only of its own ways, its own moral standards, and its own wealth. It is among the bursting granaries of the Middle West and about the giant factories of the Great Lakes that the economic and moral life of the nation is being concentrated more solidly every year. The Bureau of the Census publishes every ten years a map on which the exact geographic centre of gravity of the American population is marked with a cross. This is of great assistance in explaining the changing attitude toward foreigners, for the cross has been slowly moving west and is now in Indiana, in the heart of the Mississippi Valley. In its own way the Pacific Ocean is also centrifugal and looks to the Far East, that overflowing reservoir of humanity. Here again we find a new atmosphere, make new racial contacts, and attack problems unknown to the rest of the country.

Each of these three regions has its own attitude toward foreign affairs. The first wishes to keep in touch with Europe, but in the second, ideas are confused and suspicion is mingled with instinctive disapproval. Sheltered behind its two mountain ranges and two oceans, it dreams of a separate existence, for to it the outside world is vague and distant. Such extreme provincialism exists nowhere else, not even in France. California, the third zone, is forced to take an interest in the outer world, however; for it always feels uneasily that it must guard the frontier of the white race which passes along its shores. Whenever the Federal government has to decide on the foreign policy of the whole country, there is great rivalry between these three points of view, and either the most powerful or the most directly interested carries the day. To outsiders this sometimes gives the impression that the policy lacks unity.

There is just one country, but one can hardly call it foreign, that can lay claim to a place apart in the foreign relations of the United States. It is not France, alas, in spite of La Fayette, but Great Britain. In France, for some unknown reason, we persist in believing that the Americans and English hate each other and are only waiting for a favourable opportunity to do each other a bad turn. Some of our newspapers repeat this stupid tale to us regularly every morning and assure us that if we will only wait we can slip between these rivals and profit by their quarrels. At the Washington Conference the French delegates acted on this assumption, and look at the result! Now this whole idea is exploded and twenty-five years out of date, for it misconstrues entirely the attitude on the American side of the Atlantic.

Two persons out of every three in the United States will, I admit, run down the English and tell you that they are lazy, antiquated, and deceitful. "Perfidious Albion" still exists, but the speaker is probably an irreconcilable Irishman; and in any case this claptrap talk is largely habit. When you really know the Americans, you discover that this traditional attitude does not express their underlying thoughts. It is now over twenty-five years since they ceased to look upon England as an evil influence.

Up to the end of the nineteenth century, this dislike of the English was classic. It had been inherited from the past. It was taught in the school-books and commented on by college professors. The press excited it, and it was fostered in such circles as the navy. The burning of Washington by the British army in 1814, and the partiality shown by England for the South during the Civil War, were still pretexts of bitterness and rage. If England was at war, the Americans gloated over her troubles with positive glee. If a diplomat wished to succeed, or a politician to flatter a popular audience, the patent method was to twist the lion's tail. American *amour propre* was always enormously pleased.

This hostility is now replaced by a new attitude which overlooks the quarrels of the past, and instead emphasizes the similarity of origin of the two nations. When the flood of Latin-Slav and Jewish immigrants began to overwhelm the eastern States about 1890, the Anglo-Saxon Americans began to appreciate the bonds of language, custom, and religion which linked them to British civilization. In any case this sentiment had always survived vigorously among the New England Puritans, who, though Anglophobe in politics, were thoroughly Anglophile in other ways. Even influential men, who adopted a stern attitude in diplomatic relations with His Majesty's government, did not hesitate to pride themselves on their British origin, and when in London never considered themselves foreigners. The alien and Catholic menaces became important at a time when there was nothing contentious in British policy toward the United States, and therefore it was only natural that the tradition of hostility and disputes should be replaced by a feeling of kinship.

The real bond lies in the fact that they have a common civilization. As is to be expected, this feeling is widespread among the Anglo-Scottish Americans, but curiously enough it is not confined to them. There are many descendants of other races without a trace of English blood who have become so Americanized that they have adopted the British outlook and traditions. Many Americans of Scandinavian, German, or Dutch descent are almost more at home in London than in their own countries of origin. Ever since the dust of old quarrels was laid, England has been regarded with the prestige of an old-fashioned but authentic birthplace.

We might go even further and say that quite apart from racial affiliations, those who have succeeded or wish to succeed believe that without the manners of the original race no one can obtain access to the upper circles of society. Snobbery works for the British, for it is considered good form to despise the "Irish" and the "dagoes." On the other hand every one admires the British King, the Prince of Wales, and the English aristocracy, and British statesmen are received with marked deference. If a real foreigner speaks disparagingly or ironically about the English, he is soon made to feel that he has been as tactless as if he had been criticizing family affairs. If you wish to flatter the American dislike of foreigners, just speak slightingly today of the French, but never of the British!

We have already shown that this chosen race by divine right in America is a matter of long standing, and that by an unwritten law the highest posts are nearly always reserved for those of Anglo-Scottish and Protestant descent. There has never been a Catholic president, and very few who have not been of pure Anglo-Saxon origin. Undoubtedly many foreigners have been elected to the House of Representatives, and with considerably more difficulty to the Senate; but though there are many German names among the important government officials, there are few ending in "ski" or "vitch." If an office carries with it political and social prestige, British origin is, if not an essential, certainly an advantage. Among university presidents, club men, and business executives (though among the latter the Jews are powerful), racial origin must be studied if we are to understand the influences that are guiding American destiny.

This is a sort of secret doctrine, a tradition handed down anonymously, no one knows how or where; and in times of crisis one gets the impression of a powerful but indefinable influence behind the scenes, exerted by a few dozen or a few hundred men not in the public eye. Many of them, indeed, may be quite unknown. They are the benefactors of Protestant churches, philanthropic millionaires, university presidents, leading lawyers and bankers, politicians and society men; but they and the Jewish bankers of Wall Street are listened to in high places. Their influence is not generally political, and in a sense they are not working for an Anglo-American alliance; for many of them even consider themselves anti-British. Nevertheless, by their determination to keep the United States Protestant and Anglo-Saxon, they guarantee for Britain an undisputed and privileged place.

The realization of this hidden influence would come as a shock to the Americans, for officially race privilege is not supposed to exist in their democracy, and yet, paradoxically in this country of equality, the moral authority of certain men and certain circles is largely an affair of education and breeding. The Hays, the Roots, the Lodges, the Hugheses, and many other Americans of British intellectual stamp, have done more to guide the policy of their country than all the Bryans and Al Smiths. I cannot say whether this will last. It will certainly end if the non-Anglo-Saxon element imposes a new civilization on the country, but so long as the theory of Protestant and Nordic superiority persists, the Italian and Slav and the unassimilated Irish will be considered second-class citizens, and the British point of view will never be entirely foreign.

Political relationships are influenced by this racial affinity, and though the English and Americans may often act like enemies, they are always brotherly enemies. These two nations can never be absolutely friendly, nor yet absolutely antagonistic. A formal alliance is out of the question so long as the Irish are in politics, but the thought of war is considered sacrilege by both sides. France can arouse great enthusiasm at times in the United States, England never; but the English position is really much stronger, for in spite of the lack of demonstrativeness, it is based on the solid foundation of family relationship.

We must now examine British sentiment toward America, which seems to be instinctive antipathy since the War, although counterbalanced by a clear understanding of the necessity for collaboration. Taken individually, the English look upon the Americans as badly brought-up children; yet in any important negotiations their statesmen seem to have made up their minds to agree to all American demands without protest. Repeated concessions, followed by recuperation through the masterly play of their trump card, have been more or less the history of the last thirty years.

As soon as there is a third party to the deal, every one is cordial again; and whenever they sit side by side in international conferences, their fundamental resemblance inevitably brings them together. One can feel a spontaneous sympathy between them in the way they attack problems, in their instinctive reactions, and in the emphasis they place on certain things. They automatically oppose the other delegations, whether they are German, French, Latin, or Slav. It is doubtless partly due to the skill of the British diplomats, but also because they speak the same language, talk together, and live in the same clubs and hotels. Apart from the personality of Lloyd George, this similarity was very noticeable during the Peace Conference, and was even more striking at the Washington Conference; for Lord Balfour seemed to be perfectly at home, while the French delegation stayed isolated in their hotel, met no one, and were not understood. This clannishness which appears automatically in international circles is partly due to the fact that the Americans are ill at ease when away from home. They feel the need of interpreters, and the English, who have been everywhere for years, can be of great service as guides, intermediaries, and brokers. Outside of Europe, the Americans find the countries under British rule the most congenial, and so without attempting to combat British commerce they accommodate themselves to its standards, honour, credit, and order. Their common civilization is really at the bottom of their co-operation all over the world. The United States saw this when it first became a world power after the Spanish-American war, and although the two countries might have indulged in bitter rivalry, they came on the contrary to a closer understanding.

Even in Europe, where the situation is very different, they need an interpreter badly, for even with the direct relationships that have grown up between the United States and the Continent, scores of European things reach the New World only through the medium of England. There is no denying it, the Americans are never entirely at ease with Continental peoples. They always have a vague fear of deception and cunning; so they turn to the easy method of adopting the British point of view, though no one has ever tried to force it on them. They absorb it through the cables of the British news agencies, through the editorials in the London press, and through conversations in the London clubs. Their informant may still be "perfidious Albion," but he is a Protestant advisor, and they trust him far sooner than a "Machiavellian Italian" or a "cynical Frenchman." We are therefore safe in saying that in many matters the Americans follow the trail blazed by the government in London. If the English support or oppose a country the Americans are sure to turn in the same direction after a time. France has had this experience more than once—to her advantage after the Entente Cordiale, and to her disadvantage during the reparations controversy.

This influence is very subtle, for England certainly has not taken America in tow. When England wishes to use this broad *entente* to gain a point on some matter that particularly concerns her, America is apt to leave her in the lurch without compunction. Ever since the War, Great Britain has associated herself with the United States in a policy in extra-European affairs based on the community of their interests as members of the white race, and in this she has been assisted by the Dominions. England would have liked to carry this collaboration a step further and work with America in a common Continental policy. She had hoped, by bringing the League of Nations under the control of the two Anglo-Saxon powers, to supervise the European nations and prevent any one of them from outstripping the others. The Washington government, however, was not ready to go so far, for it had refused all solidarity with the Old World. The British Empire was interesting only as a non-European power, a useful world force which America is careful not to injure. However, if they collaborate too intimately in defence of racial interests which exceed the limit of Britain's power, it may be that the United States will in the long run endanger the unity of the British Empire.

CHAPTER XXIV

FRANCO-AMERICAN RELATIONS

FRANCE has a place of her own in the sentiments of the American people, for no country is more passionately loved at times, and none more severely judged and belittled. The Americans always go to extremes, first in one direction and then in the other, so that their relations with France are always based on illusion. With England, on the other hand, there is no sentiment, but a deep sense of family security.

The roots of the Franco-American friendship go far back into the past, to La Fayette and his romantic gesture, which the Americans with pious gratitude remember to this day. French intervention in the War of Independence, however, was not entirely due to the love of liberty, but also to spite against the English, who in the eighteenth century were the common enemies of the French and the rebels of the thirteen colonies. The English have now forgotten their old quarrel; so hostility to Britain is no longer a bond, and the political alliance based on the illustrious names of La Fayette and Rochambeau is rather antiquated. The praise of these heroes may still be a fit subject for oratory, and indeed it goes down well in after-dinner speeches; but French negotiators have discovered on several occasions that they were on a completely wrong track when they used it as a serious argument.

A second affinity between the two democracies is that both were originally inspired by the same school of political idealism. The formulas are not identical, but both pay the same lip-service to liberty, equality, and the will of the people. The vocabulary and principles of the eighteenth century are even more out of date in America than they are in France, but in America they are still used with telling effect at political conventions, banquets, and other formal ceremonies, although the modern collective organization of commerce requires very different rules.

When Americans come to France and see us persisting in our individualism and preferring liberty to discipline, they are almost shocked; for they are really more at home in countries like Switzerland and Germany, where rules are rigidly enforced. They do not say so, but they cannot altogether conceal their feelings. What many of them like about France is its freedom and easy-going atmosphere, its indulgent regard for leisure and the poetry of the past which still survives in the present. But they keep France for holidays, to be looked back on as a pleasant respite in their lives of material activity. When with their charming simplicity these friends of France praise her, they seldom touch on what she herself considers the essence of her civilization. Those who understand and love the soul of France are rare exceptions. They are generally people who have been wounded in their own country by principles and methods to which their temperaments are not suited, and who prefer to live in exile in France, where they are thoroughly at home. In Paris we have many of these uprooted spirits, who are more French than the natives and would realize themselves exiles if ever they were to return to their own country. But they are not representative of America, and we have made many mistakes on this score in the past.

The causes of the antipathy between the two peoples are unfortunately more obvious. We often ask ourselves what an ordinary American, especially one from the West, can find to love in France—the real France, not the round of pleasures that Paris offers him. Values are so different; the Cartesian philosophy, which has left its impression on

ten generations of Frenchmen, is so opposed to Bostonian
Puritanism and the sentimentality of Wesley. French
morals, based on family traditions and a sense of proportion,
find no echo in the Protestant preachings, which define
virtues and vices very differently. Most Americans, therefore, even those most friendly to the French, are quite
sincere when they consider them immoral. When the American forces left for France in 1917, many families trembled
for the purity of their "good, clean boys," and they have
ever since accused the French of teaching them the meaning
of "wine, woman, and song." The realism of French
thought, which is not content with mere words in its judgment, is not a desirable form of intelligence to them, but
almost shocking in its cynicism. "Cynical Frenchman" is a
phrase which keeps recurring as a sort of reflex. Like the
English, they are thoroughly realistic in their actions, but
they do not think it is good form to acknowledge it.

This contrast of ideas is even more marked when it comes
to methods of work. The Frenchman is superior only when
he can work by himself, free from strict discipline and organized co-operation. Therefore he is out of date to the
American, who considers that the French system leads nowhere and that it merits his indifference and disdain.
Whether it is a case of factories, banks, or offices, his opinion
is always the same. When he considers French education it
is easy to see that though he may admire it, he does not like
our methods, which appeal primarily to individual initiative.
In this they are more closely allied to Germany, and though
they occasionally do appreciate the French university and
the work it turns out, it requires considerable effort for them
to accommodate themselves to it personally. From the very
beginning, Franco-American friendships must overcome this
feeling of instinctive disapproval, even where the best will
in the world exists.

Viewed from this angle, the geographic distribution in

the United States of friends and adversaries of France is clear enough. She has countless supporters in the eastern States and the great cities of the West and South. In no other country is found such admiration or affection for France, expressed with such devotion, sincerity, and even enthusiasm, and with such delicacy and charm. It is a disinterested friendship, the attraction of cultivated minds without ulterior motives.

Unfortunately this friendship is far from being a popular movement, for the well-wishers of France are individuals, and her antagonists are collective. It is only too evident that the Anglo-Saxon civilization as expressed in institutions, groups, and doctrines, is not akin to the French. A Methodist or a Baptist minister instinctively condemns French morality, the merchant is irritated by French business methods, while the tourist takes away a superficial impression of slow elevators and telephones out of order. Although the British army became sincerely Francophile during the War and seems to have remained so, it is disquieting to note that the American soldiers took back doubtful and even, at times, bitter impressions of France, and that their home-coming in the spring of 1919 coincided with a premature reawakening of hostile feeling. The truth is that the Americans and the French have great difficulty in understanding one another; they are so totally different. France's best points escape the hasty observations of the passing tourist, for the refinements of her civilization do not lie in telephones or trains, and so escape the notice of simple folk who are over-anxious about creature comforts. Personally I do not agree with those who believe that we need only show France to the Americans for them to fall in love with it.

To this lack of understanding, which is quite as important as the ill will, we must add the hostility of the foreigners in the United States. We have referred to the German influence, and it is considerable, especially in the West and the Middle West, where they are so interwoven in the fabric of the population that it is often difficult to distinguish them. The British propaganda may be even more effective without appearing so, for it is not regarded as foreign. Without apparently touching the French, they have done them an enormous amount of harm at times in America; nor are the Italians, Irish, or even the French Canadians always ready to serve the French cause. For religious reasons, as when France was condemned by Rome, or else through political jealousy, it often happens that their influence favours her adversaries, until there seems to be a concentration of ill will with France as the target, and against which she can rely on only a few scattered individuals for assistance. Editorials in the leading newspapers, news items from France, French characters in novels and plays, allusions to the country in sermons and political speeches, all show a distinctly hostile attitude during these periods. It would be childish to attribute it all to the organized propaganda of enemies, for it undoubtedly reflects the spontaneous feelings of the people.

These estrangements come in waves which increase to a maximum and then die down, to recur later after an intermediate phase of neutrality, favour, or even enthusiasm. The painful atmosphere which has existed ever since the War is nothing new. At the time of the Dreyfus Case France went through a similar castigation, and as the vicissitudes of the notorious trial happened to coincide with the wreck of the *Bourgogne,* it became the pretext for an inexplicable and uncontrolled outburst of rage. About 1904 the Entente Cordiale caused, or possibly coincided with, a reawakening of sympathy in both America and Great Britain. During the War this sympathy increased to enthusiasm—enthusiasm, in fact, scarcely expresses the passion of the Americans for France and her cause. This admiration, which even the French found excessive, did not last long, but it is a good illustration of the way in which Franco-American relations are always extreme and insecure. It is difficult to construct a solid policy on such a basis. Still, with alternate good days and bad, we can always hope for better times in the future.

One thing at least is certain, and that is that America fought Germany alongside France, and for France, according to many of her soldiers; for this was the sentiment that carried millions of men across the Atlantic. All the same, there were other reasons that in 1917 brought the American nation into the War, although three years before, and even six months before, she would not hear of it. Unless we solve this enigma, we cannot hope to fathom Franco-American relations, nor yet Anglo-American relations.

If you ask an American why they came into the War, he will almost invariably reply that it was through a sense of duty. The cause of the Allies was just, and the Americans realized it and came to their aid without a trace of self-interest. They felt they were setting out on a crusade. This explanation is sound enough as far as individuals are concerned, and France should not forget that in so far as pure sentiment had any part in the affair, the sentiment was for her and not for Great Britain.

One of the direct causes of American intervention is really superficial, as it was the result of circumstances. The government at Washington was exasperated in the extreme by the repeated provocations of Germany on the sea, just as they were with the British in 1812. They finally refused to tolerate it any longer, for after having protested again and again that they would intervene, they had to carry out their threat in the end in order to save their face. There are certain infringements on the freedom of the high seas that the United States is as unwilling to accept in the twentieth century as she was in the nineteenth.

Still, at decisive moments nations do not act without profound political reasons; and in this case it was neither for France nor for Belgium that America went to war, but for her community of interests with Great Britain. To be more explicit, they wished to maintain throughout the world the superior position of their common Anglo-Saxon civilization. To have allowed the power of Germany, which is based on very different principles and methods, to extend beyond Europe would have meant the breaking up of an international economic system which the United States considers essential, and even worth going to war to defend.

This explanation is in keeping with the American economic interests that we have endeavoured to outline in the second part of this book. It in no way diminishes the merit of their disinterested emotions, but it does account for their post-war attitude. When the matador has driven his sword up to the hilt in the bull he goes off, for his object is attained. In the same way, once Germany had been vigorously checked, the world program in defence of Anglo-Saxon civilization was realized, and from that moment America lost interest in Europe, which since then has only provided opportunities for financial and philanthropic intervention, and as such returned to its real place, which is only secondary in American preoccupations. Since the Armistice the only important collaboration of the United States with a European power has been with Great Britain, when at the Washington Conference they shared with the British Empire the defence of the white race in the Pacific, and later aided "the City" in restoring the pound sterling to its place as an international currency—the associate, but not the rival of the dollar.

As far as Europe is concerned, the United States has to all intents and purposes resigned, and is now taking special care not to let Europe become too intimate. In their attitude toward the War they deny anything that could legitimately lead to solidarity.   When they were asked to sign the Covenant of the League of Nations, the American people recoiled, panic-stricken.   When the question of settling inter-Allied debts was discussed, any mention of the great things accomplished in common on the field of battle was coldly put to one side, as if they were eliminating useless documents in settling up their accounts.

How many times have I heard the following conversation, always the same:

"But after all, we were allies?"

"Excuse me, we were not allies; we were simply associates."

"At any rate we fought together for a common cause."

"No, the American people never made common cause with the Allies.   They came to their aid because they thought their cause was just, and it is their duty now to make certain that the Allies use the victory in accordance with justice."

After the Armistice the French made the mistake of thinking they could bring into practical discussion the comradeship which the Americans had felt for a while.   They thought that they were dealing with allies, but they found judges instead, judges who were determined to bestow their impartiality on conquerors and conquered alike.   Earlier in this book we questioned whether a solid commercial or financial relationship could exist without reciprocity.   From the moment that the Americans refused to admit that they benefited from the military efforts of the Allies, and especially of the French, they denied the moral equality between the brothers-in-arms.   This has vitiated all Franco-American political relationships.

CHAPTER XXV

AMERICA AND THE YELLOW RACES

UNLIKE Europe, the Pacific is of direct interest to the United States. In the Far West the Chinese and Japanese have stuck like leeches and focused the attention of the whole country on themselves. They are like the flotsam left by a dangerous tide which had to be kept out at all costs. The question is far more important than mere politics, for it involves the rivalry of two of the most powerful branches of the human race. It is much more serious than Europe imagines, for she merges imperceptibly into Asia, in contrast to America, whose Pacific coast is a world frontier. Looking westward over the limitless blue ocean from the heights of Cliff House, San Francisco, the impression is inspiring! A gulf opens out before us, and we feel that we are on the very brink of the white man's territory, which must be shared or defended. Such are the feelings of the Californians, feelings which we of the Old World, absorbed in our own quarrels, are making no attempt to appreciate. We should try to understand, however; for if we think only of nationalities, we shall be left behind by those who think in terms of the entire white race.

The rest of America considers the yellow race question as an exclusively Californian affair, although in reality it is international when compared with the purely domestic negro deadlock in the South. If unrestricted immigration from Asia had been allowed, the American shores of the Pacific could hardly have remained a white man's country. The governing class would have been western, but the lower grades—labourers, farmers, and shopkeepers—would have

been captured by the East.   Such a composite social structure would have been beyond the pale of western civilization.
If ever the Far East becomes so powerful that she can
force the United States to allow her emigrants to enter
freely, then the invasion which was first encouraged and
later checked will probably recommence.   The relationship
between the races is extremely delicate in this part of the
world, for the present solution is as local and one-sided as it
is in Australia, and therefore neither international nor
stable.   So the Californians are uneasy, for they have the
uncomfortable feeling that they may only have postponed
the final settlement of the problem.

From the very beginning it has been a question of
economic jealousy in daily life.   In the opening up of new
territory the Asiatic workmen proved invaluable, and in
many trades were preferred to Europeans and especially to
the American-born.   The American may be more skilled,
but he is more expensive and harder to manage.   For heavy
labour the Chinese coolie is unsurpassed.   He is the human
ox *par excellence;* also, with him the human side of the bargain can be neglected and his work contracted for like so
much merchandise, in large or small quantities.   Naturally,
therefore, he was sought after by the employers.

This was the beginning, and perhaps it is the keynote
of the "Yellow Peril."   Whether it is a case of the farm,
the mine, or even the factory, unless he is protected by
arbitrary legislation, the American workman is always forced
out by the overwhelming advantages of his competitor.

It is not that the Asiatic has any greater technical skill,
but simply that he is ready to accept a wage which would
not keep a white man alive.   His standard of living allows
him to work, if not for the bottom price, at any rate for a
very low one.   He manages to survive and even to prosper
under the most mediocre living-conditions, for he can endure exceedingly long hours of work and bad lodging.   As

Lafcadio Hearn tragically expresses it, "Asia can under-live Europe."

The white workman fights an unequal battle, because he moves on a different plane. He is better equipped for manufacturing, but only when conditions are such that his normal output can be obtained. He may have benefited by his years of progress, but they have made him a prisoner to healthy living-conditions, good food, comforts, and recreation, all of which are superfluous to his rival. After all, this is what we call civilization; and to defend it he requires a salary so high that even the minimum is prohibitive. If he does not receive it, his social status inevitably declines, which means that the high level of civilization in America is threatened by the co-existence in the same market of labour of different races. Whenever the market is unrestricted, it is the poorest who survive; for they are the most adaptable. The lower classes then change in character, and whole professions are wrested away from the superior race, until a time arrives when the latter finds that it is living in its own country like an army of occupation among foreigners.

This would be inevitable in California if the whites were not protected. Certain trades did, of course, benefit by the yellow race. The planters were richer possibly and certain unprofitable occupations might never have developed at all. The fact remains, however, that the future of the white race in this part of the world was compromised. As we have shown in another chapter, this danger, although it was foreseen, did not arise in the case of immigrants from Eastern Europe, because they could be assimilated, but if assimilation had been impossible, as in the case of the yellow races, a caste system would soon have developed. Once the healthy current of assimilation fails to circulate from the lowest to the highest classes, both the unity and the moral strength of society is jeopardized. A new class of political problems soon appears, for when there is no unity of race, equality before the law becomes difficult, and the dream of a democratic community has to be abandoned. A distinction must be made between citizens and serfs. As we have seen in the South, the mentality of the whites becomes aristocratic and exclusive, whereas the unassimilated population, especially if it is from a civilized country, is likely to form a disturbing if not a dangerous element, almost like a foreign body in an organism. A class of "Uitlanders," as they used to call them in the Transvaal, is created; and if they are given political rights, they can undermine the unity of the whole nation.

It is in reality the physical integrity of the race which might be compromised by too intimate contact with the East. With the example of the southern States so close at hand, they are forced to reflect that once they allow the seeds of the yellow races to be implanted, they will not be able to control their growth in the future. A sort of race religion has been created on the Pacific Coast, much as in Australia, where the white man's country is defended as sacred. All Anglo-Saxon communities, especially those outside of Europe, seem to be imbued with this doctrine; but in California it amounts to a passion. The power to determine their own political and social structure means nothing if they cannot control the selection of the humanity of which they are to be composed. This defence of the race is carried to such extremes that it is no longer a question of self-interest, but of emotions that may inspire a most dangerous type of demagogy.

During the last three-quarters of a century two waves of yellow immigration have threatened the coast of America west of the Rockies, and both have been checked by the only practical method; namely, by erecting an impenetrable dike. As long as this dike is intact, serious danger is averted; but we must not lose sight of the fact that the balance it maintains between the races is only political and therefore artificial.

Just as the discovery of gold originally brought the Chinese to Australia, so it was the gold rush that attracted the first Asiatics to California, about 1850. By 1852 there were 25,000, by 1860 35,000, and by 1890 they had reached their maximum of 107,000. They were peaceable, willing, and easy to get on with; so at first they were received with favour in this new, empty country that was being so rapidly developed. The pioneers were pleased to have them, but ten years had not elapsed before they were jealous of them. The Chinese were accused of lowering wages, of having different customs, and above all, different vices; but the decisive argument against them was that they were unsuitable for assimilation. A policy was originated which is still continued. By the treaties of 1868 and 1880, the government reserved the right of limiting immigration from the Far East; and after 1870 they were denied naturalization. The law of 1882, which has been renewed every ten years since, absolutely forbids the entry of Chinese coolies. After 1890 the effects of this policy began to be felt, and the 107,000 Chinese inhabitants fell away to 90,000 by 1900 and to 62,000 by 1920. The desired object had been attained, and in the light of seventy-five years' experience, we can now pass judgment on the method adopted.

Once we agree that fusion between the white and yellow races must not take place, we must also admit that the formation of a heterogeneous racial block is bound to be dangerous. If the Chinese had been allowed in without restrictions, a second coloured problem would have arisen. The danger seems less apparent as physical aversion is possibly not so intense, but it would really have been more serious, because the Chinese is so much more civilized than the negro, his competition is keener, and the source of his immigration is almost inexhaustible. Now that the danger has disappeared, at any rate for the present, we can study the attitude of the American and analyze his hostility into economic fear and mere aversion.

Now that he is no longer considered a peril or even a menace, the Chinaman has become quite popular. This seems extraordinary, but it is a fact. The frightful vices of which he was accused are now forgotten, and his virtues are lauded as well as his peaceful disposition. The guides who take you through Chinatown in San Francisco are very well disposed toward the Chinese; in fact, Thomas Cook and Sons and other tourist agencies would prefer to import Chinese rather than let their American colony disappear. And it is not only in the capital of California that we note this good will. In international politics the American government has made itself the champion of Chinese independence as opposed to the ambitions of Japan and other powers. The missionaries too look with approbation on this immense nation, which they hope to win over to the Protestant faith and American civilization. Events show that the Chinese are acceptable in small numbers, even though they cannot be assimilated. As a matter of fact they assimilate much more than is realized, for their wages soon rise to the general level; they adopt American customs and no longer wish to live as they did in China. Chinatown will not be a curiosity much longer.

The Japanese situation has not progressed to the same point, but it arouses much more bitterness. In 1890 there were only 2,039 Japanese in the United States, but when the number of Chinese was beginning to decline, the Nipponese were called in to replace them. After the annexation of Hawaii in 1898, many Japanese in these islands migrated to California; and their colony, which numbered only 24,000 in 1900, rose to 111,000 by 1920. Of this number, 93,000 were on the Pacific Coast and 72,000 in California alone.

In California the Japanese began by being coolies, but

they very quickly passed to the stage of skilled workers, shopkeepers, market gardeners, and small landowners. They are excellent settlers, and if they were not prevented, they could probably capture and fill up the whole country quite easily in a few decades. By 1904 this possibility began to alarm the Californians, who agitated for the laws excluding the Chinese to be extended to the Japanese as well. In 1906 the California Board of Education ordered the Japanese to send their children to schools specially reserved for the yellow races.

This movement was very similar to the anti-Chinese agitation, but it had a political aspect which did not exist in the case of China. By 1905 the Japanese had beaten Russia and had become a first-class power in the Far East. At first the Americans were sympathetic, but public opinion suddenly turned against them. From being a progressive people struggling against reactionary Russia, the Japanese were now considered as suspicious immigrants aided by an ambitious government. The problem thus entered a new phase, into which the Chinese controversy had never penetrated. The Japanese are both susceptible and proud, and in particular they resent being classed with other Asiatics, a point which the Americans never seem to comprehend. The Federal government views the matter from the political angle and realizes this aspect of the difficulty, but the Californians, who are directly interested, think of them only as Easterners who must be excluded. The ticklish point is that domestic politics are always reacting on foreign policy.

By 1924 two-thirds of the Japanese in California had gone on to the land, and the remainder consisted of shopkeepers, domestic servants, and professional men. It was therefore on the farms, especially in certain areas where they had concentrated, that their presence was considered a menace. By 1919 no less than 458,000 of the 3,893,000 acres of arable land were in their possession. In certain counties, such as San Joaquin, Colusa, Placer, and Sacramento, they owned more than half the land and monopolized certain crops. For example, they cultivated 89 per cent. of the celery, 83 per cent. of the asparagus, 79 per cent. of the seeds, 76 per cent. of the onions, 66 per cent. of the tomatoes, 64 per cent. of the cantaloups, and 50 per cent. of the beetroots. Their methods of invasion are well known: first of all, they eliminate the white agricultural workers by accepting extremely low wages; then, when they are the only farm labourers left, they gradually increase their demands. Finally they disarm their employer by means of a strike, and replace him by buying or renting his farm. The day comes when the whites in a county perceive that they are no longer in the majority. The Japanese have sprung up everywhere, and their homes are swarming with babies. The very atmosphere is changed.

An American farmer isolated in the middle of this foreign population finds competition very difficult if not impossible, for with all the machines in the world, his output still depends on the intensity of his efforts, and this is not the same for both sides. The following description written by a witness is positively terrifying: [1]

"The American who feels the 'Yellow Peril' acutely is the independent small farmer—the man with one or two hundred acres off which he seeks to get a living, and a small competence for himself and his children. He has, let us say, been growing berries or sugar beets or grapes or vegetables on his place for many years, all of which he has been selling in competition with other Americans whose standards of work and living have been the same as his own, or nearly so. His farming neighbours work ten or twelve hours a day at the most. They send their boys and girls to school for the greater part of the year (and please remember that here in California the greater part of the year is work-time on the farm, thanks to the unusual climate). Their wives work around the house, and per-

[1] *Must We Fight Japan?* by W. B. Pitkin, pages 205 and 206.

haps tend a few chickens, but rarely toil in the fields save when there is a shortage of help at harvest time. And the whole family takes Sunday off whenever it can.

"Into a community of such people there comes a keen and thrifty Japanese. For a year or two he may work around as a farm hand, partly for the sake of making money, but chiefly in order to discover the quality and promise of the soil in the district. Finally he rents a piece of the ground and then appear wife and children, and often too a small army of friends, all of his same race. All of these fall to, working at a pace that bewilders and horrifies the Americans thereabouts. Fourteen, sixteen, and even eighteen hours a day in the fields are the schedules frequently observed in Japanese communities. And the Japanese are not visibly injured by it. They seem to be a stock that has been selected through centuries of stern competition for their ability to stand such a strain."

These few lines graphically describe the "Yellow Peril." This is not ordinary competition, for it is impossible for the white man to follow his rival on to the ground which the latter has chosen. Even suppose his physique would stand it, he could do so only by renouncing his level of civilization. Wherever there is any question of this rivalry, be it in California, Australia, or Polynesia, it is always the same, always an economic competition which finally substitutes one race for the other. If the white race is not protected, it will be eclipsed. A whole series of laws in California have attempted to defend it. A law in 1913 and another in 1920 (the latter the result of popular initiative) forbade the Japanese to own land. Nevertheless, they were able to establish themselves by means of various subterfuges. Also, in imitation of the miscegenation laws of the South, marriage with persons of "Mongol origin" was declared illegal, not only in California, but in most of the States of the Far West.[2] The American courts then refused nat-

[2] California, Utah, Nevada, Montana, Arizona, and Oregon.

uralization to the Japanese. By all these measures it was hoped that they could be kept beyond the pale of society. They could live in the United States, prosper there, and enjoy themselves; but they would be reduced to the status of a lower caste and legally forbidden to mingle with the higher, although in actual practice they were quite capable of doing so.

When these local remedies proved insufficient, evidently the only method was to dam the inundation at its source. California has always wanted a law against the Japanese, analagous to that which excludes the Chinese. On account of the susceptibilities of the Japanese, the American government negotiated in 1907 the Gentleman's Agreement, by which Japan would retain the right of issuing passports to its nationals for the United States, but would undertake not to use this to let in coolies, labourers, and other manual workers. Immigration was thus limited to those whose economic competition was less dangerous. In so far as the whole country is taking up the idea of a closed America with her racial integrity jealously protected, just so far will the efforts of the Californian radicals overcome the prudence of the Federal government. We can follow the transformation through its various stages. The law of 1917 introduced the principle of exclusion of certain Asiatics, and later, at the Peace Conference, the Americans refused to indorse the Japanese proposal of abolishing all distinctions based on race or nationality. Finally, by the immigration law of 1924, they gave up all attempt at conciliation and completely forbade immigration from Asia, including Japan, by keeping out races that were not allowed to be naturalized.

The Washington government was anxious to tone down this measure, and would have preferred the system of quotas, which would have admitted only 146 Japanese per year. But California wanted it and would be satisfied only with the assurance that there should be no immigration whatso-

ever of races that could not be assimilated. The doctrine is
perfectly clear, and as has been pointed out to all the Asiatic
nations, it is not a question of diplomacy but of sovereignty;
and the matter is settled not by treaties but by legislation.

This has been understood by the common-sense Japanese, who have even seen the reason for their exclusion;
but what their pride cannot pardon is that they have been
classed with the other Asiatics in a common interdiction.
The Chinese, with their thirty centuries of civilization, have
no need of western consideration. In their lofty detachment they despise both our praise and our blame. Japan,
on the other hand, has come forward only recently, and
therefore wishes special diplomatic recognition. This is a
question of status, and the Americans by overlooking this
have humiliated and wounded them quite unnecessarily.

Now, however, the door is shut, and the Japanese problem in the United States will go through the same stages
that the Chinese did before it. The nervous whites are
haunted by the presence of 100,000 Asiatics whose birth
rate far exceeds their own, but they forget that the atmosphere of the United States is fatal to large families. Also,
the Japanese colony is rapidly adopting American costume,
language, and customs. Their American-born children become citizens, although they can never be assimilated. The
peril now seems to be overcome, and as they can no longer
come in great numbers, the bitterness against them has begun
to die down. They are not loved, but the problem has lost
its sting.

It is interesting to note how these problems of domestic
politics, insignificant in themselves possibly, are able to
agitate the foreign policy of the whole white race. From
this point of view, California is the vanguard; and through
her, America is involved in questions which are the very
antithesis of those perplexing Europe, and which we must

admit are in spite of their local character, very serious. All
that America has been able to do on the Pacific Coast—not
even Australia has done more—is to trace out a frontier,
arm it, and defend it. As we shall see in the next chapter,
the political consequences of this are many and complex.

CHAPTER XXVI

THE UNITED STATES, THE DOMINIONS AND THE PACIFIC

THE contacts which we have outlined in the two previous chapters are less between nations than between civilizations, or between different levels of humanity which are out of adjustment. The problems are racial and social rather than political, and our standard method of looking at them from a diplomatic or military angle has proved both restrictive and misleading.

The Americans are accustomed to a high standard of living which prevents large families, makes production expensive, and destroys the relationship between their wage level and that of other countries. They are able to maintain their advantages because of the immensity of their territory, because they are shielded from both armed and peaceful invasions, and because the density of their population is still very low. Facing them on the opposite shore of the Pacific, Asia tends more and more to the other extreme, with a heavy birth rate, a modest standard of living, and also a degree of civilization that is quite advanced. Rich and unoccupied territories like California have a fatal attraction for the yellow race, and even though their western frontier may be closed, one feels that they lie below the level of human sea which threatens to break through and submerge them. This, then, is the burning question of the Pacific, the "Yellow Peril," and America is possibly the most seriously menaced.

It is not only in California, Oregon, and Washington that we feel this human pressure, but in all the vast territories on the shores of the Pacific which have been settled by small white populations. With no attempt at concerted action, all these countries have reacted spontaneously in exactly the same way; for they have surrounded themselves with barriers to keep out immigration from the East. British Columbia could not rest until it had obtained from the central Canadian government the right to close its gates, and for many years Australia and New Zealand have arbitrarily excluded all Asiatics by drastic legislation. If the present *status* can be maintained in these Anglo-Saxon countries, their destiny as part of the white civilization can be considered as settled. It is the same evolution as in California.

Once, however, we leave the massive continents of Australia and America and turn to the various islands in the Pacific, we find that the white race has lost its advantage. It has political but not racial control, for not merely has it failed to populate any of the islands, but it has been unable to defend the native population against the invasion of the yellow race.

In 1850 Hawaii had 67,000 Polynesians out of a total population of 70,000, but by 1924 they amounted to only 21,000 out of 307,000. Alongside of them had sprung up 21,000 half-breeds, 125,000 Japanese, 25,000 Chinese, 40,-000 Philippinos, 27,000 Portuguese, and 34,000 Americans, the latter including 15,000 soldiers and sailors. What had happened was exactly what California had always feared. Once the yellow race had been introduced, it was impossible to control it. The majority are now Asiatic, and it is too late to exclude them; for the original inhabitants are not sufficiently numerous to form more than a precarious screen against their dangerous neighbours.

With this experience before them, the countries situated in temperate climes and away from the Far East, if they have been colonized by immigration, have managed to exclude the Asiatics and keep themselves racially uniform. On the other hand, the plantation colonies in tropical climates, with sparse native populations, have not been able to keep the yellow race in check. Once they are admitted, they swarm, owing to their prolific birth rate, and prosper by their genius for work.

From this we see that these countries must be defended even before the enemy has been admitted. In the Pacific the separation of the two races is indicated by the zones in which all penetration by the yellow race has been forbidden. The racial frontier which protects California, Australia, and British Columbia depends entirely on immigration laws that require sovereignty on the part of each country in order to be carried out. They are not applicable except in so far as those who pass them are in a position to apply them. In the last analysis it is a question of force, diplomatic force if there is sufficient prestige, or military force if necessary.

One of the most significant movements in the past twenty years in this part of the world is the common policy that has been evolved by all the Anglo-Saxon countries on the Pacific. They have seen that their interests harmonized, and that the most vital program for all of them is the defence of their common front against the yellow races. The method which they all follow closely consists of exclusion within their own territories, and a policy of keeping the yellow races far enough away by forming a buffer zone consisting of a series of military bases and intermediary races. This is the Australian policy, and it is shared by California. The racial point of view, which means the protection of their standard of living, is so clear in each case that little by little it dominates the political point of view as well. Possibly no Australian or Californian would admit that this is really more important than the Union Jack or the Stars and Stripes, but in his heart of hearts he knows it. It is this which makes the doctrine of a white Australian so important and carries its influence far beyond its borders.

"White Australia," declares a writer of the Antipodes,[1] "is not a political conception. It is a gospel. It counts more than religion, or even than the flag, for the flag floats over British citizens of all colors. It is more important than the Empire, because the majority of the people in the Empire are black, brown, or yellow; pagan, polygamous, and even cannibal. The doctrine of a white Australia is based on the necessity of choosing between existence and suicide." Though this quotation may appear extreme and hysterical, yet any one who has lived in Australia will admit that it expresses the latent sentiments and obsessions which thrive in this atmosphere of vague, persistent fear. "When danger threatens the race and the civilization that the flag symbolizes, political ideas are apt to become crippled and distorted, and one then realizes that there exist things even more important than the political structure of the nation, or the fatherland itself." This statement may be sacrilege, and no doubt would be contradicted in both Australia and Canada; yet a change is taking place obscurely in the loyalties of both Dominions.

These remarks apply only to the Anglo-Saxon countries bordering on the Pacific, which owe their keen sense of racial values to their British origin. They take these matters very seriously, for they consider intermarriage not merely undesirable but positively scandalous. Once we leave the English-speaking countries, this point of view changes; for neither in Mexico nor in South America is there the same exclusiveness. Here the Asiatics are welcomed and even sought. These races are not concerned with their own precise boundaries, and, in any case, one can hardly say that they are incontestably in the domain of the white race. It is quite a question whether in the event of a dispute with Japan, the Latin-Americans would side with the United States. This feeling of racial solidarity between the nations

[1] *Japanese Expansion and American Politics,* by J. F. Abbott.

of the Pacific is strictly limited to the United States and the British Dominions, all of which are passing through a similar economic evolution. It is, therefore, only logical that they should rely on each other. Not that political sentiments are at all likely to draw them together, for in fact before they come closer they must overcome various obstacles. Neither the Australians nor the New Zealanders have any traditional friendship for the Americans, but, on the contrary, are as jealous as poor relations, and are excessively loyal and British in their customs. Yet the more this small colony of 6,000,000 whites, isolated at the other end of the world, realize their terrifying situation, confronted by the "Yellow Peril," the more they respect the might of America. To a lesser extent a similar psychological reaction is taking place in British Columbia and possibly throughout the whole of Canada.

If we may be permitted to state what no one else will say but which many think, or at least feel subconsciously, this is the attitude that is evolving. The British Dominions on the Pacific in general rely on their mother country to defend them eventually against an Asiatic aggressor, but here we have a delicate and unprecedented difference. They feel that their security depends also on another condition, on the collaboration of the entire white race in this zone to defend western civilization. This is why the Australians and the Canadians, the latter for other reasons as well, are so intent on keeping on good terms with the United States and will not hear of any solution on the Pacific that is not agreed to by America. When Mr. Hughes was premier of Australia he summed up the whole policy in a sentence when he said that he saluted with joy the launching of every new American battleship.

This means that Australia needs a permanent protector, and that she looks upon America as an alternative. Canada in her turn knows that she can depend on America, who will never tolerate the slightest attack on either her territorial integrity or her racial status.   In actual practice, therefore, Canada has a complete guarantee without counting on England at all.   When certain Canadian statesmen declaimed to militarist Europe that in America they have eliminated force as a factor of defence, the truth is that they have not honestly analyzed their actual position.   Canada's security does repose on force, but on the force of her neighbour.

This attraction is not without its dangers.   In no sense does it mean a diminution of loyalty to the British Crown, but this very community of interests between the Dominions and the United States is in itself disquieting.   In a speech delivered in Canada which awoke vigorous protests from the British press at the time, Sir Auckland Geddes bluntly described the danger of this intimacy: "The British Dominions which look out on to the Pacific feel that in Washington there is an instinctive understanding of their difficulties, which when they come to London they have to explain laboriously to Downing Street.   When the Dominions look to the mother country and find no satisfactory understanding, they are apt to look to Washington, and Washington, being not devoid of eyes, will look back to them."

From now on the problem of the Dominions, and with it that of the whole British Empire, is that no policy embracing an anti-American point of view will ever be accepted by such great partners as Canada and Australia.   When the Anglo-Japanese Alliance terminated in 1921, the Foreign Office wished to renew it.   They looked at the matter from a diplomatic and European point of view and relegated racial sentiment to second rank.   It was owing to the insistence of Canada, later seconded by Australia, that London was persuaded to abandon this alliance, which the American public considered most unsuitable for a white nation.   The Washington Agreement is, in reality, an *entente* of all the white nations of the Pacific to keep Japan *in statu quo*.

Those who expect to see England and the United States rivals for the domination of the seas are absolutely on the wrong track.   Instead, they have arrived at a common Anglo-Saxon program, with the important qualification that for the first time possibly the inspiration came not from London, but from Washington with the connivance of Australia and Canada.   The visit of the American fleet to Sydney and Melbourne in 1925 was the confirmation of this union.   In the Pacific this demonstration was regarded as a solemn warning that white America would back white Australasia against any aggression from the Far East.

Certain onlookers, who judge America by European standards, and in their haste expect an evolution to be accomplished before it is well begun, believe that the United States is waiting for the dissolution of the British Empire in order to take its place.   This is absolutely wrong.   As we have already shown, America finds British activities throughout the world useful to her economically, and there is nothing at present to indicate any political ulterior motive that might offset this policy.

To them Australia and New Zealand are important markets, nothing more; and as for Canada, they already feel that they and the Canadians are one and the same people. The situation is unique.   The existence of a frontier, their different flags, and the fact that politics in each country are swayed by different impulses, are all secondary considerations compared with the essential fact that on both sides of this purely theoretical and unguarded line is to be found the same civilization—American, not British—the same language spoken with almost the same accent, and the same customs.   The most important link of all, however, is the standard of living which rivets the Canadians economically and socially to the Americans.   Canada would never consider linking up with Europe at a lower standard, and this is a practical argument against which neither sentiment nor politics can avail.

Although the Canadians are faithful to the British crown and flag, yet for years they have admitted to themselves that they could not possibly run counter to the United States, and leaving all sentiment aside (for sentiment would be rather against the Americans), they would have to adopt a policy of collaboration with the rest of the American continent. The Americans on their side do not appear to harbour any ambitions of territorial conquest or political domination over their neighbours. They are not land-hungry, although Europe will never understand that their imperialism has nothing to do with land-hunger.

They are quite content to look upon Canada as an economic annex of their own in which they are at liberty to make money. They are quite reciprocal in this and are on the most friendly terms with their neighbours. "They are good people and just the same as we are," they will tell you. "Let them come if they wish; the door is open, and we would not offend them for the world." In point of fact, the northern States are full of Canadians, and when Americans cross the frontier they do not notice that they have left their own country until they meet a haughty and supercilious Englishman in the streets of Toronto, Ottawa, or Montreal. It is useless to prophesy as we have been doing for nearly a century that Canada will one day separate from England, for the day has come already. Political allegiance may last indefinitely, and the Canadians will never go over spontaneously to the United States; but from the point of view of culture and the other bonds which formerly linked them to Great Britain, they no longer wish to gravitate about a focus in the Old World.

In the nineteenth century Great Britain was the leader of the white race everywhere except in Europe, for even French activities in Africa were of only secondary im-

portance. During the past few years we have seen the
United States called on, less by men than by circumstances,
to assume her share of responsibility in the Pacific zone.
The British government seems to have partially abandoned
to them the international defence of the race in Canada.
Meanwhile a change in relative influences has shifted the
centre of gravity, not only of the British Empire, but of the
whole white race itself, for its richest territory is no longer
in the Old World. By an attraction not unlike the movements of heavenly bodies, the Dominions tend to gravitate
about a new centre; and as a result Europe is likely to lose
not merely her material following but even her moral prestige; for in the past it was through Great Britain that she
exercised her main influence in distant parts of the world.
We are therefore contemplating the rise of a new constella-
tion, dominated not by politics but by racial, economic, and
social considerations.

This has been predicted in England for years. Around
1900, Chamberlain, Rosebery, and Charles Dilke realized
that racial ties were likely to become more important than
politics, and even then they contemplated the possibility of
the centre of the Empire moving away from London, without, however, disintegrating the Anglo-Saxon empire. It is
questionable whether the American public appreciates its
new *rôle* as leader of a part of the white race. In the
eastern and central States, where interests are national or
provincial, the matter is never seriously considered; and in
the South they are engrossed in their own local problems
created by their exasperated racial susceptibilities. It is only
in California, Oregon, and Washington, and on the western
slope of the Rockies in general, that white-race consciousness in opposition to the yellow race brings any feeling of
international solidarity. Even there, however, they are
startled if you ask them if they would consider themselves
allied to Australia if she were attacked by Japan. Only a

few thinkers have considered this possibility; yet they all invariably and almost instinctively reply, "We would not abandon Australia, and we believe the whole country would be behind us." We are therefore justified in assuming that they have not sought after the *rôle* of leader and protector which Great Britain has held for so long, but which fate now seems to be offering to America. Nevertheless they cannot escape it, and they have even begun to fill it. It is therefore always possible that the form of the British Empire may change in the future.

This race feeling, which is working toward a new grouping of peoples, is an Anglo-Saxon conception; but it is more drastic in America and the Dominions than in Great Britain. Neither South America nor continental Europe is anxious to adopt the policy of exclusiveness on which these ideas are based, and they will eventually refuse to be dragged into an ethnic system founded on racial contempt and hostility and likely to create tender sensibilities and hatred. The Americans will become sooner or later the guiding force in the Anglo-Saxon family, but the day when they will be the leaders of the whole white race is much further off.

CONCLUSION

CHAPTER XXVII

EUROPEAN VS. AMERICAN CIVILIZATION

THE America that Columbus discovered was to our ancestors geographically a new world. Today, as a result of the revolutionary changes brought about by modern methods of production, it has again become a new world, and furthermore we have still to rediscover it.

Having first cleared away all hampering traditions and political obstacles, the American people are now creating on a vast scale an entirely original social structure which bears only a superficial resemblance to the European. It may even be a new age, an age in which Europe is to be relegated to a niche in the history of mankind; for Europe is no longer the driving force of the world. The old European civilization did not really cross the Atlantic, for the American re-awakening is not, as is generally supposed, simply a matter of degrees and dimensions; it is the creation of new conceptions. Many of the most magnificent material achievements of the United States have been made possible only by sacrificing certain rights of the individual, rights which we in the Old World regard as among the most precious victories of civilization. In spite of their identical religious and ethnic origin, Europe and America are diverging in their respective scales of value. This contrast was brought to a head by the War, which installed the United States prematurely in an unassailable position of economic supremacy. To America the advent of the new order is a cause for pride, but to Europe it brings heart-burnings and regrets for a state of society that is doomed to disappear.

From an economic point of view, America is sane and

healthy. Her prosperity in spite of possible setbacks rests on her vast natural resources and on the unexcelled efficiency of her means of production. Thanks to the abundance of her raw materials, her conquest of wealth has reached a point unknown elsewhere. To the American, Europe is a land of paupers, and Asia a continent of starving wretches. Luxury in every-day consumption and the extension to the many living conditions previously reserved for the few— these are new phenomena in the history of mankind, and are undoubtedly evidence of splendid progress. But what is absolutely new about this society which is accomplishing such marvels is that in all its many aspects—even including idealism and religion—it is working toward the single goal of production. It is a materialistic society, organized to produce things rather than people, with output set up as a god. Never before in history have social forces converged on so vast and so intensive a scale, but even the extent of the created wealth is less remarkable than the dynamic force of the human impulse that has brought this wealth into being.

Europe squanders her man-power and spares her substance, but America does exactly the reverse. For the past half-century, and especially during the last ten years, the Americans have been concentrating on the problem of obtaining the maximum efficiency of each worker. As a result of the use of machinery, of standardization, and of intensive division and organization of labour, productive methods have been renovated to a degree that few Europeans have ever dreamed of. In this super-collectivism, however, lies grave risk for the individual. His integrity is seriously threatened not only as a producer, but as a consumer as well.

If the aim of society is to produce the greatest amount of comfort and luxury for the greatest number of people, then the United States of America is in a fair way to succeed. And yet a house, a bath, and a car for every work-man—so much luxury within the reach of all—can only be obtained at a tragic price, no less than the transformation of millions of workmen into automatons. "Fordism," which is the essence of American industry, results in the standard-ization of the workman himself. Artisanship, now out of date, has no place in the New World, but with it have dis-appeared certain conceptions of mankind which we in Europe consider the very basis of civilization. To express his own personality through his creative efforts is the am-bition of every Frenchman, but it is incompatible with mass production.

We must not imagine that thoughtful Americans are un-aware of the peril which is threatening their manhood, but it is too much to expect them to sacrifice their machines; for they give production priority over everything else. Hav-ing refused to save the individuality of the factory worker, they shift their defence to other grounds. During the day the worker may only be a cog in the machine, they say; but in the evening at any rate he becomes a man once more. His leisure, his money, the very things which mass produc-tion puts at his disposal, these will restore to him the man-hood and intellectual independence of which his highly organized work has deprived him. This change in the cen-tre of gravity in the life of the individual marks an absolute revolution in the ideas on which society in Western Europe has been built up. Can it be possible that the personality of the individual can recover itself in consumption after be-ing so crippled and weakened in production? Have not the very products, in the form in which they are turned out by the modern factory, lost their individuality as well?

One of the finest attainments of American democracy has been to give much the same things to her poorest and rich-est citizens alike. The banker has his Rolls-Royce and the workman has his Ford. The banker's wife has her Paquin gown, and the working-girl chooses a similar one from the enormous quantities produced after the minimum of delay. The same applies all through the list. This generalized comfort is possible, first, because production is concentrated on a limited number of models repeated *ad infinitum,* and secondly, because the public is willing to put up with it. Thus we are forced to conclude that the price that America pays for her undeniable material progress is the sacrifice of one aspect of civilization.

Thus they are advancing in one direction and retrogressing in another. The material advance is immeasurable in comparison with the Old World, but from the point of view of individual refinement and art, the sacrifice is real indeed. Even the humblest European sees in art an aristocratic symbol of his own personality, and modern America has no national art and does not even feel the need of one.

Once it is admitted that their conception of society is materialistic in spite of the idealism of its leaders, it is only logical that the doctrine of efficiency should become the central idea of the country. Today in America no sacrifice is too great to be endured for this sacred principle. There is no possible escape. Big profits overshadow liberty in all its forms, and the exercise of intelligence is encouraged only if it fits in with this common aim. Any one who turns aside to dabble in research or dilettantism is regarded as almost mentally perverted. Hence a growing tendency to reduce all virtues to the primordial ideal of conformity.

This point of view is not imposed by the upper classes or the government, but by the great masses of the people themselves. In the universities the majority of students are satisfied if they memorize an array of ready-made facts, and they seek from their professors not culture but the fundamentals of a successful career. In nothing does America more resemble Germany than in this discipline of thought. It may lead to splendid material results, and it is undoubtedly a marvellous aid to economic achievement; but under it originality and individual talent, and often art and genius, rebel or are stifled. France has the same instinctive fear of American methods as symbolized by Ford as she had of the German system on the eve of the War. Although she fully realizes that by the triumph of these methods the productivity of the world will increase tremendously, that things which now lie latent in our grasp, restricted and materially sterile, will blossom anew in the conquest of wealth, yet she hesitates to pay the price. She recalls with the force of a warning the quotation from Lucretius: *Propter vitam vitae perdere causas.*

An important transformation of society results from this concentration of energy on the one supreme object of mass production. The individual, having become a means rather than an end, accepts his *rôle* of cog in the immense machine without giving a passing thought to the effect on his personality. Religion, also enrolled in the movement, exalts production as an ideal akin to the mysticism of life and of human progress. The ideal of "service" sanctifies this collaboration and its superb material rewards. Caught between the atrophied individual and the over-disciplined community, the family finds its field of action greatly restricted; for in the eyes of the apostles of efficiency, the family is regarded as a barrier impeding the current. Though the Catholic Church still defends it, believing it to be one of its strongholds, yet society as a whole no longer relies on the home for the early training of the nation. It is to the public schools, the churches, to the ten thousand Y.M.C.A.'s and other associations for education and reform, to the press, and even to publicity that they look instead for the education of the masses. They pay little heed to the need of preserving for the jaded individual either the refuge of the family circle or the relaxation of meditation and culture. On the contrary, they consider them as obstacles in the way of progress. In the absence of an intermediate type of social institution in which co-operation is moderated by freedom, American society tends to adopt an aspect of practical collectivism. This collectivism is approved of by the upper classes and is whole-heartedly accepted by the masses; but it is subtly undermining the liberty of the individual and restricting his outlook to such an extent that without so much as regretting or realizing it, he himself assents to his own abnegation. In this respect the American community is closer to the ancient civilizations in which the individual belonged to the City-State than is the social fabric of Western Europe which has evolved from the Middle Ages and the French Revolution. The dreams of Rousseau have at length been realized, but not by the methods or under the conditions that he imagined, but strange to relate by a régime of industrialism that he could not possibly have foreseen.

Those who seem to suffer most under this discipline are the foreign-born of the upper classes, but certain mature Americans also protest against it. The youth of the country makes no objection, and there is no reaction of the individual against this moral tyranny. The nation is not individualistic in mentality, and it therefore accepts this collectivism as part of itself; and the régime really suits it. The material advantages are so great, the security so perfect, and the enthusiasm of collective action in accomplishing stupendous tasks so overwhelming, that in an almost mystical abandon, other considerations are neither heeded nor missed.

But can the individual possibly survive in such an atmosphere? In her enthusiasm to perfect her material success, has not America risked quenching the flame of individual liberty which Europe has always regarded as one of the chief treasures of civilization? At the very moment that America is enjoying a state of prosperity such as the world has never known before, an impartial observer is forced to ask whether this unprecedented abundance of wealth will in the long run lead to a higher form of civilization.   Europe, where industrial mass production was initiated, hesitates, terrified by the logical consequences.   Will she end by adopting them?   On the contrary, are they not incompatible with the old-established civilization which so expresses her personality?   Some who are eager to rejuvenate industrial Europe look to America for inspiration and guidance; but others hold back, deeming the past superior and preferable.

When we visit America, we see Europe from a new perspective.   It seems different from what we had imagined, and very different from the impression gained from the reproaches of Oriental thinkers.   In the light of the American contrast we see that material pursuits have not entirely absorbed the soul of Europe, and that it can still appreciate free and disinterested thought and spiritual joys which can often be obtained only by renouncing comforts and fortune.

The chief contrast between Europe and America is not so much one of geography as a fundamental difference between two epochs in the history of mankind, each with its own conception of life.   We have the contrast between industrial mass production which absorbs the individual for its material conquests, as against the individual considered not merely as a means of production and progress but as an independent ego.   From this unusual aspect we perceive certain traits that are common to the psychology of both Europe and the Orient.   So the discussion broadens until it becomes a dialogue, as it were, between Ford and Ghandi.

INDEX

THE END